COMPARATIVE GOVERNMENT AND POLITICS

COMPARATIVE GOVERNMENT AND POLITICS

A. Bhatt
Ravi Ranjan

ANMOL PUBLICATIONS PVT. LTD.
NEW DELHI-110 002 (INDIA)

ANMOL PUBLICATIONS PVT. LTD.
Regd. Office: 4360/4, Ansari Road, Daryaganj,
New Delhi-110002 (India)
Tel.: 23278000, 23261597, 23286875, 23255577
Fax: 91-11-23280289
Email: anmolpub@gmail.com
Visit us at: www.anmolpublications.com

Branch Office: No. 1015, Ist Main Road, BSK IIIrd Stage
IIIrd Phase, IIIrd Block, Bangalore-560 085 (India)
Tel.: 080-41723429 • Fax: 080-26723604
Email: anmolpublicationsbangalore@gmail.com

Comparative Government and Politics

First Edition, 2010

PRINTED IN INDIA

Printed at Mehra Offset Press, Delhi.

Contents

Preface

Like any other subdiscipline of comparative political science, there are many issues related to the study of regime type, regime transition, and democratization. The abundance of quality and type of regime over many languages, regions, and aeras makes it incredibly difficult to systematically study these phenomena. This is true not just cross-nationally but also domestically. We are often unable to pinpoint the exact causes of regime transitions, that cannot properly identify what type of regime the polity then becomes, and have a fantastically difficult time agreeing on proper definitions of democracy and democratization. It is even more taxing to compare non-democratic regimes. These polities have little in common across nations other than the rote suppression of constituent rights. Even this occurs at different levels and with different motivations. How will we ever be able to capture such subjective, and often inaccessible, individual predilections and their importance to regime formation? Evidently, the study of both democracy and non-democracy is equally tenuous.

Developing countries and transitional economy countries must constantly bear in mind that government financial management plays a major role in the implementation of policies aimed at promoting national economic social and other developmental goals. Government financial management encompasses all or part of the processes and functions of planning and programming budgeting, budget execution and accounting audit and evaluation. It is aimed at ensuring that to the maximum practical extent, a government's financial resources are used lawfully, efficiently and effectively and with transparency and accountability to the legislature and the people.

—Author

1

The Evolution of Comparative Political Analysis

Political Economy

Under what political and economic conditions are *efficiency* and *equity* jointly sustainable in an economy with low barriers to trade and capital movements? In different ways both the UK and the German economies are efficient – leaving the current global financial crisis out of the discussion. But the UK has been unsuccessful in producing equity and Germany has been more successful, although in the last decade and a half the gap between median-and low-income workers in Germany has substantially increased, coinciding with a decline of the collective bargaining coverage of low-income workers and their labour market protection.

So the big question is: why did the German political economic coalition (in the broad sense) of the 1980s, which underwrote protection for low-income workers, give way to a new coalition that ceased to do so? One of the most interesting aspects of the answer is that unions are as central to the new coalition as they were to the old.

Feasible Coalitions and Distribution in Germany and the UK

The German landscape has changed in the past decade in significant ways, both in terms of the operation of the labour market and the political and industrial coalitions that support it. A little background information is necessary to understand the system. Lijphart (1984) classified the political systems of advanced countries into two types, consensus and competitive:

- Consensus systems have proportional representation in their electoral systems, multiple 'representative' political parties, coalition governments and an involvement of interest groups in policy-making; parties are representative in that interest groups close to the party have defined roles in party policy-making.
- Competitive systems have majoritarian, first-past-the-post elections, typically two major 'leadership' parties, one-party government and with interest groups kept in the lobby; parties are leadership parties in that the leader is typically given power to make policy – and parties are often defined by their leader in the eyes of the electorate.

Varieties of Capitalism (Hall and Soskice 2001) classifies advanced countries into Coordinated Market Economies (CME) and Liberal Market Economies (LME). The ideal-type CME has strong associations representing business and labour; an emphasis on vocational training with transferable occupational and company-specific skills; co-determination within companies; collective bargaining coordinated across industries; block shareholders and patient (long-term) capital. The ideal-type LME emphasises flexible labour markets; unilateral management control; general education and skills; an absence of social partners; and diffused shareholding. There is a more or less perfect match between consensus political systems and CMEs and between competitive political systems and LMEs.

Germany, at least very broadly, was a CME and also a consensus polity at the start of the period covered by this research and certainly in the 1980s; but, while Germany is probably still best described as a CME with a consensus political system today, there are significant changes in the way both its capitalist and its political system work. The UK is still an LME with a competitive political system: if anything it has become more so.

Although consensus politics slows down reform because it is negotiated out by the different interests involved, research suggests that a consensus approach to politics is unlikely to change in a major way. The only change in a CME from consensus proportional representation (PR) to competitive majoritarian since the general adoption of PR in the first quarter of the twentieth century has been in Italy; this was associated with the exceptional circumstances of the break-up of the Christian Democracy party.

An important implication of the consensus political system in general and PR in particular is the centre-left bias of the system. The high proportion of centre-left government coalitions in consensus-PR systems (nearly 75 per cent of government years in the second half of the twentieth century) stems from the need nearly always to form coalitions and the preference of centrist voters for centre-left coalitions that could impose high taxes on higher-income groups. Middle-income groups in CMEs – with relatively compressed 5:1 earnings ratios – tend to have common interests with lower-income groups over education and health (Iversen and Soskice 2006).

Centre-left coalitions are reinforced by the fact that parties in PR consensus systems are representative, with close relations to economic groupings of voters cemented by institutions representing those voters and with a voice in the relevant political party. This has been particularly the case in CMEs, where associational activity is important. An implication is that parties of the right cannot easily move to the centre of the political spectrum without losing voters: if these parties could move to the centre and commit to centrist policies, centrist voters could have centrist coalitions.

But the centre-left bias works out very differently in CMEs in continental Europe than in Scandinavia. Manow (2009) shows that, in Scandinavia, coalitions have been between Social Democratic parties and agrarian parties, often with tacit centrist party support for minority governments. But in CMEs in continental Europe, power has been to a major degree shared between Christian Democratic parties and Social Democratic parties. Centrist voters are prepared to vote Christian Democratic or to vote for centrist parties which form coalitions with Christian Democratic parties because Christian Democratic parties are based on economic groups across the spectrum, with social as well as business wings. The internal compromise position within Christian Democratic parties thus accepts taxing higher-income earners and redistributing to middle-and lower-income voters. This in turn requires Social Democratic parties to be not too far to the left of this position if they are to be attractive coalition partners for centrist parties. And this in turn explains the contributory basis to social security in continental Europe (modifying redistribution) by comparison with tax-financed social security in Scandinavia.

The traditionally different structure of the provision of social services and education is also explained by a position of internal compromise. In effect the state provision of social services in Scandinavia, through a high proportion of female public-sector employment and the absence of tax subsidies for homeworkers, represents an egalitarian solution compared to the greater emphasis in continental Europe of home and charitable provision. Similarly, the split provision of secondary education separates children from different class backgrounds on the continent in a way that the single school system in Scandinavia does not. Despite the more inegalitarian nature of welfare states on the continent, both continental and Scandinavian welfare states have traditionally been more effective than those in LMEs.

These broad results are supported by three factors:

- Unions were linked to Social Democratic and to a lesser extent Christian Democratic parties, so that there was no political coalition available to attack the institutional nature of the industrial relations system.
- The interests of larger and also more advanced businesses, especially in manufacturing, in the CME environment reinforced this: needing a cooperative and skilled workforce, large companies in particular have traditionally supported representative employee bodies in which the long-term interests of employees – whose skills give them power within the company – can be supported in exchange for cooperation and peer-monitoring. Thus a major sector of business has had an interest in an insurance-based welfare state and an effective industry-wide industrial relations system, including industry bargaining over wages. This extends too to the broad system of vocational training which provides a large proportion of the workforce with relatively occupational-specific skills.
- Middle-income workers with occupational and often company-specific skills support an insurance-based welfare state, since relatively long tenure means that if jobs are lost

it takes time to find a new appropriate one. This is particularly the case for older workers; hence median voters would not be in favour of dismantling the welfare state.

Broadly speaking, until reunification in 1990, the German system provided relatively good jobs with high security for most workers in manufacturing, the public sector and the higher-skill parts of the service sector; somewhat less good jobs in the more traditionally low-skill services, but still with some security; and a relatively high proportion of women were care-workers at home. Employment problems were taken care of by early retirement, and social security contributions paid for this. The bifurcated education and vocational training systems channelled children into different employment paths. This setup was supported by an implicit and sometimes explicit political coalition of social and Christian democracy; by a coalition of employer associations and unions; and by supportive skilled workers and middle-income voters. Although the distribution of income was far from equal it could be described as a solidaristic compromise. It is this broad compromise which has begun partially to unravel in the past decade.

The relation between a liberal market economy and a majoritarian polity was and has remained more clear cut in the UK. Majoritarian systems almost inevitably involve two major parties (centre-left and centre-right) competing for the median vote. There is a centre-right bias in governments:

- The distribution of educational competencies is sharply unequal at the lower end of the spectrum, so that middle-class electors see the welfare state as directed towards these groups.
- Given general skills and a more flexible mid-career labour market, there is less concern among middle-class voters for an insurance-based welfare state to maintain living standards in the event of unemployment.
- Middle-class voters are more concerned that a centre-left party in power will raise taxes on the middle classes to spend on the welfare state, than they are concerned that a Conservative party will move right and cut taxes and public expenditure. It follows that middle-class voters would only be prepared to vote Labour with a leader such

as Tony Blair, whom they believed had the interest of the middle class at heart. This is reinforced by low voting participation rates among lower-income groups. In addition, business is in general hostile to the welfare state; and weakened unions have had little influence.

Policy stances in the UK have had three major characteristics over the past two decades:

- Labour policies have not been significantly more left-wing than Conservative policies over this period; instead the major appeal of both parties has been to middle-income voters.
- Because of the need to appeal to middle-income voters, and because of their perception of the welfare state as geared to lower-income groups often outside the labour market, welfare state policy and reform have focused on welfare-to-work.
- Neither Conservative nor Labour policies have been of comfort to the unions. Structural economic policy has been driven by the goal of flexible labour markets.

Germany's Changing Political Economy in the Last Decade

One picture of Germany over the past decade is that it has moved from a solidaristic, coordinated market economy with stakeholder corporate governance and a consensus polity to an individualistic, liberal market economy with shareholder values enforcing short-term profitability and a competitive polity. Carlin and Soskice (2009) and Hancké and Johnston (2009) show this vision to be very wide of the mark. Instead, a hybrid has emerged: a successful, modern, export-led economy operating on coordinated market economy lines, together with a flexible labour market for the low-skills sector. Behind this emergence has been an important shift of both political and industrial coalitions, and some modification of the rules of the political game.

The prolonged economic slowdown in Germany since the mid-1990s has played a large part in precipitating the strategic policy shift to bottom-end labour market flexibility. It has also stimulated the industrial and political coalitional realignments that made the shift possible. In addition, this slowdown was maintained directly and indirectly by the nature of the German macroeconomic demand-management regime, contrasting with recovery in the UK and US recovery in the post-2001 period. Moreover, while coordinated wage restraint by unions was beneficial for exports, it appears to have had adverse macroeconomic effects in Germany.

Since the mid-1990s, after the initial boom caused by reunification, both monetary and fiscal policy have operated conservatively. This reflected the need to fulfil the conditions of the Treaty of Maastricht through restraining public expenditure increases; and the deflationary impact of the rise in the D-Mark in 1994 was augmented by cuts in employment as companies attempted to rebuild profitability from the low levels of the 1980s to the levels needed to finance new investment in a global financial market. From 1999 onwards, membership of the European Monetary Union (EMU) meant that the Bundesbank had no control over interest rates; and fiscal policy was not used in a counter-cyclical way in 2001–03 to counter the recession of that period as it was in the US and UK. Fiscal conservatism is common to advanced countries with powerful, but not fully coordinated, wage-and price-setters. This is now a widely held view in monetary policy. Basically, the argument is that powerful wage-setters will adopt more moderate wage demands if they believe that fiscal policy is unlikely to respond to increased unemployment. If there are many wage-setters the fiscal stance of the government is irrelevant to the behaviour of the individual wage-setter because the small wage-setter has no influence on aggregate unemployment: hence the UK and US can adopt a discretionary fiscal policy. Or if there is a (more or less) encompassing wage-setter, it will know it has a dominant influence on unemployment and will therefore have a perfect trade-off between wages and unemployment (Soskice and Iversen, 2000; Soskice, 2008). Thus, it is not accidental that Germany has had a conservative position on fiscal policy.

This conservatism reinforces the operation of wage behaviour in Germany. Because German fiscal policy is unresponsive to unemployment, large unions are highly responsive to the employment concerns of their members. The large wage-leading unions are most powerfully represented in large companies in the export sector; the major exception to this is verdi, representing the large public and services sector, whose key members are skilled workers and technicians with relatively long tenure. These unions have adopted wage restraint, carefully calibrated against world price developments to boost exports and maintain company profitability so that their key members' employment is not at risk. However, this wage restraint has, counter-intuitively, increased deflationary pressures in the German economy. This is because the demand-boosting effects on employment from exports – which have benefited union members – are more than counterbalanced by the adverse effect on domestic demand, given that wage increases are broadly similar across the economy with its high collective-bargaining coverage. The price elasticity effect on exports is less than the income effect of the real wage restraint on domestic demand. This contrasts with the small open CMEs of Scandinavia, Belgium, the Netherlands or Austria, which have all enjoyed relatively low unemployment, and where positive export effects outweigh negative domestic-demand effects.

Slow growth and rising unemployment, together with the classic resort to early retirement, put pressure on the public-sector deficit in Germany. Successive German finance ministers, with the exception of Oskar Lafontaine (1998-99), took very seriously the rules of the EMU Stability and Growth Pact that the deficit should not rise above 3 per cent of GDP. This led to fierce debate about changing early retirement rules, the pensions system and the system of unemployment benefits. The vigour of the debates was precisely because the polity was consensus-based and wide political agreement to change was required. And they had an unexpected and unwelcome economic consequence. Those who were employed became anxious about the future value of both unemployment benefits and pensions, increasing their savings to compensate. This magnified the deflationary pressures. Germany got caught in a slow-growth, rising-unemployment equilibrium. Unemployment can be pushed up by a slow growth in demand. All this requires, assuming economies have to be on real-wage bargaining schedules or upward-sloping labour supply curves, is that the real exchange rate depreciates, permitting the relative decline in real wages. A parallel but opposite course was taken by the UK, where real exchange rate appreciation allowed real wages to rise and unemployment to fall. The German system (like the Japanese and for similar reasons, aside from the banking sector) experienced a combination of slow growth, strong export performance, high household savings levels and rising unemployment.

Restructuring the Advanced Sector

Strong export performance was not only the result of wage restraint in the export sector. Major structural changes took place within companies in the advanced sectors of the economy. What is interesting is that the 'institutions' of the coordinated market economy have all changed significantly yet retain recognisable forms and functions:

- the consensus-based organisation of companies, in which the works council plays an important role in co-determination;
- the vocational training system, and the higher levels of vocational education in German higher education, including Fachhochschulen and many university departments, especially in the Technical Universities;
- the internal-external system of wage determination, and the role played by trade unions and employer associations;
- the patient capital system of corporate governance.

While some caution against over-generalisation is needed, the broad changes are:

- further alignment of the interests of companies and their skilled workforce while reducing the number of semiskilled workers, often by outsourcing;
- integrating the leader of the works council into company decision-making;
- concentrating on ensuring long-term, risk-corrected, rates of return required by world financial markets, without moving to Anglo-Saxon methods of short-term management;
- a more company-oriented view of the benefits of vocational training while continuing to support the system, for example tailoring specialisations in the last two years of an apprenticeship to company needs but concentrating more on relevant general skills in the first two.

Interestingly, changes have been brought about by cooperation between works councils and management. Given that the average-skilled worker is looking for long-term tenure, the interest of the works council has been to help management meet long-term financial goals. This has often been against the interests of less-skilled employees. And thus there has been a corresponding divergence of interests between works councils in the advanced sector, representing skilled workers, and trade unions representing semiskilled as well. But while companies have if anything got closer to their works councils, large companies still remain strong supporters of trade unions. While they wish to expand the range of agreements with their works council, they are generally opposed to the idea of getting rid of industry bargaining. For companies do not at the end of the day want wage levels bargained out on the basis of individual company profits, which would lead to lower returns on investments and leave them vulnerable to the threat of industrial action at the company or plant level. Behind the continuing relation between large companies and employer associations, on the one hand, and trade unions on the other, is the fact that unions themselves have shifted to giving more power within the union to works council chairs in the large companies. This power shift within trade unions is important in understanding the new coalitional structures.

Reshaping the Welfare System in Germany

The bulk of rising unemployment in Germany fell on less-skilled and less-educated workers. It is generally true that these workers bear the brunt of labour market dislocations, arguably because employers have less incentive to develop company-specific skills in them. But in CMEs this effect is magnified institutionally, for skilled workers are core union members and in effect median voters. Especially in larger and more advanced companies, which depend heavily on a skilled cooperative workforce, the jobs and tenure of these workers are increasingly protected by works council rules, and management is usually happy with this result.

Unemployment has risen to quite unaccustomed levels, standing at 8.6 per cent in March 2009 according to figures from the German Federal Labour Office – the unemployment rate in West Germany was lower than that of the US for almost all the period from the mid-1950s to 1990. In the absence of the strong export-led growth of much of that period, the existing strategy of using early retirement to keep down unemployment is largely incompatible with Germany's desire for fiscal restraint. Whatever one may think about the logic of conservative German fiscal policy, it is central to understanding the strategic switch initiated by the Social Democratic Party (SPD) and, in effect, supported by the Christian Democratic Union (CDU).

The strategic switch was to cut back on pensions and unemployment benefits, as well as on health expenditure. Among other things, standard unemployment benefits were to last for a shorter period, there were to be more restrictive conditions on jobs that could be rejected by benefit recipients, and claimants would be moved into means-tested assistance after a period. More dramatically, a major move towards flexibility at the low end of the labour market began, consisting of low-paid 'mini-jobs' (paying less than €400 per month or requiring less than 50 days' work per year). What is interesting is how it was possible to push these complex measures through in a consensus polity with a centre-left bias.

Reconfiguring Industrial and Political Coalitions

This strategic policy shift required multiple changes in the German polity. It required a shift in the industrial coalition between unions and employer associations as well as a shift in the broad political coalition. Since both coalitional shifts required – or were premised on – changes in the underlying goals of the participants, it implied changes in those participants. The research is based on Carlin and Soskice (2009) and Hancké and Johnston (2009, forthcoming).

A new industrial coalition has slowly been emerging, based on unions (with the leaders of the major works councils being of particular importance), large companies and employer associations in the export sector. No one is technically excluded by such 'social partnerships', but in practice less-skilled and less-educated workers, small companies, the Handwerk sector (small, high-quality artisan producers), and the eastern Länder are. This new industrial coalition if anything gains by the development of flexible labour markets at the low end of the economy: at least in principle it reduces the cost of less-skilled sheltered sector services, thus raising the real earnings of skilled workers. Moreover, since most longer-term unemployed workers are low-skilled, skilled workers are unlikely to fall foul of the welfare reforms.

The series of reforms launched by Gerhard Schröder in 2003 and known as Agenda 2010 required the SPD to move rightwards along the political spectrum, and – before the Grand Coalition formed in 2005 – to carry the Greens with them. Although it did not technically require CDU and Christian Social Union (CSU) votes in the Bundestag, it would have been difficult to push the new strategy through in the face of stiff opposition; and in both the SPD and the CDU, and even more in the CSU, there was an important left or social wing. The same was true of the Green party. The reforms also required Bundesrat approval. Such major party shifts are very difficult without changing the nature of the party. Indeed, although Schröder got the majority of the SPD to support him, it led to a fracture of the party, and contributed to the formation of the Linkspartei as an electoral vacuum developed on the left and some of those on the left of the SPD moved out. The SPD is now identified as a more centrist party with a substantial decline in electoral support while electoral support for the Linkspartei has grown to double figures: very crudely, and allowing for continuing fluctuations, the SPD now represents about 25 per cent of the electorate and the Linkspartei 15 per cent.

The shifts in the CDU and the CSU are if anything more complicated. Because there is no 'left-wing' home for CDU and CSU social-wing politicians – they obviously cannot move to the Linkspartei – the tensions within the Union are greater. The free market liberal wing of the CDU has become less powerful; the new leadership of the CSU gives greater weight to its social wing and Angela Merkel as leader has become a moderator across factions within the CDU and between the CDU and the CSU.

From a UK perspective, the basket of reforms originally in Agenda 2010 should have been quite acceptable to the 'middle-class' voter or skilled worker. Why then has it been so evidently difficult in Germany to construct a balanced political coalition around them? What they do is to move Germany from a solidaristic society to a more segmented society: put crudely, it may seem a little surprising that the protected two-thirds at the top of the segmented society should not be happy with the increased real incomes which come from, in effect, withdrawing protection from the bottom third.

The difficulty can possibly be explained by two factors. First, research on the political institutions of a consensus polity underlines the notion of a representative party in which different social groups (or their political representatives) have an organisational right to be heard. Schröder upset this balance in moving the centre of gravity of the SPD to the right. And, as previously explained, the CDU has had major difficulties in following suit as its left-leaning wing has no other potential political home.

Second, research – on the German production regime – on the nature of skills in German labour markets shows that highly skilled workers with long-tenure employment may be nervous about unemployment because of the length of time they think it will take to find appropriate alternative employment, even though the probability of losing their job may be low; and the older they are the greater their concern. Thus, even though they are well protected by their works council, the previous guarantee of adequate unemployment benefits for an adequate length of time and early retirement for older workers was of great importance. Indeed, so strong was the pressure inside the CDU and CSU that the Grand Coalition modified the rules on the duration of benefits and on early retirement.

Bringing Together the Pieces

Germany over the past decade was identified as stemming from the decline of unionisation in Germany, and more generally the winding back of institutional protection, especially at the lower end of the economy. This lessening of union influence can be seen as a response to the infeasibility of the previous solidaristic, export-led and early retirement model, the infeasibility of which only emerged clearly with the decline of European growth in the 1990s after German unification. The depressive effects of real wage restraint in Germany (but not the smaller countries of Europe) and the maintenance of a conservative fiscal policy (unlike the UK and the US) were also factors. Looking back at the 1980s in Germany, trade unions, integrated with business in a strong vocational training system, were part of the solution, not the problem. This is in contrast to the UK during that period, when the Conservative government's attack on trade unions, designed to force business and its largely semiskilled workforce to become more competitive in a world characterised by skill-biased technical change, effectively reduced trade unions to bit players in the skills development of the workforce.

Identified characteristics of German private-sector businesses that help create a climate in which apprenticeships can flourish. These characteristics can be summed up as: the ability of business to cooperate; the maintenance of patient capital; and a continued demand for a depth of skills in workers. As explained above, the advanced sector in Germany has continued to drive Germany's high value-added export success along classical German lines, specialising in markets in which success depends on a skilled and cooperative workforce, with company-industry technologies and both industry/occupational and related company-specific skills. This requires block-holder share ownership capable of both self-evaluation and a long-term perspective. In addition, companies have a strong incentive in a range of areas (technology transmission and innovation systems, and collective bargaining) to retain close relationships with other companies and with business and employer associations. This explains why German companies appear still to display the characteristics the research.

UK companies share few of these characteristics. Their comparative advantages (in high value-added sectors) are in markets that require high risk-taking, the ability to draw in and, if necessary, push out employees with specific skills, and the freedom to structure rewards without external interference. The incentive structure for top managers in such companies is influenced by diversified shareholders, who pull out if they are concerned about inadequate performance. Add to this the fact that UK companies in lower value-added markets are typically concerned about low costs and you have a British business environment that has few of the characteristics needed for an effective apprenticeship system. As for the question of minimum wages, it is not difficult to see why minimum wages fit well with governmental capacity in the UK. It is because they can be imposed directly by government and do not require business cooperation or commitment. Though not so immediately easy to see, minimum wages also have an important political function for a Labour government in signalling to party activists that it is concerned to reduce poverty – although even here there is a silver lining for the middle classes as their children work their way through tertiary education.

Conversely, a minimum wage sits uneasily in environments dominated by collective bargaining as in many northern European countries. Indeed Germany is the only northern European economy with extensive collective bargaining that has (and only very recently) passed minimum wage legislation, albeit only in a few sectors. But even here the legislation requires both the employer association and union in a sector to apply to impose 'minimum wages' on a sector. In effect, a collectively agreed minimum wage is extended to all companies in a sector whether or not they are members of the sectoral employment association. Thus it is a very German form of minimum wage.

Policy Conclusions on Sustainability

Of the world's large economies, Germany has long been closest to showing how equity could be complementary to efficiency rather than traded off against it. Core in Germany to that complementary, and central to this research programme, is a vocational training system that both raises productivity and safeguards real wages and employment tenure. The success of the German apprenticeship system depends on a complex web of political and economic institutions that ultimately generate commitment from businesses and confidence among apprentices. And it is the absence of such an institutional web that prevents effective apprenticeships developing in the UK.

But in the past decade and a half, Germany has in effect discarded the system as it operated for those at the bottom of the labour market, by deregulating and deunionising that part of the market. Moreover, since acceptance into private-sector apprenticeships requires good behaviour and diligence in schools, it is at least tempting to link the contrast between the relatively high IALS scores on literacy and numeracy of less-educated German adults, and PISA scores, with a decline in apprenticeships. Since educational performance is positively correlated with family income, it is not difficult to see this as a vicious circle for less advantaged families. The genesis of deregulation and deunionisation in Germany has stemmed from two factors: sizeable inflows since 1990 into the West German labour market from the former Communist states, none of whom passed through the German vocational training system; and negative external demand shocks combined with the absence of compensating drivers of domestic demand. This is of course part of a much wider problem that Germany and Japan have generated for the world economy by excess savings.

The most straightforward way to reverse this policy direction is through public-sector provision of a wide range of social services along Scandinavian lines, and the creation of flexible employment opportunities for women. If these jobs are sufficiently flexible, this will also raise earnings in low-paid sectors, such as retailing.

Aside from the fact that Germany is likely to need a strong driver of domestic demand during a prolonged period in which demand for exports of capital goods will remain sluggish, an expansion of public-sector employment will require an expansion of apprenticeships. So long as these are made contingent on appropriate school performance this can act as a catalyst to raising school standards.

The most important question is whether there is a restructuring of the current political and industrial coalition that will support such changes. There are three reasons for thinking that there is. First, there is now a large potential workforce and electorate of younger educated women who want opportunities to move in and out of the labour force with some guarantees of continuing good employment; this has proved difficult for the private sector to provide in Germany, and the public sector fulfils this function well in Scandinavia – explaining in part the higher Scandinavian reproduction rate.

Both the SPD and the CDU are beginning to compete for this expanding section of the electorate. Second, if skilled male industrial workers become more worried about their jobs, this offers in effect additional social security if it enables their wives to earn reasonable incomes. And this will be a powerful voice in the key unions in the industrial coalition. Finally, the SPD in particular has been badly damaged by the new coalitional structures of the last decade (despite the central role of Schröder in their formation). This offers a way of recapturing support from the Linkspartei.

Comparative Political Analysis

Like any other subdiscipline of comparative political science, there are many issues related to the study of regime type, regime transition, and democratization. The abundance of quality and type of regime over many languages, regions, and eras makes it incredibly difficult to systematically study these phenomena. This is true not just cross-nationally but also domestically. We are often unable to pinpoint the exact causes of regime transitions, cannot properly identify what type of regime the polity then becomes, and have a fantastically difficult time agreeing on proper definitions of democracy and democratization. It is even more taxing to compare non-democratic regimes. These polities have little in common across nations other than the rote suppression of constituent rights. Even this occurs at different levels and with different motivations. How will we ever be able to capture such subjective, and often inaccessible, individual predilections and their importance to regime formation? Evidently, the study of both democracy and non-democracy is equally tenuous.

Aside from failures to generally identify and quantify regime type, there is the implicit recognition of trust as a main catalyst for the breakdown of autocracies and the initiation and consolidation of democracy. However, the concepts of trust, or legitimacy, are extremely abstract and though we may attempt to tackle them methodologically, we will never reach a understanding of this psychological variable and its impact on political outcomes. When so much of the literature relies on such an undefined concept, it makes putting faith into the theories and explanations of regime scholars a bit harder to swallow.

More specifically, operationalizing variables such as democracy or democratic consolidation usually requires a tradeoff. In order to be parsimonious we often must make the arbitrary decision to set regime off type as, for example, a continuous 3-6 point scale variable. While this makes our models easier to handle it might not necessarily reflect the real world; in reality there are many different variations of each regime type creating a penumbra of various shades of political grey. However, it would also be a mistake to endlessly quantify regimes { we would simply spin out of control never to meaningfully test this variable again. A middle ground, if one can be appropriately identified, could be the best for testing levels of regime type and democratization. Much of the current literature attempts to discover such a place and hopefully we are getting closer. After examining Samuel Huntington's widely accepted work on the 'third wave' of democratization it is difficult to argue that his theories are less than well thought out. But it becomes clear that while attempting to explain the different eras of democratic conversion we have so many different possible causes that we can find no tangible answers. A mix of both endogenous and exogenous factors probably cause democratization but these factors differ not only between countries but within. Take, for example, the list of possible contributors to democratization on pages 37-38 (Huntington 1991). Then take a moment to mull over Huntington's immediately following statement, "The theories relating these factors to democracy and democratization are almost always plausible. Each variable and theory, however, is likely to have relevance to only a few cases" (1991:38). Great. So is democratization a generalizable phenomenon or would it serve us well to move away from the quantitative research and back toward qualitative area studies? Are there an innite number of causes that can only be explained in one country at a time? If the work of Huntington confronts such issues, it is safe to say that the work of many other researchers echoes the same sentiment. Yes, democratization is a difficult dependent variable to study. Perhaps it is a great example of a subdiscipline that would largely benefit from a combination of empirical and qualitative work.

Huntington's lengthy discussion of declining authoritarian legitimacy is another area that may benefit from such a fusion. His opening line to this section, if rather discouraging, reads, "legitimacy is a mushy concept that political analysts do well to avoid" (Huntington, 1991:46). If, as this section goes on to detail, legitimacy is so important to understanding shifts from autocracy to democracy, is regionally different, and declines naturally over time how in the world can we model such a thing? Though Huntington provides extensive qualitative work on the issue, quite convincingly I would argue, there is a lack of empirical evidence. Again, our field today is one of quantitative work. Is democratization going to be relegated to the world of the case studies forever? The inclusion of economic development, while significant in most studies of regime transition, is a prime example of a concept that is difficult to compare cross-nationally. While modernization theories became the dominant explanations for democratization in the mid-twentieth century, we are discovering today that these explanations do not always hold empirically. Instead, the unique patterns of industrialization, wealth, levels of taxation, education, and growth rates are all interrelated and heavily impact a country's democratic path. Again, however, these unique patterns are specific to only one or a few cases (Huntington 1991). Rather than economic development (traditionally a measure of GDP per capita) focused on as the causal factor for democratization, it is here described as leading to other social goods (such as education, literacy, etc.) that then work in tandem to produce democratization (Huntington 1991:106).

Along with the unruly nature of democratization, in this work the author chooses to define democracy on the basis of elections as opposed to some of the other widely accepted specifications of democracies as attitudes, civic structures, and institutions. This definition of democracy is a minimal one (Huntington 1991). However, for Huntington it is so defined because it allows us the opposite view of non-democratic systems: all of the electoral hallmarks of democracy are absent in autocracy. It is as simple as that. Where we often have difficulty pinpointing non-democratic regimes for comparison, Huntington works to show us that a simplification of democracy may work to allow for an equally simple view of autocracy. But things quickly become more complicated as we must differentiate between democratization and liberalization. How can you tell these two phenomenon apart? Will they look the same in all countries? Next we must make the distinction between democracy and stability. Again, how do we measure these things across borders? Lastly, do we treat our regime types as dichotomous or continuous variables? What about democratically elected leaders who don't actually hold any power and are instead installations of another group (Huntington 1991:11)? These are just a few examples of the many problems that arise when defining democracy and democratization. Huntington goes on to show us just how complicated questions of the concepts of democratization can be, without even addressing the methodological side of the puzzle. As you can imagine, operationalizing these concepts and modelling them in a way that accounts for changes over time, the often dichotomous nature of the dependent variable, the likely country-group similarities, and the possible multicollinearity of such intertwined observations is quite a difficult task. Let's turn to a discussion of the Przerowski et al. paper that faces just such methodological conundrums.

This is another paper that shows us how complex the relationships between democratization and its causal factors can be. The authors and that several independent variables bear weight in explaining democratic endurance but they do so dependent upon different levels of each other. In other words, there are mediating and often collinear relationships between the variables. Like Huntington, Przerowski et al. and that international (exogenous) factors are important to democratic endurance. For example, if there are more democracies in any one particular year, fledgling democracies are more likely to survive (Przerowski et al., 1996:3). This is directly related to Huntington's diffusion hypothesis; if the countries around you are democratic then you probably are too. This is one of the easiest hypotheses to measure and should have broader implications for the democratic peace. The authors also find that the institutions of a nation are very important for democratic endurance. In other words, Przerowski et al. find that democracies are more likely to succeed in countries with parliamentary rather than presidential systems. This is especially interesting, as countries who have previously had military regimes are more likely to adopt presidential structures (Przerowski et al., 1996:6). But this is a time bound discovery, Countries in which monarchy was abolished (France in 1848 and again in 1875, Germany in 1919) and colonies that rebelled against monarchical powers (the United States and Latin America in the late eighteenth and early nineteenth centuries) replaced monarchs with presidents. Countries that emerged from colonial domination after the Second World War typically inherited parliamentarianism from the colonizers" (Przerowski et al., 1996:6).

With Huntington we are able to differentiate between three distinct, time dependent waves of democratization. With

Przerowski et al., we see that time affects the types of institutions a nation chooses as well as the levels of economic development in a nation. These factors help to explain democratic endurance. But this begs the question: will democratization and democratic endurance look the same for nations in the future or are we relegated to studying retrospective cases? This question is not unique to this particular sub-discipline and speaks to the overall generalizability of our theories. As another point, the concepts that are intrinsically linked to the authors' findings are difficult to pinpoint. They point to a pattern of political learning as the basis for structural choices: countries may see that parliamentary systems work best for retaining democracy but they still choose presidential institutions because of past experiences and legacies. This is quite interesting but I'm afraid that it is very difficult to parallel institutional endurance to democratic endurance without more formalized models. When the authors state that, "countries that adopt presidential institutions when they transit to democracy are stuck with them" (Przerowski et al., 1996:7) they are doing so based on an examination of only two countries' experiences. This is a very bold and a very broad statement. Despite their statistically significant models I am inclined to think that this is an area where a larger is required to make any law-like allegations. In sum, the conclusion that economically developed countries who adopt parliamentary systems are the most likely to see enduring democracy is an interesting mix of modernization and democratization theories. But without a larger sample of countries to test, I hesitate to apply of these findings cross-nationally.

The Epstein et al. paper (2006) is a direct response to Pzerowski et al.'s claims in the above mentioned work. Specifically, the authors reference PACL's work stating, an increase in per capita GDP-is not a causal factor in the process of democratization. Rather, they argue, the positive association between income and democracy results from the reduced likelihood of more modern countries sliding back, as it were, into undemocratic forms of government once having (randomly) become democratic (Epstein et al, 2006:441).

The authors reject this wisdom on the grounds that the previous findings were based on a simple dichotomous dependent variable. Here, however, the authors extend the category of regime by including 'partial democracy' in their models. Will this make a difference in the findings? Will the modernization theory still be rejected based on this new regime classification? If so, it teaches an important lesson to the field. A closer and more thorough examination of our dependent variables may lead to better operationalization. The authors employ the complicated methods of PACL including the newly classified regime measures. One question drives them; they want to know what makes countries democratic and what keeps them that way.

While this is an exciting edition to the literature, the issue of identifying partial democracies is also a difficult one. Deciding only to include a third measure and not a fourth or fifth may have further implications. When disaggregating regime type, there is necessarily some arbitrary assignment of the range of polity scores given to this middle classification. The Polity IV data set is employed (-10 to +10 point scale) and the partial regime category is defined as those polities with scores ranging from +1 to +7. Though this is entirely reasonable, it is also safe to say that another group of researchers may and it pertinent to measure partial democracies from-1 to +6, or some other some change of range, thereby altering the results entirely. This is a common issue for political economy and as we saw with the discussion of both Huntington and Przerworski. It can be corrected but that will only come as a result of a large, common body of knowledge with standardized measures. Unfortunately, we are not there yet.

Wisely, Epstein et al. also consider the historical legacies of democratizing nations by using a measure of previous democratization. Two other independent variables are employed in an attempt to make the model as full as possible. These include a log of trade openness, and another variable capturing the "resource curse" hypothesis (which argues that "countries deriving a large share of national income from easily extractable natural resources tend to be undemocratic and unstable) (Epstein et al., 2006:557). The authors run a number of difficult statistical models including tobit analyses, hazard models, duration models and Markov regressions. The results report that PACL initially misinterpreted the standard errors of their Markov model, leading them to report the impact of GDP on democratization as insignificant (Epstein et al., 2006:566). The introduction of the partial democracy measure helped highlight this mistake and the authors believe the inclusion of such a variable should become a standard in the field (Epstein et al., 2006:566). This work should highlight how difficult it is to model the complex concepts of regime and democratization. The amount of work done to simply reappraise one particular element of an author's argument is overwhelming. And, unfortunately, no one but the individual researcher and his or her research design/data are available to back up the findings.

So far what we have seen is a mixture of both complementary and contrasting theories and data. Author Barbara Geddes seeks to rectify some of the deepest contradictions that exist between theoretical approaches to regime type and transition. With Huntington fresh on our minds, it is interesting to note that, " since 1974, identified by Huntington (1991) as the beginning of the "third wave" of democratization, 85 authoritarian regimes have ended" (Geddes, 1999:115). Obviously, then, it is still difficult for us to make generalizations about the processes of democratization and democratic endurance. This is mostly our inability to capture inter-regional differences in the actual processes of democratization (Geddes, 1991: 117). What can we do to x this problem? Geddes attempts to rectify this by providing systematic explanations for the differences between types of authoritarianism. We have attempted to classify different democratic systems at great length but have neglected defining authoritarian regimes because of the conceptual difficulty inherent in doing so. She classifies each regime as personalist, military, single-party, or amalgams of the pure types (Geddes, 1991:121). Though it is another positive step to even try and disaggregate authoritarianism into individual regime characteristics, it also may be bit arbitrary. Other intermediary classes of authoritarianism arguably exist. Making disctinctions is necessary in order to maintain parsimony but we may be making that model vs. real-life tradeoff. It is not necessarily undersirable to do so; the alternative may be the inability to statistically examine real-world phenomena. That certainly wouldn't get us anywhere.

In response, Geddes addresses these classification issues by emphasizing control over access to power and influence rather than by formal institutional characteristics (Geddes,1991:123). This is an excellent decision as it captures the more announced elements of individual regimes rather than the often rigid structures we use for cross national comparisons. And although she must adopt traditional assumptions regarding the nature of power (i.e. leaders want to maintain power and they will please constituents in order to do so), she tweaks them to the unique perspective of autocrats. This mostly includes the latter assumption; we must empirically analyse the different levels of support needed by different autocratic regime types because there does not exist an across the board need to pay attention to constituents' demands (Geddes, 1991:125). Perhaps sometimes leaving institutional explanations for ones that better capture the psychological tendencies of executives is a useful change.

Through a thorough examination of both game theoretic and regression analyses, Geddes is able to conclude that "strong evidence supports the argument that economic development increases the likelihood of democratic politics. Available evidence also supports the claim that authoritarian regimes are more likely to break down during economic crisis, though some forms of authoritarianism are more susceptible to economic downturns than other" (Geddes, 1991:140). Her work helps us understand the different paths democratic transitions may take in light of the specific nature of their authoritarian legacies. The concepts and methodological issues, though existent, are addressed in ways that give us hope. We needn't believe that the contradictory theories of our field can never be rectified.

Regardless of the difficulties comparative political scientists face, the field is of extreme importance and must continue to be pursued in earnest. Each of these authors has contributed a great deal of insight into his or her held and serve as solid examples of the benefits of continued scholarly dialogue. Identifying what triggers the switch to democracy as well as what will make democracy last may lead to a more peaceful and verdant world. In order to do this, we must find a field wide standard for defining our concepts. This may be possible if we continue to collaborate and empirically explore regime transitions and democratization. The qualitative.elements of the field are extremely important as they are able to capture the deep historical, sociological, and often psychological underpinnings of our outcomes. Questions of trust may be answered by including tenets of the broad literature on the subject found more generally in comparative politics. Drawing on the methods this sub-field has learned to employ, we may be able to better incorporate measures of legitimacy into comparative political models and thereby increase their explanatory power. In sum, the theoretical development of regime, regime type, and democratization has advanced greatly since the 1950s and 1960s. However, if we would ultimately like to come to conclusions that are law-like and irrefutable we must keep pushing forward; political science has not yet reached the same scientic standards found in the hard sciences. Yet no matter what the issue, it can be resolved. We must have faith that work in this area will lead us to a better understanding of the world around us.

Social Movements, Revolutions and Civil Society in Comparative Politics

Although the subfield of Comparative Politics claims an extraordinarily broad scope of analysis, certain sociopolitical issues are generally regarded as more intriguing or more important than others. Political revolution is one such issue. In some ways, revolution is the most fundamental research topic for Comparative Politics, for a domestic transition of regime-types typically affects entire populations in more salient ways than any other political phenomenon. Moreover, the particularities of each revolution invite the comparativist to search for patterns of social behaviour. Theoretical constructs from other social sciences have been borrowed, compared, and refined to fit the particular research questions. Classical democratic theories are continually modelled, quantified, tested against one another, and remodelled accordingly. Thousands of case studies and hundreds of cross-national comparisons have been the product of comparativists' dire yearning to answer the question: Why revolution? Indications of progress in solving this timeless riddle are evident in the elucidated parameters and integration of the relevant research. As scholars have cultivated diverse approaches to solving the riddle, a collaboration of their findings has shed light upon certain macro-theoretical deficiencies as well as measurement issues that must be addressed in order to maintain the scientific integrity of comparative solutions.

In his 1965 seminal work on the dilemma between collective action and rational choice, Mancur Olson suggested that "only a separate and 'selective' incentive will stimulate a rational individual in a latent group to act in a group-oriented way" (2). This dilemma became known as "Olson's problem," the "free rider problem," or "the Collective Action Problem" among subsequent researchers, and remains a major logistical obstacle in comparative studies on revolution despite more than four decades of research.

What social forces and/or personal incentives compel individuals to risk their lives in revolutionary attempts? Given that collective action is necessary for any successful revolutionary effort, the inclination to "free ride" must be either dismantled by social "virtues" or perceived as disadvantageous for the personal aspirations of revolutionaries. Most scholars in the comparative subfield have approached the issue from the latter hypothesis, for which individuals' incentives for participating in the revolutionary effort are preferable over the free rider alternative. However, scholars are quick to point out that the appeal of a "free ride" is inextinguishable when the alternative involves risking one's life. This theoretical dilemma has led scholars to overlook the fundamental link between individuals' instigations of revolutionary efforts and the social constructs that help determine the outcomes of such efforts.

Jeffrey Berejikian's 1992 article, "Revolutionary Collective Action and the Agent-Structure Problem," reveals the ongoing theoretical difficulties in accounting for the free rider problem. Berejikian explains how two distinct approaches have come to dominate the comparative research on revolutions: Methodological Structuralism and Methodological Individualism. The former is essentially the application of neo-institutionalism to the study of revolution, as epitomized in Theda Skocpol's States and Social Revolutions (1979). Methodological Individualism, on the other hand, is a rational choice approach exemplified in Samuel Popkin's book, The Rational Peasant (1979). Both approaches fail to draw a link between agents and structures, or, between individuals' motivations to revolt and collective revolutionary efforts. Popkin concentrates exclusively on the agent, while Skocpol's focus is almost entirely on the structure. As a consequence of implicitly denying the other's legitimacy, both methodologies fail to provide solutions to the free rider problem.

At the heart of the agent-structure problem is the fact that agents and structures are ontologically inseparable (at least in the context of this research topic). Social structures are made up of individuals, who are concurrently agents of social activity. Both methodological structuralism and methodological individualism approach revolution by means of conceptual reductionism, focusing on either the agent *or* the structure. The interaction between agents and structures is fundamental for the outcomes of each: individuals affect social structures and vice versa. Agents, structures, and their interactions are all embodied in a single human being, just as they are in a widespread social movement.

Skocpol's focus on structures leads her to extrapolate class preferences across individuals of the particular social class. This leads to some theoretical problems. Although peasants may collectively benefit from a successful revolution, individual peasants are unlikely to affect the outcome of the revolutionary effort. In addition, peasants are likely to benefit from a class revolution even if they were not participants in the revolutionary struggle. Free riding is arguably the most rational option for the individual peasant. Berejikian addresses the contradiction that arises from Skocpol's theoretical gap:

"The assumption of rational maximization as a decision rule on the part of individual peasants does not logically lead to the conclusion Skocpol's analysis assumes, namely, that peasants will collectively act to address their class-defined goals and aspirations. Thus, while the structural hypothesis directs itself to explaining the timing and scope of peasant revolts, the individualist assumptions implicit throughout would seem to argue for a nonevent" (649)

To provide further evidence of the "missing link" in Skocpol's analysis, Berejikian mentions several historical examples for which Skocpol's enumerated structural conditions for revolutions have not led to a peasant revolt. These findings imply that social class interests are best understood as overlapping individual interests. However, comparativists must keep in mind the fact that individuals will always have incentives that are not class-oriented, such as personal safety during a time of war.

Methodological Individualism, as portrayed in Popkin's Rational Peasant, also fails to provide a coherent theoretical explanation for a revolution's surmounting of the free-riding inclination. Popkin's defence of rational choice theory in the context of revolutions relies upon the rationality of maintaining a positive reputation among members of a community. In other words, a peasant will join a revolutionary effort if refusal to join would result in his ostracization among fellow villagers. However, this concept of rational participation in a revolutionary effort is unable to explain the incentives for those individuals who joined the revolution before it became so socially obligatory that refusal incited ostracization. Social pressure to revolt derives from individuals, and its effectiveness depends, in part, on the number of individuals applying the pressure.

Unlike Skocpol, Popkin explicitly confronts the inclination to free ride. His use of social pressure to justify the rationality of revolting, however, implies that structure does indeed affect the agent's incentives. Conversely, according to Berejikian, Popkin frames revolutionary efforts as, "the aggregation of intentional individual actions, rather than permissive structures, accounts for revolution" (650). In contradiction to the Popkin's focus on the individual, social pressure is a structural component that Popkin views as influential upon individual rationality. In addition, Popkin's complementary justifications for rational revolt rely upon the manipulation of private incentives regarding collective goods. For a peasant revolution to gain sufficient support, all peasants must accordingly recognize their direct participation in the revolution as necessary for the final outcome of collective good distribution. Not only is this consensus improbable, it is incomplete, for it emphasizes economic rationality without acknowledgement of the uselessness of economic outcomes for those who lose their lives in the struggle. The real dangers of revolution alter the dynamics of incentive structures typically employed in rational choice models. The free riding tendency is especially appealing (or "rational") when participation in collective revolt sharply increases the likelihood of violent death.

The conceptual obstacles exposed by Berejikian can essentially be described as the effects of utilizing a narrow approach without regard for the insight of alternative approaches. The result of using a narrow approach is a failure to account for the interactions between agents and structures. This failure is revealed in the theoretical deficiencies of both Methodological Structuralism and Methodological Individualism, specifically, in their failure to adequately address the free rider problem in the constructs of their theories. While the structural approach overlooks individuals' incentives to revolt in spite of the likely insignificance and high level of personal risk, the individualist approach is unsuited for explaining the original collective formation of a revolutionary effort, as it fails to address the structural context for which revolution is amenable.

The conceptual obstacle of explaining collective action and the free rider problem has been the topic of much scholarly literature over the past two decades. Despite the vast amount of theory and research intended to model collective action, however, Mark Lichbach concludes that "...most scholars recognize that the marriage between the CA (Collective Action) research program and conflict studies has largely failed" (1994 9). The obstacle that has yet to be surmounted, according to Lichbach, is the formulation of a "useful modification of a solution to the free rider problem" (30). Finding a solution to the free rider problem is not the obstacle, as around two dozen different solutions have been developed and refined in theoretical works. The difficulty lies in modelling a solution for use in testable comparative models. The mere presence of so many different solutions has caused conceptual dilemmas for any research seeking to analyse the causality chain of social occurrences.

Each solution to the "Rebel's Dilemma" is somewhat predictable, as they require strategic planning on behalf of the rebelling parties. This predictability ensures that the regime in power—whose interests must lie in direct opposition to the rebels—will attempt to counteract the strategies (or "solutions") employed by the rebels. Therefore, gauging the usage and effectiveness of such strategies is extremely difficult, especially for empirical and cross-national research. Moreover, the solutions are not mutually exclusive, but rather mutually dependent, in some regards. Lichbach explains: "Any one solution must be an incomplete explanation of the CA... The major difficulty is that each solution presupposes the existence of at least one of the other solutions...

While each type of solution might be necessary to either create, maintain, or transform CA, taken independently, none is sufficient" (23). The vast amount of research addressing the collective action problem has clarified some of the ways in which the dilemma may be overcome in practice, but has not resulted in an applicable component for a comparative research model.

Nonetheless, the findings of the CA research program should not be disregarded in comparative studies of revolution. The first measure that should be taken by comparativists wishing to implement these findings is the acquisition of thorough knowledge about the specific societal circumstances of the revolution or revolutions under analysis. Upon acquiring comprehensive information on the relevant societal conditions, certain solutions are likely to emerge as more accurate depictions of the particular rebels' strategies than others. Researchers can reduce the number of potential solutions in regards to social context and further predict which ones were most influential over the course of particular rebellions. However, they must also keep in mind that "in practice, CA problems are overcome by combinations, mixtures, adaptations, and modifications of the two dozen sets of pure solutions" (Lichbach 27). The social context is crucial in determining which combinations or hybrids of solutions are likely to be effective. In fact, the effectiveness of different solutions relative to the social context is, to Lichbach, more important than the "missing link" between rational choice theory and collective action. He explains:

"...the problematique of the CA research program, as I see it, is to determine the conditions under which a particular CA solution is adopted and the conditions under which a particular solution is effective. In short, we bypass the initial problem of why rational people rebel and never reach the ultimate problem of aggregate levels and outbreaks of rebellion. A midrange approach best elaborates CA ideas"

This approach is not only better suited for integrating CA research into comparative studies, it also provides a more conducive medium for testing CA research in empirical models. Necessary for the advancement of integration between CA research and comparative politics is systematic evidence directed at gauging the specific components of the many CA solutions. This evidence has not been a top priority among the rivalling structural and rational choice approaches, for "...those who have applied CA theories to conflict have focused almost exclusively on the initial problem of whether anyone who is rational will actually participate in protest and rebellion". A more productive course would include an explicit assumption that rational people do rebel, and would aim to identify the most effective strategies used to garner support by providing evidence, rather than mere logic. The evidence is currently trailing far behind the theories regarding conceptual solutions to the free rider problem.

Modelling the solutions to the free rider problem is clearly a difficult task for comparativists. Measurement issues add to the difficulties, as traditional empirical data generally obscures personal motivations and group strategies. Although survey evidence may be appealing for certain research questions on the topic, such data is generally unavailable and unreliable, due to the psychological tendency of misinterpreting personal motives. Any quantitative approach to the issue must be grounded upon intensive qualitative observations of particular societies in order to ensure the validity of the models. Cross-national studies on revolutions are especially prone to yield spurious findings, given the importance of the social context for this particular subject. Such comparisons should not be avoided altogether, however, for the scientific integrity of any comparative research demands the falsifiability of theories. The specific methodological caveats of this research topic are discussed below.

A prime example of the importance of thorough case-level analysis is portrayed in E. Spencer Wellhofer's 2003 article, "Democracy and Fascism." Rather than accept the traditional reasoning for the rise of fascist regimes, Wellhofer examines the particular circumstances surrounding the rise of Italian Fascism in 1919-21. The extensive research on the fall of Weimar Germany and rise of the Third Reich has led to the overgeneralization of conclusions, with the German case as the basis for explanation. For example, the formation of particular interclass alliances was generally accepted as a universal requirement for the rise of a fascist regime, due in large part to the interclass coalitions of the Weimar Republic. Wellhofer's analysis reveals that the rise of Italian Fascism occurred under much different societal circumstances than the rise of the Third Reich. As part of his in-depth analysis of the Italian case, Wellhofer tests the most prevalent theories addressing a link between civil society and democratic sustainability. Exhibiting the importance of cross-approach analysis, Wellhofer includes in his model a test of the rational choice explanation, which is measured according to voting demographics and elections. The format of this piece is intellectually satisfying because it includes the necessary thoroughness of case-specifics as well as tests of multiple alternative explanations. Moreover, the results vindicate the case-level analysis in that they reveal a unique case that does not "fit the mold" of Weimar Germany. Wellhofer is careful not to generalize his conclusions, aside from the encouragement of case-level analysis preceding cross-national research models of revolution.

Wellhofer's article also emphasizes the particularly rich diversity of civil society across nations. For the same reasons that make the topic of revolution unfavorable to cross-national generalizations, civil society is impossible to measure without a keen knowledge of specific societal attributes. Robert Putnam's article, "Bowling Alone," is latent with some of the basic conceptual and measurement problems that scholars should avoid. This article lacks both a research design and a systematic depiction of evidence. Ad hoc conglomerations of evidence are presented to support the author' claims, yet the sources of evidence are never validated as being representative of the implied trends. Moreover, Putnam's reliance on a few very specific indicators of civil society strength (Elks Club membership, Boy Scout membership, etc.) makes his conclusions vulnerable to social transitions over time, which are not necessarily indicative of fluctuations in the strength of civil society. A more inclusive, systematic approach would produce more reliable findings.

Norris et. al.'s article, "Who Demonstrates?" takes such an approach in examining the strength of civil society. The indicator of civic fortitude is participation in demonstrations. This variable's strength is its compatibility with cross-national comparisons and time-series analyses. Norris et. al. do not provide the in-depth case study analysis that most research on civil society demands. The authors' dependent variable, however, depicts interesting trends across nations and other independent variables, such as economic factors. The particular social context certainly affects the extent of participation in demonstrations, and this article helps expose some of these structural and economic influences. As the focus of this article is not civil society per se, demonstration participation may be an imperfect indicator of civic engagement. However, the research design is clearly stated, the evidence used is systematically acquired, and the results certainly cast doubt upon Putnam's contention: that civil society is atrophying in the U.S.

Comparative research on revolution and civil society is as methodologically problematic as it is intellectually appealing. The empirical standards of social science, as expounded by King, Keohane and Verba in Designing Social Inquiry, suggest some especially difficult standards for research on revolutions. These standards are tremendously important, however, and should be followed as closely as possible. One particularly stringent DSI standard that poses unique challenges to revolution research is falsifiability. KKV suggest that "...to make sure that a theory is falsifiable, choose one that is capable of generating as many *observable implications* as possible. This choice will allow more tests of the theory with more data and a greater variety of data, will put the theory at risk of being falsified more times, and will make it possible to collect data so as to build strong evidence for the theory". Since revolutions can only be studied after they occur, and research is highly dependent upon the particular social context, researchers face a particularly difficult challenge in formulating conclusions that can be tested against other cases. Nonetheless, this challenge is necessary for progress to ensue, so creative ways of ensuring falsifiability are beneficial to the subfield. For example, Lichbach explains that CA theories are not considered to be either right or wrong, but rather better or worse than one another for explaining social phenomena. Better theories essentially falsify worse ones because they reveal that the worse theory is not the best one in existence. This process leads the conditioning and refining of theories in a competitive environment.

Unit homogeneity, as described by KKV, is another measurement obstacle for cross-national research on revolutions (KKV 91). The importance of social context inhibits the generalization of findings due to unit heterogeneity. Even case study research must take caution when extrapolating its conclusions across time, as social transformations may alter the effects of different variables within the same nation. Another important issue of consideration is the fact that correlation does not imply causation, despite the appeal of drawing such a link. The mere presence of two dozen solutions to the CA problem reveals that a spurious link can easily go undetected when the variables do not specifically gauge the factors for which they are intended. In addition, KKV's warning: "...do not select observations based on the dependent variable so that the dependent variable is constant," is often violated in revolution research. When the occurrence of a revolution is the topic of inquiry, researchers often compare nations that witnessed a successful revolution against those who did not. Such comparisons should only be made after the selection of cases and testing of hypotheses; otherwise the case selection will be biased.

The vast array of comparative research on revolutions and civil society has led scholars to endorse and enforce the rules of comparative research. These rules are necessary for the integration of research, and thus the advancement of the subfield. While revolution is an especially intriguing topic of comparative politics, it presents particular obstacles that must be addressed in the research design. The high level of interest in the topic of revolution has most likely encouraged the strict enforcement of social science "rules" upon the relevant literature. This is a positive feature of the research topic, albeit an additional obstacle for scholars to surmount.

The Complex Issues of Comparative Political Economy

What role do economics play in politics and vice versa? To what extent are these two fields dependent upon one another? Are conclusions about political economy generalizable? The study of comparative political economy must account for these difficult puzzles in every theoretical approach, research design, and empirical analysis. Each time a researcher defines her concepts or operationalizes his variables a multitude of complex, causal factors must be included. Unfortunately, the exact nature of the relationships between these variables is hardly ever known. It follows that regardless of the individual phenomenon under study, there are common issues that all of the political economic papers, the sub-discipline generally, and the greater comparative field must face together. Misspecifications, arbitrary classifications, and vague definitions are often not about a particular researcher's shortcomings. Instead, it is regularly the result of trying to make cross-national comparisons in the face of multiple cultural, institutional, and sociological contexts. In other words, the definitions of concepts are often times contextually dependent. Historical factors create unique industrialization patterns that must be factored into the current national contexts. Furthermore, the fact that cultures matter is extraordinarily difficult to model. How does one empirically measure or express cultural tenets? This, along with other abstract concepts such as partisan ideology or individual policy preference, are integral to studying comparative political economy.

Unfortunately, conceptual issues alone do not plague the literature. Because of our complex concepts and theories, our research may be limited to small studies and specific time spans. In addition, it is difficult to create parsimonious models that do not involve multicollinearity. This is truly an obstacle to generalization. It remains that much of the work in political economy is heavily dependent on (historical) case studies; this qualitative area is an island left within a largely empirical field. Zuckerman (1997) may be right. Perhaps to rectify the lack of appropriate methodologies for our research we must shift from our focus on causal relationships to a search for specific, process mechanisms. Currently, the body of literature on comparative political economy holds both promise and dismay. Will we ever answers to our questions?

David Cameron, a foremost researcher in the field, presents a comparative analysis of public welfare systems in his 1978 piece The Expansion of the Public Economy. Though dated, this piece stands as a solid example of the comparative potential of political economy. Specifically, he examines what gives rise to the welfare state in advanced, industrialized nations. His empirical examinations result in the conclusion that political and institutional theories best work to explain the existence of an extensive welfare state. Yet despite his efforts and contributions, Cameron also falls prey to conceptual and methodological difficulties. For instance, regarding the political explanations Cameron states that, two aspects of politics may influence the magnitude of expansion of the public economy: (1) the effect of electoral competition in "bidding up" the scope of expenditure programs; and (2) the effect of variations in the partisan composition, and presumably the ideological preferences, of government (Cameron, 1978:1246). Although a mostly institutional paper, both of these categories of political explanation strike me as variants of sociological approaches. There are obvious drawbacks in attempting to explain economic and political outcomes this way. The largest being that the complications caused by sociological approaches tend to create more questions than provide answers; attempting to compare cases cross-nationally from a sociological vantage point is more difficult than comparing institutions.

Furthermore, properly measuring these concepts cross-nationally may be impossible, as cultural preferences often arise from endogenous and almost infinite mechanisms. Setting a continuous range of 'ideological preferences' to be used in comparisons would be arbitrary at best. Though Cameron mentions the importance of these tenets, he does not explicitly propose a way to empirically address their unwieldiness. It seems that he operationalized ideological preferences by measuring the percentage of parties in the government's electoral base (Social Democratic or Labor parties)(Cameron, 1978:1254). These parties only truly apply to a handful of Western European countries. Some of these are even regionally grouped. Are the preferences of these two parties constant across borders? Can we draw generalizable conclusions from the use of this variable? Furthermore, how does Cameron capture the amount of 'bidding up' going on? An inclusion of more major party labels or a measure of total policy earmarks given to certain patronage groups could be better indicators of these issues. Perhaps these problems are simply a function of the limited amount of time and number of cases.

Regardless, Cameron's most important ending is certainly institutional in nature. The author posits, the best explanation of why public authorities in some nations have expanded their control over the appropriation and allocation of resources while those in other nations have not is international in character. Among the nations considered here, the expansion of the public economy was most closely associated with a relatively high exposure to, and dependence upon, external producers and consumers" (Cameron, 1978:1255).

In other words, the amount of trade dependence works best to explain the existence of the welfare state. This explanation, called the openness of the economy, "rests on the following governmental structures: (1) the formal relationship among levels of government within a nation-in particular, the existence of multiple, independent centres of public authority; and (2) the degree of fiscal centralization" (Cameron, 1978:1248). But he also states, within his political explanation, that voters are likely to provide short-term support for candidates when they see a surge in real income. Politicians participate in a 'political business cycle' pumping public funds into the economy just before an election (Cameron, 1978:1247). It is difficult for me to understand how this is not an institutional explanation. Though the specific structures of national electoral cycles are not mentioned, electoral systems, in my mind, are institutions. Separating these two concepts to be measured separately may present problems. Perhaps it is Cameron's political explanations that are actually driving the amount of 'trade openness' in a country. Is one measure simply a proxy of the other? A clarification of the exact definition of institutions used may provide more insight into this potential problem. Maybe more importantly, with a study focused only on advanced, industrial nations will we ever be able to compare these findings meaningfully to third world or otherwise underdeveloped nations? Basing our theories on outcomes from such similar nations might exclude the ability to explain across all regions and nation types. Only further tests will reveal the true efficacy of these explanations.

If Cameron's findings are correct, we might expect to find the so-called international explanations working to analyse the size and presence of the welfare state in most, if not all, of our advanced, industrialized nations. However, Lange et al. (1991) place a different emphasis on the existence of trade interdependence. Specifically they ask: has increased trade interdependence resulted in a decrease in the impact a political party may have on domestic economies? If Leftist parties are indeed associated with higher levels of welfare spending, will welfare programs begin to decrease as left and right ideals converge in a new political economic context? Here the authors argue that increased trade interdependence has not led to the convergence of left and right ideologies (Lange et al, 1991:541). Instead, endogenous, as opposed to exogenous, explanations may account for the 'state' of the welfare state. This plays on a huge body of historical literature associated with the role and size of political parties in Western Europe, especially Scandinavia. The presence of Leftist parties has often told us much about the political and economic systems of a particular country. In our present-day study of political economy, however, it is right for researchers to question how useful these older practices may be. These authors take on this task.

To begin Lange et al. nd that, "the results suggest that while economic interdependence had a marked impact on the macroeconomic strategies in all of the advanced industrial democracies, the effects of differences in the degree of openness between individual countries have been much smaller" (Lange et al., 1991:554). In other words, economic interdependence may be important but trade openness does not markedly change a nation's policies. This may indicate that regardless of the domestic party situation, measures of interdependence will be running the show. Unfortunately the authors also tell us that, "the effects of interdependence may be more a function of financial integration than trade openness, but it is extremely difficult to test this proposition empirically" (Lange et al., 1991:555). Are the concepts the authors wish to test too difficult to accurately capture in a model? From a methodological standpoint, the results they obtain are rather statistically weak. This, like Cameron's piece may be a nod to a very small (15 countries) or of the short time period under observation (1960-1987). For example, a discussion of current Leftist corporatist states highlights the existence of multiple policy preferences in the face of rather advanced trade interdependence. However, there are only several viable corporatist states and they mostly exist in one particular European region, sharing similar histories and economies. I am inclined to think that perhaps our authors are inadvertently testing on the dependent variable: the case selection reflects what they hope to find. These conclusions and examples illustrate the point that it is very difficult to empirically evaluate our political economic concepts. Yet, this should not, and does not, stop the field from grinding forward.

Another sticking point highlights the difficulty of generalizing political economic theories. The authors, "used the trade openness of national political economies as a measure of the degree of their vulnerability to changes in the global economy" (Lange et al., 1991:553). Lange et al. do not go on to provide a more thorough explanation as to how this variable was operationalized. Not all nations are going to respond in the same way to the same levels of trade openness.

I would think that Great Britain might have more trade openness than France but that France's traditionally regional, high-end product production model would leave them more vulnerable in the face of trade openness than Britain. My apologies if I am missing a more announced or implicit argument regarding the use of this variable, but it seems, again, a bit difficult to apply cross-nationally. Without an historic understanding of the trade systems of the nation in question, the same variable may have very different implications for different regions. The conclusion that the left still exists and that there has not been total partisan preference convergence in the face of globalization and trade interdependence is certainly intuitive. The authors leave us with, In sum, these results conform well with the hypothesized partisan separation over government supply-side strategies for enhancing competitiveness and flexible adjustment in world markets. The stronger the combined political and organizational power of labor, the more extensive were government interventions with respect not only to directly redistributive measures and labor market policies but also to industrial and investment strategies" (Lange et al, 1991:562)

In sum, this work, again, falls prey to larger conceptual and methodological issues. Some of the operationalized variables do not seem to be captured with any degree of specificity. It is also another example of research that must rely only on advanced, industrialized societies. Just like Cameron, the models are attempting to capture particular, ideological stances that may actually be the product of a region's culture rather than its institutions. In the end the best the authors can over is a cautionary statement against ruling out viable Leftist party preferences and impacts; institutions cannot be expected to expel the differences between left and right ideologies.

Hopefully the above discussion of work by Cameron and Lange et al. has exemplified some of the difficulties associated with applying concepts and methods to multiple national contexts. Let's not forget that there are also triumphs to be had. Paul Pierson's work, The New Politics of the Welfare State shares in the struggles of the field but also provides a great deal of insight on this topic. As progress moves forward, it makes sense that we would expect work in political economy to move toward welfare program retrenchment as domestic and international issues shift to deal with burgeoning populations and globalization. Yet this is not necessarily true. What accounts for the maintenance, and sometimes expansion, of social welfare programs? A critical link to understanding the welfare state and potential policy retrenchment lies in Pierson's distinction between the processes that create welfare policy and those that take these policies away. This is an excellent place for subsequent researchers to begin empirically evaluating both processes as separate from one another. However, Pierson also mentions the difference between welfare policies being 'popular' when enacted and being 'unpopular' when repealed. Is this necessarily always the case? Can we build a measure of popularity/unpopularity regarding policy initiation/ retrenchment into our models or is this immeasurable? Collecting survey data on such issues may suffice, but we should take time to address this issue before moving on with future modelling.

Importantly, Pierson's findings include explanations found in both of the last two papers: "A combination of economic changes, political shifts to the right, and rising costs associated with maturing welfare states has provoked growing calls for retrenchment" (Pierson, 1996:145). But as we see with his inclusion of four country-level cases studies, though theoretically feasible, this is not the reality of the modern welfare state. Instead, we see moderate reforms or in some cases social program expansion. As usual, I must ask, is there something inherent in each of these countries, though he does pair most-like cases together for comparison, that allows us to explain the popular ideological distaste for retrenchment? Could we make this into a viable quantitative paper or are Pierson's institutional explanations rooted too deeply in culture and history? Perhaps the lesson we can take away from this initial evaluation is that neither quantitative nor qualitative explanations suffice alone. Perhaps KKV is right: we must combine these logically connected approaches to produce meaningful causal theories.

Another group of authors, Stephens et al. (1993), do not shy away from the issues plaguing their field. They almost immediately state that there are significant problems with the methodologies, conceptualizations, and operationalizations among the sub discipline of comparative political economy. I couldn't have said it better myself! They also quickly point out that there is a large degree of collinearity between commonly employed explanatory variables (Stephens et al., 1993:712). The remedy: using the largest possible and conducting studies on pooled data over time. Furthermore, bad independent variables, the authors feel, should be deleted based on statistical, substantive, and theoretical criteria (1993:716). While a worthwhile recommendation, we also must remember that the omission of explanatory variables can be risky territory. Though continued disagreements in the sub-discipline should be addressed in order to create a better body of knowledge, we need to be quite conservative in our omissions as they may lead to misspecication. Mostly, the authors seem to champion the cause for more parsimonious and better models.

But for all of the talk about these great concepts, the authors still fall victim to conceptual and methodological issues. Here, we will be examining our dependent variable, existence of the welfare state, across several party types and mitigating structural setups. "A single, carefully constructed measure is far preferable to a composite index of convenient but inappropriate indicators," (Stephens et al., 1993:716). This is absolutely true but who is to solve the issue of which indicators are inappropriate and which are not? What about collapsing measures into a single variable to serve as a proxy? Is this allowable? The authors go on to present a number of very complex hypotheses that focus on institutional factors regarding power sharing and parties. They include three separate indexes as their dependent variables using, as always, advanced, industrialized nations with a small and a constricted time period (post WWII). Could it be the time period that is a effecting the results? Perhaps expanding the model to include cases prior to WWII would provide us with more insight? Their findings show that the contrast between Christian Democracy and Social Democratic parties provide strong confirmation for the refinements of the political class-struggle argument (Stephens et al., 1993:734). But the constitutional structure is also significance all three main explanations of welfare state emergence. Though this paper is not perfect, it is perhaps proof that facing the problems of comparing cross-nationally by empirically addressing common conceptual and methodological issues can increase the explanatory power of our models and find connections amongst previously competing theories.

Unfortunately, I am constrained here by both space and time. Yet it should be obvious that comparative political economy remains one of the most complex sub-disciplines of comparative political science. Its historical legacy, combined with time and sample size limitations calls for creative approaches to some of its biggest puzzles.

All of the authors discussed above have significantly contributed to the literature in this field by employing the critical thinking skills expected of every liberal arts researcher. Continued empirical modelling along with solid theoretic development is perhaps the best prescription for any methodological or conceptual ills that plague the literature. Whether or not there will ever be one, single consensus in this area remains to be seen. I am inclined to believe that the multiple explanations employed here are not mutually exclusive but neither can they be compressed into some 'one-size-fits-all' package. The unique face of every nation will not allow for this. However, we can continue to expand our body of knowledge and examine our quantitative and qualitative work for signs of patterns and improvement.

Political Economy

Political economy originally was the term for studying production, buying and selling, and their relations with law, custom, and government. *Political economy* originated in moral philosophy. It developed in the 18th century as the study of the economies of states—*polities,* hence *political* economy.

In late nineteenth century, the term "political economy" was generally replaced by the term economics, used by those seeking to place the study of economy upon mathematical and axiomatic bases, rather than the structural relationships of production and consumption (cf. marginalism, Alfred Marshall).

History of the Term

Originally, *political economy* meant the study of the conditions under which production or consumption within limited parameters was organized in the nation-states. The phrase *économie politique* first appeared in France in 1615 with the well known book by Antoine de Montchrétien: *Traité de l'economie politique*. French physiocrats, Adam Smith, David Ricardo and Karl Marx were some of the exponents of political economy.

In 1805, Thomas Malthus became England's first professor of political economy, at the East India Company College, Haileybury, Hertfordshire. The world's first professorship in political economy was established in 1763 at the University of Vienna, Austria; Joseph von Sonnenfels was the first tenured professor.

In the United States, political economy first was taught at the College of William and Mary; in 1784 Adam Smith's *Wealth of Nations* was a required textbook.

Glasgow University, where Smith was Professor of Logic and Moral Philosophy, changed the name of its Department of Political Economy to the Department of Economics (ostensibly to avoid confusing prospective undergraduates) in academic year 1997–1998, making the class of 1998 the last to be graduated with a Scottish Master of Arts degree in Political Economy.

Current Approaches to Political Economy

Contemporarily, *political economy* refers to different, but related, approaches to studying economic and political behaviours, ranging from the combining of economics with other fields, to the using of different, fundamental assumptions that challenge orthodox economic assumptions:

- *Political economy* most commonly refers to interdisciplinary studies drawing upon economics, law, and political science in explaining how political institutions, the political environment, and the economic system—capitalist, socialist, mixed—influence each other. When narrowly construed, it refers to applied topics in economics implicating public policy, such as monopoly, market protection, government fiscal policy, and rent seeking.

- Historians have employed *political economy* to explore the ways in the past that persons and groups with common economic interests have used politics to effect changes beneficial to their interests.
- "International political economy" (IPE) is an interdisciplinary field comprising approaches to international trade and finance, and state policies affecting international trade, i.e. monetary and fiscal policies. In the U.S., these approaches are associated with the journal *International Organization*, which, in the 1970s, became the leading journal of international political economy under the editorship of Robert Keohane, Peter J. Katzenstein, and Stephen Krasner. They are also associated with the journal *The Review of International Political Economy*. There also is a more critical school of IPE, inspired by Karl Polanyi's work; two major figures are Susan Strange and Robert W. Cox.
- Economists and political scientists often associate the term with approaches using rational choice assumptions, especially game theory, in explaining phenomena beyond economics' standard remit, in which context the term "positive political economy" is common.
- Anthropologists, sociologists, and geographers, use *political economy* in referring to the neo-Marxian approaches to development and underdevelopment postulated by André Gunder Frank and Immanuel Wallerstein.
- New political economy students treat economic ideologies as the phenomenon to explain, per the traditions of Marxian political economy. Thus, Charles S. Maier suggests that a political economy approach: *interrogates economic doctrines to disclose their sociological and political premises....in sum, [it] regards economic ideas and behaviour not as frameworks for analysis, but as beliefs and actions that must themselves be explained*. This approach informs Andrew Gamble's *The Free Economy and the Strong State* (Palgrave Macmillan, 1988), and Colin Hay's *The Political Economy of New Labour* (Manchester University Press, 1999). It also informs much

work published in *New Political Economy* an international journal founded by Sheffield University scholars in 1996.

Disciplines related to Political Economy

Because political economy is not a unified discipline, there are studies using the term that overlap in subject matter, but have radically different perspectives:

- Sociology studies the effects of persons' involvement in society as members of groups, and how that changes their ability to function. Many sociologists start from a perspective of production-determining relation from Karl Marx.
- Political Science focuses on the interaction between institutions and human behaviour, the way in which the former shapes choices and how the latter change institutional frameworks. Along with economics, it has made the best works in the field by authors like Shepsle, Ostrom, Ordeshook, among others.
- Anthropology studies political economy by studying the relationship between the world capitalist system and local cultures.
- Psychology is the fulcrum on which political economy exerts its force in studying decision-making (not only in prices), but as the field of study whose assumptions model political economy.
- History documents change, using it to argue political economy; historical works have political economy as the narrative's frame.
- Economics focuses on markets by leaving the political—governments, states, legal frameworks—as givens. Economics dropped the adjective *political* in the 19th century, but works backwards, by describing "The Ideal Market", urging governments to formulate policy and law to approach said ideal. Economists and political economists often disagree on what is preeminent in developing production, market, and political structure theories.
- Law concerns the creation of policy and its mediation via political actions that have specific results, it deals with

political economy as political capital and as social infrastructure—and the sociological results of one society upon another.

- Human Geography is concerned with politico-economic processes, emphasizing space and environment.
- Ecology deals with political economy, because human activity has the greatest effect upon the environment, its central concern being the environment's suitability for human activity. The ecological effects of economic activity spur research upon changing market economy incentives.
- International Relations often uses political economy to study political and economic development.
- Cultural Studies social class, production, labor, race, gender, and sex.
- Communications examines the institutional aspects of media and telecommunication systems, with particular attention to the historical relationships between owners, labor, consumers, advertisers, and the state.

Comparative Political Analysis

Three approaches have dominated the study of comparative politics: institutional, rational choice and political culture approaches. In this essay I will be addressing a series of question and topics within each literature—seminal works, assumptions, strengths and weaknesses, and applied areas of research.

Institutional Approach

The study of institutions has been central not only to the field of comparative politics, but to the political science field as a whole. Many authors have argued that institutions have shaped political behaviour and social change. These authors have taken an "institutionalist" approach which treat institutions as independent variables.

In the last twenty-five years the field of comparative politics has experienced the emergence of the "new institutionalism," which developed in reaction to the behavioural perspectives that exercise a significant influence on the field during the 1960s and 1970s. The new institutionalism body can be divided into three analytical approaches: historical institutionalism, rational choice institutionalism, and sociological institutionalism. These three theoretical islands developed independently from each other. I will provide a review of the three analytical approaches.

Historical Institutionalism

This approach developed in response to group theories of politics and structural-functionalism (Hall and Taylor 1996). Historical institutionalists sought to expand both approaches by "borrowing" existent ideas and adding new assumptions to them.

From group theory, historical institutionalists borrowed the assumption that conflict among rival groups for resources is at the heart of politics (Hall and Taylor 1996). From the structural-functionalists, historical institutionalists borrowed the assumption that the state is made up of interacting parts.

The big contributors to this approach are Steinmo and Thelen. Steinmo and Thelen see institutions as a constraint upon individuals and their choices (Koelble 1995). They argue that institutions are a determinant of choices and preferences. Steinmo and Thelen critique the rational choice approach for viewing institutions as a constraint upon individuals but not as determinants of choice.

Historical institutionalists define institutions as the "formal or informal procedures, routines, norms and conventions embedded in the organizational structure of the polity or political economy" (Hall and Taylor 1996). When it comes to the one of the big questions of institutional analysis, how institutions affect the behaviour of individuals, historical institutionalists use two approaches – the calculus and the cultural approaches.

The calculus approach emphasizes the aspects of human behaviour that are based on strategic calculation – individuals seek to maximize their goals given by their preference and they act strategically in the pursuit of those goals (Hall and Taylor 1996). It is important to note that preferences and goals are exogenously to the analysis. Institutions affect human behaviour mainly by providing actors decreasing the level of uncertainty about the behaviour of other actors by providing information, rules and norms.

The cultural approach argues that human behaviour is not fully strategic; rather it is bounded by an individual's worldview. This approach does not see individuals as utility maximizers, but as "satisficers" whose actions are dependent on context rather than strategic calculation (Hall and Taylor 1996). Also, institutions provide moral or cognitive templates for interpretation which in turn affect the identities, self-images, and preferences of individuals.

Historical institutionalists are attentive to the relationship between institutions and ideas. They emphasize the importance of institutions but they do not posit institutions as the only causal force in politics; other factors play a role such as socioeconomic development and diffusion of ideas. Some of the weaknesses of this approach is that it does not incorporate some aspects of individual decision making to its analysis. Some of the strengths of this approach include its emphasis on the effect of political struggle on institutional outcomes and how institutional outcomes then affect political struggles. This approach should be more useful to the analysis of institutional development and policymaking (Koelble 1995).

Rational Choice Institutionalism

The rational choice institutionalism was born out of the study of American congressional behaviour (Hall and Taylor 1996). These scholars were trying to explain why congressional outcomes were considerably stable and they decided to look at institutions. They found that institutions of the Congress lowered transactions costs among legislators making the passage of legislation stable.

Some of the big names of this approach are North, Levi and Rothstein. North and Levi respond to the historical institutionalists and sociological institutionalist's view that individuals act upon bounded rationality. They argue that if individuals do not realize their interest, it is because they do not have complete information and are subject to transaction costs (Koelble 1995).

Rational choice institutionalists assume that individuals have a fixed set of preferences and they behave in manner that maximizes the attainment of these preferences. One of the unique assumptions of rational choice institutionalists see politics as a series of collective action problems (Hall and Taylor 1996). Individuals are constraint to take actions in the absence of institutional arrangements that pose guarantees complementary behaviour of other individuals.

Some of the weaknesses of the rational choice institutionalism include: (a)rational choice institutionalists are unable to provide an adequate predictive theory of action since it does not specifies how preferences come about and why they vary from individual to individual; (b) sociological institutionalists argue that the rational choice institutionalists view that individuals create institutions in order to further their goals is incorrect because individuals cannot choose among institutions and rules; (c) rational choice institutionalism ignores social structure. The rational choice institutionalist approach ought to be more useful for the analysis of interactions between organizations and individuals (Koelble 1995).

Sociological Institutionalism

This approach emerged from organizational theory. These scholars wanted to challenge the view that some parts of the world reflect a formal rationality while some others reflect culture. They argued that the "institutional forms and procedures used by modern organizations were not adopted simply because they were most efficient for the task at hand ... instead... these forms and procedures should be seen as culturally specific practices" (Hall and Taylor 1996).

Sociological institutionalists define institutions more broadly than any other approach. Powell and DiMaggio define institutions not just as "rules, procedures, organizational standards, and governance structures, but also as conventions and customs" (Koelble 1995).

They go further and make the assumption that institutions define "rational actors." When it comes to the relationship between individuals and institutions, scholars use the cultural approach to explain outcomes. They argue that institutions affect behaviour of individuals by socializing individuals into particular institutional roles and individuals consequently internalize norms related to these roles.

One of the weaknesses of this approach is that it does not explain how institutions originate. Another weakness is the operationalization of culture. Some of the strengths of this approach are: (a) it is able to explain how institutions affect individuals' preferences or identities; (b) it provides an explanation how actors choose strategies from culturally-specific repertoires (Hall and Taylor 1995).

Rational Choice Approach

The rational choice approach derives from the neoclassical economic model and it has been applied to a variety of subfields of political science including interest groups and bureaucracy, formation of coalition in government, electoral politics and so forth.

Many scholars have contributed to the rational choice approach. Mancur Olson was one of these scholars. In his The Logic of Collective Action (1965), Olson emphasizes strategic interaction and the individual decision making process. Olson argues that "rational, self-interested individuals will not act to achieve their common of group interests" (1965:2). Olson explained that rational individuals will not act to achieve a common goal because he knows that his efforts will not have an effect on the situation, and he will be able to enjoy any improvement brought about by the other actors whether or not he supports the organization.

Members of a group have a common goal but they have no common interest in paying the costs of providing that collective good. These assumptions led scholars to investigate conditions under which individuals will come together in an effort to influence government or each other (Levi 1997). Olson also brought up to light the discussion of the fee rider problem which called into question the assumption that interests are automatically translated into organization.

Douglas North is another contributor to the rational choice approach. North emphasis on transaction cost theory, economic institutionalism, and the role of relative bargaining power have stimulated investigation of the variation in state action and state outcomes.

The model of rational choice conceives individuals as goal-oriented actors who act to pursue the best available outcome. This approach is methodologically individualist and purposeful action (Kim 1997) but it also focuses on the aggregation of individual choices. Thus all group choice ultimately is explained by individual choice.

One of the core assumptions of the rational choice theory is that individuals are rational actors. This assumption is the subject of much criticism. There is little agreement on what it means to be rational. Levi suggests that the most useful assumption of rationality for the field of comparative politics research is that "individuals act consistently in relation to their preferences" (1997:24).

Another assumption is that individuals act strategically in order to attain their goals. Here an important evaluation or consideration of behaviour of other relevant actors takes place before decision-making process. In order to make decisions, a strategic player should have expectations about other players. Another key assumption regards the forms of constraints on human behaviour. Constraints come in two major forms. First is scarcity of resources. An individual that wants to spend his vacation time in Hawaii, cannot realize his objective if he does not have the capital to afford the trip. Another source of constraint is institutional or organizational. Institutions shape individual choices in order to produce equilibrium outcomes. On the other hand, some may also argue that institutions may facilitate action.

According to Margaret Levi, the strengths of the rational choice approach includes: (a) it has the capacity to produce testable theory; (b) its ability to make sense of a correlation or a set of events by providing a story that indentifies the causal mechanisms linking independent and dependent variables; (c) its universalism that allows us to make generalization that are applicable to cases beyond those cases of immediate investigation.

Among the weaknesses of this approach are: (a) the approach seems inadequately sensitive to the historical, political, and cultural contexts (Levi 1997). As a matter of fact, political culture scholars argue that the conceptual weakness of rational choice theory can be corrected through the use of political cultures; political culture when conceptually clear and empirically defined is able to specify the whole range of human objectives or goals (Lane 1992).

Political Cultural Approach

Political culture has been used a conceptual umbrella that wraps around values, perceptions and beliefs, dealing with every political phenomena. Political culture emerged out of the need, emphasized especially by Almond, to deepening and broadening the scope of political explanation. The goal of political culture was to explain the diversity among and continuity within states (Lane 1992). The origins of the modern political and cultural analysis can be related to the Political Culture and Political Development (Pye and Verba 1965). Political culture has also adopted a psychologist or individualist approach, an example is The Civic Culture by Almond and Verba (1963).

The political culture approach, like the other approaches, faces conceptual problems. Scholars within have not reached a compromise in defining "culture." In Political Culture and Political Preferences, David Latin criticizes Wildvsky for his definition of culture. Wildavsky defines culture as "shared values legitimating social practices" (Latin 1988:499). Latin argues that by focusing only on shared values, Wildavsky misses the point that people with strongly opposed views can share a culture and people with strongly similar views may come from different cultures. Latin proposes that we should see culture as not as values that are upheld but rather as "point of concern" (idea presented initially by Thomas Metzger). Latin argues that to share a culture means to share a religion, language, or history. As one can assume, if the difficulties in reaching a common definition of culture are great, its operationalization is even greater.

Ronald Inglehart is one of the major contributors to the political culture approach. Inglehart tries to operationalize culture through levels of what he calls "civic culture." Civic culture refers to a coherent syndrome of personal life satisfaction, political satisfaction, interpersonal trust, and support for existing social order. In his The Renaissance of Political Culture, Inglehart hypothesized that societies that ranked high on this syndrome are much likelier to be stable democracies than those that ranked low.

He also argues that publics of different societies are characterized by durable cultural orientations that have major political and economic consequences which are closely linked to the viability of democracy (Inglehart 1988). He finds that "wealthier nations and those with highly developed tertiary sectors are most likely to be long-established democracies, and the publics of these societies tend to show 'civic' political culture, have less materialist values priorities" (1226).

In our unit we saw the political culture approach been applied to explain levels of democracy and postmaterialism attitudes. Edward Muller and Mitchell Seligson develop a model that allows them to make inferences about the possibility of unidirectional or reciprocal causation between civic culture attitudes and democracy. They find that most civic culture attitudes do not have any impact on changes in levels of democracy.

Their findings contrast with the assumptions made by Almond and Verba (1963) and later Inglehart, as discussed earlier, that the viability of democratic institutions is affected by individual attitudes and beliefs. Raymond Duch and Michaell Taylor in their Postmaterialism and the Economic Condition test the notion that early economic experiences have a lasting effect on postmaterialism values as proposed by Inglehart. And their findings suggest that education and economic conditions at the time of the survey are much more relevant explanations for variations in the postmaterialist measure.

Some of the weaknesses of this approach are: (a) the conceptualization and operationalization, as discussed earlier; (b) the inability to draw a distinction between subcultures and the overall political culture; (c) the inability to bridge the inferences made on the individual level to the state or system level. In my opinion the greatest strength of this approach is its potential to correct the rational choice theory conceptual flaw of not being able to identify the range of human goals. Marc Howard Ross is an advocate of the political culture approach and he points out to two features of culture relevant to comparative politics (Lichbach and Zuckerman 1997). First, people use culture to define meaning; second culture is the foundation of social and political identity which affects individual behaviour.

Conclusion

These three discussed approaches have dominated the field of comparative politics. They all have the same aim, explain social phenomena – they just have different assumptions and use different methods.

I think that these three approaches are more useful if seen as complimentary rather than as antagonistic. As Zuckerman and Lichbach indicate, no approach displays rigid and uniform orthodoxy; and they share an ontological and epistemological symmetry. (1997). In order to improve theory in our field we should embrace creative confrontations and try to absurd the best out of each school of thought.

2

Classification of Political System

Democratic or Authoritarian?

"If the constitution of a state is democratic, then every exceptional negation of democratic principles, every exercise of state power independent of the approval of the majority, can be called dictatorship."-Carl Schmitt, *The Crisis of Parliamentary Democracy*

Why do countries change their governments from authoritarian to democratic, and vice versa? This question is one of the most essential in comparative political science, but its broad scope poses many problems for scholars. Defining regime-types and classifying national governments accordingly has proven to be a major obstacle for scholars. The relevant literature has developed a unique approach, but has yet to exhibit theoretical consistency. National-level variables—such as the extent of government, the role of the elected government in overall governance, and national wealth—are unduly assessed either theoretically or empirically.

Case-studies are prevalent in the literature. Large N quantitative studies are inherently problematic in one way or another, given the rich diversity of political institutions and economic environments across nations. As evident in Geddes' work, much of the empirical work lacks unifying statistical models and relies on single variable statistics and analyses.

Perhaps a combination of qualitative and quantitative analysis is the only reasonable approach to this research question. Prior to determining the right approach, however, the qualitative components of the dependent variable must be clearly defined. Unfortunately, conceptual ambiguity remains prevalent in the literature.

Dichotomous and trichotomous measures of regime-types are inherently broad generalizations. Even these categories, however, lack clear definitions. "Democracy," according to the qualitative analyses in each of the readings, describes *liberal* democracies. A regime that does not meet the standards of democracy is described as "authoritarian," though it may or may not pass the "democracy tests" of the models. Huntington discusses the converse circumstance of a democratic regime, "If those democratic decision makers become, however, simply a façade for the exercise of much greater power by a non-democratically chosen group, then clearly that political system is not democratic", but devotes just one sentence to the most illiberal feature that has, at times, arisen in "free and fair" democracies: "Implicit in the concept of democracy, however, are limitations on power". I perceive the author's conception of these limitations to be in line with the concept of liberalism, or the limitations of government. However, these "limitations" are neither defined nor accounted for in any of the authors' classifications.

Moreover, the authors fail to recognize that their conception of democracy is necessarily that of liberal democracy. "...Popular election of the top decision makers" essentially serves as the requirement for democratic rule in the empirical models (Huntington 9). However, such electoral systems have, at times, produced authoritarian democratic regimes. Democracy—as defined by the authors—and authoritarianism are not mutually exclusive; liberal democracy and authoritarianism are. False classifications are likely if liberalism is not taken into account in the classification process, which seems to be the case for all of this week's literature. A country that meets the minimum criteria for the "democracy" category is automatically categorized as a democracy. There is no positive screening for authoritarian elements, for the authors assume (empirically, but not conceptually) that the minimum criteria for the democracy category is enough to ensure that no government that could meet these standards could ever be considered an authoritarian regime. The "façade" is undetectable.

Both qualitative and quantitative aspects of the authors' approaches are theoretically ambiguous. One example is Huntington's "façade " scenario, which is too essential to the "procedural" conception of democracy to shrug off with a single paragraph, as the authors do. How is one to determine what qualities denote a "the exercise of much greater power?" concealed behind the facades?

Contemporary Marxists make a persuasive argument that according to the authors' descriptions, the United States' government is not a democracy, but a façade. A "much greater power" than that of the elected government may reasonably be considered the control of the monetary system (in a system of fiat currency, as we have today). Are the IMF, the World Bank, or the Federal Reserve "democratically chosen"? Of course not. Nor are the Supreme Court, the UN, NAFTA, NATO, the EU, etc. Yet all of these governing bodies play central roles in the lives of civilians. How are we to define "power" and "democratically chosen groups? The literature makes no apparent effort to address these legitimate concerns while classifying national governments.

On the contrary, Libertarians may reasonably argue that the authors' descriptions of regime-types would imply that the United States government is not a democracy because it exceeds the "limitations on power," in the sense that it violates the principles of classical liberalism, rather than being not powerful enough, as the Marxists suggest.

Aside from conceptual ambiguities, the large N empirical analyses suffer from overgeneralization. For example, Epstein et al find that, "higher incomes per capita significantly increased the likelihood of democratic regimes, both by enhancing the consolidation of existing democracies and by promoting transitions from authoritarian to democratic systems". However, this phenomenon is probably underrepresented by the data. The economic variables are measured incorrectly by Epstein et al and Geddes, since the value of national currencies does not reflect the real worth of the unit of currency for which the values are associated. Inflation cannot be accounted for among different countries by means of an aggregate value. This way of measurement implies that the "modernization" process has no effect on the prices of goods relative to the national currency. In fact, the decreased cost of living complementing industrialization counteracts the real value of international inflation. This is due to the decreased costs of production, increased trade, and greater domestic demand. The value of a national currency in a "modernizing" nation is expected to increase domestically, relative to the international currency exchange (ceteris paribus). Therefore, the wages of industrializing nations as measured do not reflect the changes in real income of a nation, but rather the shifts of currency exchange values relative to the international community.

Democratic Transition

The now familiar research question of this week's readings, though approached in multiple ways, is that of why some countries transition to democracy while others do not. Furthermore, our authors wonder why democratic regimes flourish in some regions while they languish in others. What is it about our structures, cultures, and economics that allows for maximum democratic growth and retention? We have spread our wings since the modernization theories of the 1960s and look predominately to economic and structural explanations for democratization in the current literature. While it is broadly accepted that the level of development and governmental structure matters, and matters deeply, the authors acknowledge that it is important we empirically evaluate the claims made regarding the extent to which these things explain the rise of democracy. It is no leap to assume that each researcher must, at some point, make arbitrary distinctions in order to maintain parsimonious models. Here, that most often involves simplifying the nature of regime type into neatly packaged categories: democracy, partial democracy, autocracy, etc. Are we willing to accept this tradeoff between parsimony and reality?

The Przeworski et al. article suffers from a blatant case of such over simplification. Their classification of democracy, as per Dahl, as "all regimes that hold elections in which the opposition has some chance of winning and taking office" leaves quite a bit to be desired. It may be true that they are conservative in their estimate of regime type, but the extraordinarily broad and arguably lacking definition of democracy makes me wonder if we will actually collect observations that are useful for general comparisons at all! Using such a definition we may be comparing democratic to oligarchic or semi-repressive autocratic regimes under the guise of comparing two pure democracies. A lesser, though additional, example of simplification issues arises from their claim that "countries that adopt presidential institutions when they transit to democracy are stuck with them." I will not argue that the authors provide an interesting qualitative, and limited quantitative, background but it is mostly useful as a semantic exercise. There are many subtleties that hallmark institutional change and even without widespread structural overhaul, there may still be elements of mixed, presidential, and parliamentary systems across each regime type not rendered under Przerworski's criteria.

Geddes and Epstein et al. also simplify regime type. In these instances, each author disaggregates autocratic and democratic institutions. Geddes's paper, though very well done, must assume that three specific manifestations of autocratic regimes (military, personalistic, and single-party) represent the wide spectrum of institutional options available to autocrats. Epstein follows suit, creating a trichotomous model by setting the dependent variable, regime type, as equal to democracy, partial democracy, or autocracy. While we do not want an infinite or immeasurable amount of alternatives, arbitrary simplification may cost us the ability to apply our models to real life.

For Huntington it is the very 'clarification' of democracy that speaks to this issue. He is sure to emphasize the fact that his definition is used specifically in his book and he admits that it is necessarily a compromise among other available conceptions. On page 9 he tells us that, "the definition of democracy in terms of elections is a minimal definition." His reasons for describing the term as such are certainly convincing, but I am not sure that I am willing to buy into such an undemanding conception of such an immensely important ideal.

Despite the issues of ambiguity and the ability of researchers to manipulate definitions of regime to fit the specific question at hand, the readings in this week's unit are theoretically thick and useful. We must keep in mind that the importance of methodology can sometimes be trumped by well conceived theory. However, it is important that we find some threshold; we need common ground so that we are not setting arbitrarily simple definitions for terms that are extraordinarily complex. Coming to a consensus about such issues within the democratic transition literature should be one of our main priorities. Without fulfilling our responsibilities to rectify this shortcoming in the literature, I worry that we will not properly develop a generalizable understanding of democratic transition and endurance. After all, is it not comparison that we are interested in, in our field?

Capitalism, Socialism, and the 1949 Chinese Revolution

The 1949 Chinese Revolution was a transformative, epochal event, not only for the Chinese but for the rest of humanity, as well. If the 1917 Bolshevik Revolution in Russia (that resulted in the creation of the Union of Soviet Socialist Republics or Soviet Union) inaugurated an international competition for the hearts and minds of people all over the globe, the Chinese revolution raised the stakes of that struggle. The popular media, academics, political leaders and others in the "West" produced an understanding of this struggle as between "capitalism" and "communism," although these terms are rarely defined in more than loose and unusually flexible terms, and in spite of the fact that the Chinese revolution was shaped by domestic struggles with a long history within China, much more so than by global struggles between two super-systems.

Nevertheless, the intensity of the *perceived* global struggle between super-systems was shaped, in part, by the fact that communist ideology, as represented by certain statements of Vladimir Lenin, the central intellectual and political figure of the Bolshevik Revolution, was understood as grounded upon an idea of worldwide revolution — all nations would, according to the logic (teleology) of this (orthodox) version of Marxism, ultimately succumb to communism. (The Soviet leadership expressly supported the idea of "worldwide revolution" and took steps to help achieve this objective, including organization and leadership of the Communist International or Comintern, although C.L.R. James, among others, argued that Stalin's political machinations sabotaged international solidarity within the communist movement.) The threat to "spread the revolution" created, at the least, the illusion of a mortal conflict (mortal from the standpoint of the elites who stood to lose if the resolution went against them). In other words, this idea of worldwide revolution and the efforts by Soviet leaders and communists in other countries to make it a reality presented little room for compromise between the opposing camps (on the one side, the supporters of the existing social system in the Western nations and, on the other side, the communist movement). Thus, the communist victory in China (the most populous nation on Earth) created a stronger sense of threat in one camp and of impending victory in the other. It also contributed to the way this bipolar struggle came to overshadow all other international relationships and many domestic conflicts within nations, as well.

The conflict was mystified by both sides: it took on the dimensions and intensity of a religious crusade that permeates all aspects of social life. Indeed, if societies are really formations of social and environmental processes, all interacting and shaping one another, then the introduction of this polar conflict into the fibre of existing social relationships could not help but impact virtually every society (or social formation) and transform numerous cultural, economic, and political processes within those societies. The mystified (metaphysical) nature of the conflict served both sides: those who wanted to defend the status quo (the moral, political, and economic arrangements that predominated) in the "Western" nations were able to promote *anti-communist* attitudes and actions by depicting the other side as opponents of freedom, goodness, democracy, and light; while those who supported the goals of the Comintern could rally greater support for overturning the status quo by making use of the rhetoric of the Soviet or Chinese versions of Marxism (which looked all the more prophetic and, therefore, True, in the wake of the Chinese revolution). The existence of the new "Chinese model" was particularly troubling to one side and encouraging to the other precisely because it opened the door to a "domino effect" of revolutionary change in the less industrialized world, creating the possibility of accelerated social change that might threaten the established order in the advanced capitalist nations.

Sometimes the effects of this conflict were quite unexpected. For instance, many individuals have argued that the "Cold War" (particularly the post-1949 Chinese Revolution version of the Cold War) may have been critical to the success of the Civil Rights Movement in the United States, as U.S. political leaders sought to win the hearts and minds of leaders in newly independent African nations and intellectuals throughout the "Third World" by demonstrating the openness, flexibility, and fairness of the

American way of life (including the American economic system, which was presumed to be the embodiment of capitalism and diametrically opposed to the "communist" alternative). Ironically, the Civil Rights Movement was also interpreted, within certain anti-communist circles, as a subsidiary operation of the international communist movement. Civil Rights leaders, such as Martin Luther King, were often accused of being communists (or, at the least, "fellow travellers"). Thus, the new language and logic of communism and anti-communism (mostly in rhetorical and metaphysical form) transformed the rules of social engagement over racism, as well as many other issues.

In a larger sense, the conflict between these two camps reshaped popular culture. New images and ways of thinking about the self and society permeated the media, from literature to the motion pictures. For the most part, the conflict was not waged in terms of social theories or ideas about the proper organization of society. Instead, the conflict took on a religious connotation. In the West, communism was portrayed as "sinister," even "evil." Behavioural norms were changed, influenced by images of impending threat from the communist menace, whether from without or within. Anti-communism coalesced into a form of paranoia. This paranoia was promoted in a wide range of films and books. One of the classics of this era was the science fiction film, *Invasion of the Body Snatchers*. In this and other films, the concept of threat from infiltration of family and friends was supportive of notions prevalent within the anti-communist movement that communism would capture the hearts and minds of the innocent and turn them into obedient slaves of the world communist movement.

But this cultural battle begs the question — was the struggle really between capitalism and communism? Does this notion capture the essence of the conflict in question? Or were these words simply misused tools in a conflict over more mundane issues, such as whether a relatively old and established elite would control the resources and political machinery in certain countries or whether a new elite would come to power and take their place. It would distort matters to imply that this struggle between different political and economic agencies, at a minimum it was a struggle between the governments and corporations of the West versus the government and bureaucracy of the newly formed USSR, could be reducible to either a conflict between capitalism and communism (as two distinct, non-arbitrarily defined economic systems) or a contest for control by two different sets of elites. Similarly, it would be a distortion to imply that it is not possible for the conflict to simultaneously satisfy both the capitalism versus communism condition and the contest between elites. However, it is no less distorting to begin with the assumption that either of these conditions is correct. We need to know that the Bolsheviks were genuinely interested in communism if we are to assume that the initial conflict — the USSR versus the West — was ever between capitalism and communism, as alternative, oppositional, and mutually negating social systems. This is not proven by the simple statements of the Bolsheviks about their interest in creating communism at some unspecified date in the future. We must have a clear sense of what communism is and whether or not the Bolsheviks were working to establish the conditions for the existence of such a social formation.

After all, if a new slave master were to take control of a slave plantation and tell his slaves, "My ultimate goal is to free you and to create a new form of social arrangement in which you shall never be oppressed again," would the slaves believe him? What would be necessary for them to believe him? Does it matter in terms of defining the class structure of the society whether or not they believe him? If a conflict breaks out between this new slave master and the slave masters at other plantations then perhaps this might reinforce the idea that something extraordinarily different (and threatening to the old social order) was happening. But would that conflict be sufficient to convince us, as social analysts, that this conflict was between slavery and an alternative social system in the making, much less already present, and not simply between two variant forms of slavery? In other words, what would we need to know in order to conclude that this new slave master was a "revolutionary" intent upon ending slavery (or having already revolutionized class processes, ending slavery on the plantation in question)? This question would be further complicated if instead of a single slave master, the group claiming to oppose slavery was a collective of leaders, each with a different understanding of slavery and revolution, including a subset of these leaders who understood that an immediate end to certain conditions of slavery was utopian and dangerous to social cohesiveness (perhaps arguing in favour of ending private ownership/private appropriation-based slavery in favour of state ownership/state appropriation-based slavery as a *first stage* in their new society, but not ending slavery altogether). To imply that the conflict between the West and the USSR (and the later expanded conflict between the West and the Communist Bloc) was a struggle between capitalism and communism is to imply that the "Communist Bloc" was genuinely interested in creating communism (and ending or, at least, minimizing non-communist forms of surplus appropriation and distribution, if not having already brought this dramatic change in the *operating system* for surplus control into effect).

In the West, there is a tendency to speak of the USSR, China, and other members of the "Communist Bloc" as already communist nations. If we took this seriously, we would need to believe that the software of communism, which is the control of surplus value by the workers themselves, had been implemented in the USSR, China, and these other so-called communist nations. However, this leap of faith is avoided within the discourse by defining communism in purely polemical (non-scientific) fashion as synonymous with the set of political, economic, and cultural processes that developed in the USSR under the dictatorship of Joseph Stalin (a definition of communism that is dependent upon the post hoc rise to power of a specific dictator and the implementation of his vision of society). In other words, communism is not defined based on the software of labor processes and the control over surplus labor, as in Marx's definition (which did not presuppose a Josef Stalin), but on the hardware of the physical social structures and institutions without regard to the underlying software. Thus, the discourse of the Cold War ignored the fact that the wage labor/capital blueprint which Marx defined as the capitalist mode of production (Marx's name for the capitalist operating system) was operative in both the "West" and the "East," but in the one case implemented by state-owned firms within a bureaucratic structure (the hardware of the so-called socialist bloc) and in the other case implemented by public corporations with the support of state institutions (the hardware of the Western bloc). This Cold War discourse ignored prior discussions of communism in philosophy and social science, including Marx's few references to this system. Similarly, capitalism gets defined in simple terms as the commonly recognized features of the economic and political system(s) prevalent in the "Western" nations, particularly the presence of relatively unregulated corporations operating in relatively "free" markets and popular voting for certain governmental positions (in contested elections with at least two political parties). In the most simplistic version of this polemic, capitalism is simply conflicted with "free" markets. Indeed, there is no need for the word "capitalism" since the phrase "free markets" would capture the entire meaning for purposes of discourse and analysis. For many social analysts and commentators, their definition of capitalism is ad hoc, changing over time or occasion to meet polemical demands or simply to reflect the present set of idealized characteristics of particular high income societies, usually the United States suffices as *the* model. Unlike typological work in the "hard" sciences, the typology upon which these ad hoc definitions rest are almost never subjected to much scrutiny nor required to meet even minimal standards of uniqueness (non-arbirariness) and clarity. It is as if an animal could legitimately be classified as a reptile based on the whims or polemical requirements of the particular biologist who deploys the term in his scientific analysis or policy statements, rather than based on non-arbitrary and easily identified criteria with unambiguous scientific implications.

It is interesting that despite Marx's perceived role in shaping the bipolar communism-capitalism conflict (his name is often invoked by one side or the other for polemical reasons), his multi-volume attempt at producing new knowledge about the specificity of capitalist economic processes (where the word capitalism is produced as a social concept defining a unique set of social relationships (which can occur in a variable historical context) by which certain individuals perform surplus labor and a different set of individuals appropriate this surplus labor) is ignored. Thus, it may be useless, in the context of this polemical "debate" over capitalism and communism, to try to distinguish whether or not the conflict between the West and the "Communist Bloc" was a conflict between actual capitalism and actual communism, understood as strictly defined and alternative economic systems. In the polemical debates, the terms capitalism and communism lose all social scientific meaning. The entire history of thought within which capitalism was defined as a unique economic system formed around a distinct class process and communism was defined as an alternative mode of producing and appropriating an economic surplus is absent from the arena of these debates. Think of capitalism and communism as alternative forms of software for shaping the creation and distribution of surplus value (whether in product or monetary form). But this is not the way capitalism and communism are discussed in popular discourse. Instead, in the popular rhetoric, capitalism and communism become simple proxies for two specific sets of contending social formations (distinct in many ways but not necessarily in terms of prevalent class processes).

But we cannot play so fast and loose with these concepts (or the underlying software or social codes governing who performs labor and who receives the fruits of such labor upon which the concepts are based) if we are to make sense of the internal struggles and debates within the Chinese leadership that came to power in 1949 (anymore than it would make sense to ignore the historical definitions of capitalism and communism if one wanted to make sense of the post revolutionary struggles and debates within the Bolshevik leadership). In our survey of the Chinese economy, we will attempt to gain a better understanding of what was at stake in the Chinese Revolution of 1949, of the contending visions within the leadership of the Communist Party of China (*Gong Chang Dang*) as to what constituted capitalism and communism, and whether or not there is any "objective" way to determine if China underwent a revolution as sweeping as the term communism implies (a revolution that implies a complete change of the underlying software, or operating system, if you will, shaping the relationship between direct producers and appropriators of the fruits of labor of those direct producers). This will be important as we explore the current phase of "economic reform" in China and attempt to make sense of where China is going in the future.

But first, let me be clear about something on this point. China's leadership never claimed to have inaugurated communism with the 1949 Revolution. As was the case with the Bolsheviks, China's leaders were members of a communist party but never claimed to have instituted communism — a society without exploitation— with their revolution. They claimed merely to have overthrown the political leadership of the "bourgeois" state — to have made a political revolution against a pro capitalist state — and by so doing to have cleared the way for the construction of "socialism." Socialism was understood as an intermediate stage between capitalism and communism. During this intermediate phase, the preconditions for communism would be gradually put into place to allow for the eventual attainment of communism, which some of the opponents of communism have described as a form of utopian (and therefore unattainable) society. No one ever said how long the society would have to be in this intermediate "socialist" stage, nor was the stage itself or the preconditions for communism that were to be instituted clearly defined. It was also anticipated that worldwide revolution would result in rapid growth of communist party led governments around the world and that these governments would develop socialism in a coordinated effort. Socialist solidarity was understood as an inevitable consequence of the movement of social forces that could be delayed but not permanently forestalled. Thus, the Soviet leaders saw the Chinese revolution as just another step along this road to the coordinated building of socialism. Socialism was never conceived, within communist ideology, as a system that would be developed *sui generis* in individual countries. There would not be a Soviet form of socialism and a Chinese form, for instance. This way of thinking not only caused tensions between Soviet intellectuals and political leaders and their Chinese counterparts but also caused some rather serious squabbling among leaders of the Communist Party of China (CPC), which was founded only four years after the Bolshevik Revolution, with some taking the internationalist line and others arguing in favour of the idea of a unique Chinese form of socialism.

To further complicate matters, the Chinese Nationalist Party or Guomindang — the party that was overthrown by the Chinese Communist Party and subsequently fled to the island of Taiwan— did not view itself as an instrument of a ruling capitalist class (which would be consistent with the notion of a "bourgeois" party). To the contrary, the Guomindang, many of whose leaders were openly supportive of and supported by the Soviet Union (and some, such as Chiang Kai-shek, studied in the Soviet Union), was generally described as nationalist and socialist. Sun Yat-sen, the Guomindang's Lenin, was one of the strongest supporters of the Soviet Union. And the Soviets provided the Guomindang with financial support, armaments, and advisers. (If this is not sufficient to make the ideological waters murky, then consider also that the Chinese Communist Party made nationalism an important aspect of its constitution, eliminating another potential ideological difference.) On numerous occasions the Guomindang and the Chinese Communist Party were allied, particularly in the anti-imperialist struggle against the Japanese and there were even members of the Guomindang who simultaneously held membership in the Chinese Communist Party (at least until Chiang Kai-shek began his purge of communists from the Guomindang). The Communist Party officially recognized the valuable role of the Guomindang in bringing about the transition from the monarchist regime, embodied most recently in the form of the Qing Dynasty, to a *modern* state. This, of course, begs the question of who would control that state as the Chinese nation continued along a path that both the Guomindang and the Communist Party called *modernization*. When the Guomindang, under Chiang Kai-shek's leadership (after Sun Yat-sen's death), turned against the Chinese Communist Party in 1927, assassinating most of the communist leadership (leaving a void that would be filled by the rural based Mao Zedong), the motivation may have been less ideological than part of an effort to eliminate any possible competition over control of this "modern" state. Thus, the Chinese Communist Party, who won the struggle against the Guomindang despite the aforementioned assassinations, overthrew one version of socialism in favour of another version, at least when viewed in purely polemical terms.

This leaves us with some perplexing questions. What exactly was/is socialism? What did the Chinese Communist Party leadership mean by this term? What do they mean when they use it today? Is there a narrow enough definition of the term "socialism" as to allow us to test whether one society is or is not socialist?

For that matter, in order to make sense of the aforementioned struggle between communists (who are portrayed and portray themselves as opponents of capitalism) and anti-communists, we will need to ask similar questions of the concepts of capitalism and communism? Because these terms are frequently used for polemical purposes, we often think we know what they mean and can very easily end up like the Caterpillar in Alice in Wonderland (with these words meaning whatever we want them to mean — there being no test for whether the conditions of the concept are or are not met). For our purposes, however, we will need to both understand what political and intellectual leaders in China (and elsewhere) meant by these terms and to attempt to find social scientific definitions (very strictly defined and testable terms used in a consistent manner within a consistently logical framework of argumentation) that could be used to analyse the economic, political and cultural dynamics driving change in Chinese society. These are two very different ways of talking about the concepts of capitalism, socialism, and communism.

Let us begin with the latter problem—finding a social scientific meaning of these terms. We need a social scientific definition of capitalism, socialism, and communism that can be deployed in our analysis of the Chinese economy, Chinese economic history, and the intellectual debates about China's "communist" revolution and its current transition (from what to what?).

Since the concept of communism was/is largely understood as oppositional to capitalism, then lets start with capitalism. What is this thing that the communist party leaderships (in China, the Soviet Union, and elsewhere) wanted to transcend and ultimately replace with communism? The term capitalism began its life as an economic concept, although today it is often used to describe political and cultural elements, as well. Nevertheless, a concept of capitalism that is overly general or synonymous with other widely used concepts — such as the conflation of market economies with capitalism — becomes less useful as a device for categorizing and analysing. What we want is a concept of capitalism (and communism) that is narrow and unique enough as to allow us to distinguish something profoundly different or similar between the societies under analysis (and, in a more micro context, between different social relationships within the economy).

Since Marx is often implicated in the various debates over this and related issues, it might help to get an idea of how Marx understood capitalism. Marx, in his attempt to distinguish the different social processes that shape people's lives, discussed a wide range of social relationships and processes: property, exchange, and power relationships played an important role in his analysis, for instance. However, Marx thought that many social commentators had, over time, done a great deal to analyse, even criticize, existing forms of property ownership, exchange relationships, and political arrangements. Social analysts who opposed the existing social order, capitalism, because they felt it was oppressive generally criticized these particular aspects of the capitalist societies of the day. Marx believed that even if these factors were changed — property ownership, exchange relationships, and political arrangements — it was not guaranteed that one would get to the heart of the problems created by capitalism. In particular, he believed that there existed a form of oppression that was poorly understood, rarely discussed, whose genesis had required dramatic changes in the living conditions and social status of countless human beings, and which was critical to understanding what it was that made capitalist society unique vis-a-vis other unjust societies (Marx was clearly making some important value judgments in his criticisms of capitalism, feudalism and slavery). This unique form of oppression is what he called capitalist exploitation.

But capitalist exploitation, to be understood, had to be strictly defined as distinct from other forms of exploitation. And exploitation, as an economic concept, had to be strictly defined as distinct from other forms of oppression. Marx defined exploitation as the product of a generalized social process, called class. Since capitalism is the prevalence of a specific type of class process, i.e. the capitalist class process, then we should begin by understanding this generalized concept of class before moving to the more specific instances. In other words, we want to be able to answer the question of what is a class process before answering the more specific question of what is the capitalist class process. Once we can answer both of these questions, then we will be in a stronger position to test whether or not the facts of the Chinese revolution and post revolutionary society have, indeed, been anticapitalist (as might be anticipated by the rhetoric employed by many of those engaged in the communist/anti-communist debates of the Cold War era).

In order to understand class, we will use the conceptual language that has been developed by Stephen A. Resnick and Richard D. Wolff, two noted economists from the University of Massachusetts and the founders of the journal *Rethinking Marxism*. Resnick and Wolff's reading of Marx leads them to avoid defining class as a *noun*, as is common practice. For Resnick and Wolff, the issue that Marx focused upon in his major theoretical works (*Capital*, *Theories of Surplus Value*, and *Grundrisse*) was not a struggle between classes but a struggle over class as a social process (the term process implies a continually changing phenomenon — a phenomenon that only exists in motion — a *verb*). For this and other reasons they use the term class process in describing the unique type of social interaction that Marx was concerned about in his social scientific work.

What is class process? Firstly, Marx understood that society depended, among other processes, upon human beings physically transforming raw materials and other material inputs (machinery and other products of past labor) into new and useful products. Food has to be grown and prepared. Cloth has to be created and clothing made. Construction materials and housing have to be made. And so on. For Marx this productive effort was general to all societies, irrespective of the existence and/or type of class process. All human beings do not, however, engage in activities resulting in such useful products. And even for those who are so engaged, they may, under certain conditions, consume such products in excess of the *value* of what they produce. Thus, under certain social conditions it is necessary for some workers to produce output in excess of the output they take as compensation for their efforts. This extra work has been defined by Marx and others as *surplus labor*. The extra product created by surplus labor was defined as *surplus product*. And the social value of the surplus product (as typically determined in market exchange relationships) was defined as *surplus value*. Now we have all of the ingredients necessary to a relatively strict definition of class process. Class process is the social process that results in i) human beings performing surplus labor, ii) the surplus products (of this labor) being appropriated and iii) the distribution of the surplus value (in surplus product form or in monetary form) to other human beings.

What distinguishes one class process from another? In other words, how can we distinguish capitalism from feudalism or feudalism from communism? All these are class processes in so far as they involve the production, appropriation and distribution of surplus products. The difference between the various class processes is the particular social arrangement that results in the worker performing the surplus labor and the appropriator taking possession of the fruits (the product or value) of that surplus labor. And these social arrangements have been variable over time and place. Marx spent a great many pages attempting to specify the historical process that brought into being the social arrangement that is peculiar to capitalism. It was the primary purpose behind the writing of the three volumes of *Capital*, his best known social scientific work (although less well known than his shorter more polemical *Communist Manifesto*). In a nutshell, the social arrangement that distinguishes the capitalist class process from other class processes is the existence of a free market in labor power (the capacity to work) under conditions where it is possible for someone other than the actual labourers/direct producers to take possession of the fruits of their labor. This definition tells us that capitalism, if it is to exist and be reproduced over time, requires a particular type of market, a free market in the buying and selling of labor power, and a particular type of ownership, the ownership of the fruits of the labor of an employed wage labourer by someone other than that employed wage labourer.

However, capitalism is not reducible to either markets or ownership. There must be a free market in labor power, meaning that potential labourers must have the freedom to seek employment (for a wage) in an environment where, under normal conditions, there are choices about possible employers. There must be a political and cultural environment within which it is possible for someone other than the worker who created a product to take ownership of that product. The worker is paid a wage, embodying a certain amount of economic value, in exchange for her giving up the right to own the fruits of her labor. She accepts this contract willingly and retains the right (the freedom) to quit her employment and seek employment elsewhere. That's it. That is capitalism. This simple but powerful definition provides all that is necessary to determine if the capitalist class process exists under concrete social conditions. We do not need to know who rules the state or whether voting plays a role in determining the composition of an existing legislative body. We do not need to know if there are flexible exchange rates. We do not need to know if there are gun laws. We do not need to know whether people in the country speak Putonghua or English. Of course all of these topics might be useful in any attempt to tell the story of how capitalism came to exist or not or the particular context within which it exists.

If the capitalist class process is the appropriation of the surplus value of free wage labourers (labourers who seek employment for a wage in a free market in labor power) by human beings other than the free labourers themselves, then we can easily see where some of the confusion has originated. Instead of seeing free markets in labor power as a condition of existence of capitalism, it has become a commonplace to think that free markets in general are a condition of existence of capitalism. This is very misleading, of course, since it is possible to have free markets in everything except labor power and not have capitalism. (Indeed, the presence of free markets in labor (power) is a necessary but not sufficient condition to define a society as capitalist. Simply because the capitalist class process may exist in a society does not imply that this type of class process prevails over all others, in terms of numbers of workers involved, total output generated, or any number of other possible criteria. Similarly, the existence of instances of slavery would not define an entire society as a slave society, if this economic arrangement were not typical.) China has been the site of numerous debates over and experiments with free markets, dating as far back as the Han Dynasty (202 B.C.E. to 220 C.E., when debates over state intervention versus free markets are documented) and the well-field system of the Tang Dynasty (618 C.E. to 755 C.E., or thereabouts) where output generated on that subset of peasant plots not allocated to producing in-kind rents for the aristocracy could be consumed by the peasant household or sold in village markets, but free markets in labor power have been very rare, indeed. In the antebellum South of the United States, where there was even a free market in the buying and selling of human beings, the market in the buying and selling of human labor (power) was relatively underdeveloped. Most direct producers in the antebellum South were either slaves or self-employed producers, not capitalist wage labourers. Under the system of slavery, a large number of productive labourers in the southern states of the United States existed in a condition of servitude, living out their lives in work camps as the owned property of other human beings, despite the presence of free markets in most goods and services. Indeed, most of the products created by these slave labourers were sold in markets, where buyers and sellers were relatively free to interact and engage in exchange. And the ideology of free markets was also very strong in the antebellum South. For slavery based entrepreneurs the freedom to engage in the buying and selling of human chattel and the concomitant freedom to put those human beings to productive use was no minor matter. Indeed, it was the pro-slavery forces in the U.S. Congress who led the fight for free trade and other policies that presage "neo-liberalism." Thus, there can be no doubt that markets played a critical role in the economic life of the southern states. Nevertheless, the predominant class process of the South, typically assumed to have been the slave class process (whereby the performance of surplus labor depended upon the existence of a human chattel arrangement) was clearly distinct from the capitalist class process (which is understood to have prevailed in the northeastern states of the United States), whereby workers could seek and quit employment according to their own volition.

We can also see why it might have been possible to expand the role of ownership as a condition of existence of capitalism beyond the simple condition whereby it must be possible for someone other than the free wage labourer to take ownership of the surplus value created by that labourer (and then to distribute this surplus value so as to secure the conditions for further appropriations in the future). It is commonplace to believe that private ownership in general is a defining characteristic of capitalism. But again, slavery provided wide scale private ownership and yet is an economic arrangement profoundly different from capitalism. Similarly, feudalism and self-employment (the ancient class process) often exist in the presence of wide scale private ownership.

Thus, neither private ownership nor the existence of free markets in commodities other than labor power is, in these general terms, a sufficient condition for the existence of the capitalist class process. And since we call a society capitalist if and only if the capitalist class process prevails (is the predominant source of the social surplus), then the existence of such free markets and/or private property is not sufficient for a society to be labelled capitalist. It is also the case that the absence of wide scale free markets and private property are not sufficient to determine that a society is not capitalist.

As for the more ambiguous term, socialism, the intellectual and political leader of the Bolsheviks in Russia recognized that capitalism and socialism were not incompatible. On the eve of the Bolshevik Revolution of 1917, Vladimir Lenin wrote that "Socialism is nothing but a state-capitalist monopoly used for the benefit of the entire nation and thus ceasing to be a capitalist monopoly." Thus, it appears that Lenin is defining socialism as a variant form of capitalism, rather than a different type of society from capitalism.

In support of Lenin's argument, the existence of a command economy, wherein the allocation of goods and services is largely controlled by agencies of the government, does not preclude the presence of a free market in labor power per se and, therefore, does not preclude the continued prevalence of capitalist relations in the economy. But was this the case in practice? In particular, was it the case in China that the creation of a command economy was coincident with the establishment and/or reproduction of free labor (power) markets? Were Chinese workers free to choose their place of employment or, at least, to choose where they would seek employment?

In thinking about these questions, you should give some thought to the definition of capitalism developed in this brief essay. In particular, you might want to think about how a command economy could also be capitalist. In other words, as an exercise in deploying this strict definition of capitalism, you might define a capitalist command economy as one variant form of capitalism.

On the other hand, what if workers, like generations of peasant farmers and artisans during the various dynastic periods in Chinese history, were not free to choose where they would seek employment? If workers were assigned by the government to a particular work site (danwei or commune) and did not have the freedom to quit, then what sort of economic system, in class terms, would have prevailed in China? This question is of no minor importance to our investigation of the ongoing transformation of the Chinese economy and the implications of that transformation.

Finally, you may ask why any of this matters. It's been asked before. Oddly, it is often asked by U.S. conservatives who normally would have considered the question of whether or not a particular entity is "communist" or "capitalist" to be very consequential but somehow lose interest in the question when challenged to think more carefully about the social scientific meaning of these terms. In any event, it matters because it goes directly to the heart of whether or not there is some fundamental difference between China and the Chinese economy and the "West" and "Western" economies, including the United States of America or between the various post-revolutionary states of the Chinese social formation and states during the aforementioned dynastic periods. What is similar and what is different? What has changed and what has been reproduced? If it turns out that China's communist party is engineering capitalism, rather than something opposed to capitalism, then it will certainly make some difference in how the United States and China interact. And it will also make a significant difference in the lives of the people of China.

The Road Ahead

What do we intend to accomplish with this lecture series? We begin with an historical exploration of the institutional creations and alterations that lead from the 1949 Revolution in China up to what we know as contemporary China. Historical processes are necessarily always relevant to the political, cultural, environmental, and economic processes of the present. The past is always articulated with the present. Nevertheless, our main objective is to understand the China of the current period, to be in a position to make sense of the multiple possible paths that society may take from yesterday to tomorrow. In the process, we will need to debunk some myths about China. That means necessarily stepping on some toes. For example, we will critically analyse the meaning of the terms market economy, socialism (with or without Chinese characteristics), communism, capitalism, ancientism, feudalism, exploitation, vanguard party and dictatorship of the proletariat, among others. How are these terms defined within and what role do they play in the versions of Marxian theory prevalent within the Communist Party of China and in the strategies and concrete policies of that ruling party? What is the relationship between these terms and the actual functioning of the Chinese economy, which can be understood as a complex and changing set of algorithms: an algorithm is a process that follows some sort of logic — this logic can change according to certain rules, which are, in turn, the result of other algorithms. Face it, we humans love rules. We need them. Some animals have their algorithms hard wired into their brains (and maybe to a certain extent so do we), but more so than any other creature on this planet we sentient beings seem to constantly and creatively order our lives (for better or worse) with our own consciously constructed algorithms. We sometimes produce beautiful algorithms of behaviour and interaction that serve to make life better and other times, well, we do the opposite. The possibilities for human interaction (and therefore human society) are far greater than any individual's imagination. Let us keep that in mind as we explore the specific dimensions of the Chinese social formation.

Is the transformation taking place in China likely to alter the social relations on the planet in such a dramatic fashion as to inaugurate a distinctly new epoch in human history? If so, what are the dimensions of this seachange? What new algorithms will arise in the human family? And is it inevitable or are there possible obstacles that could block this transition and lead global civilization down alternative paths?

And there is that sticky question that underlies this entire first essay in the series: Is the change in China a transition to capitalism, as many have now come to believe (even if operating from very different conceptions of the meaning of the word capitalism)? Does this matter? If it is such a transition, what is it a transition from? And does this matter?

Most of the analyses of China, including those originating within China, operate from an explicit or implicit teleology: the belief that the changes in China are following some form of Hegelian logic that leads from one stage in human social development to a higher, more advanced, and logically necessary next stage. This is a common way of thinking within the social sciences. It was not only the province of Hegel, but also of the

German Historical School, end-of-history neoconservatives, and most Marxists. People are often quite passionate about their teleologies. For the sake of full disclosure, let me say up front that I am not a believer in such teleologies. Indeed, my use of the term "ancient class process" to refer to productive self-employment is, in part, a stab at the heart of teleology.

By making the adjective "ancient" into an ahistorical term I hope to make clear that one can identify distinct economic (as well as cultural, political, and environmental) processes that can be located at various moments in temporal space, that are not wedded to a specific interval in that temporal space (in class terms, *ancient* Greece was not unique, nor was the class *ancientness* of Greece a one-to-one function of temporal location), but are rather temporally autonomous, so to speak, influencing other processes at various moments in both temporal and geographic space. Ancient producers can exist in the New York City of 2003, for example, as well as in the India of 1203. Ancient production (productive self-employment) can prevail in societies of the future, as well as having prevailed in societies of the past. There is no law of social evolution that says that ancient societies (in these terms) must be a thing of the past only. In other words, there are a large variety of social conditions that may foster ancientism, just as there are a large variety of social conditions that may foster capitalism or feudalism or slavery and the temporal dimension is in no way a restriction on the potential existence of some variant form of these social formations (or the underlying class processes). I'm not saying "stuff happens" as if it is in some way random, but that there are multiple paths to any type of social formation based on the known five fundamental class processes (ancientism, communism, capitalism, feudalism, and slavery). This is an attempt to get us to stop thinking of the world in non-thinking ways: such as separating human social evolution into an ancient world and a modern world and therefore missing certain fundamental similarities, as well as unexpected differences. We need to do the analysis. I guess that is the theme of these lectures/essays. In other words, in addition to trying to understand China, I want us to do so with an aggressive use of the conceptual framework and, as much as possible, to avoid prejudging prior to the theoretical work having been done.

Authoritarian and Democratic Techniquesz

"Democracy" is a term now confused and sophisticated by indiscriminate use, and often treated with patronizing contempt. Can we agree, no matter how far we might diverge at a later point, that the spinal principle of democracy is to place what is common to all men above that which any organization, institution, or group may claim for itself? This is not to deny the claims of superior natural endowment, specialized knowledge, technical skill, or institutional organization: all these may, by democratic permission, play a useful role in the human economy. But democracy consists in giving final authority to the whole, rather than the part; and only living human beings, as such, are an authentic expression of the whole, whether acting alone or with the help of others.

Around this central principle clusters a group of related ideas and practices with a long foreground in history, though they are not always present, or present in equal amounts, in all societies. Among these items are communal self-government, free communication as between equals, unimpeded access to the common store of knowledge, protection against arbitrary external controls, and a sense of individual moral responsibility for behaviour that affects the whole community. All living organisms are in some degree autonomous in that they follow a life-pattern of their own; but in man this autonomy is an essential condition for his further development. We surrender some of our autonomy when ill or crippled: but to surrender it every day on every occasion would be to turn life itself into a chronic illness. The best life possible — and here I am consciously treading on contested ground — is one that calls for an ever greater degree of self-direction, self-expression, and self-realization. In this sense, personality, once the exclusive attribute of kings, belongs on democratic theory to every man. Life itself in its fullness and wholeness cannot be delegated.

In framing this provisional definition I trust that I have not, for the sake of agreement, left out anything important. Democracy, in the primal sense I shall use the term, is necessarily most visible in relatively small communities and groups, whose m embers meet frequently face to face, interact freely, and are known to each other as persons. As soon as large numbers are involved, democratic association must be supplemented by a more abstract, depersonalized form. Historic experience shows that it is much easier to wipe out democracy by an institutional arrangement that gives authority only to those at the apex of the social hierarchy than it is to incorporate democratic practices into a well organized system under centralized direction, which achieves the highest degree of mechanical efficiency when those who work it have no mind or purpose of their own.

The tension between small-scale association and large-scale organization, between personal autonomy and institutional regulation, between remote control and diffused local intervention, has now created a critical situation. If our eyes had been open, we might long ago have discovered this conflict deeply embedded in technology itself.

I wish it were possible to characterize technics with as much hope of getting assent, with whatever quizzical reserves you may still have, as in this description of democracy. But the very title of this paper is, I confess, a controversial one; and I cannot go far in my analysis without drawing on interpretations that have not yet been adequately published, still less widely discussed or rigorously criticized and evaluated. My thesis, to put it bluntly, is that from late Neolithic times in the Near East, right down to our own day, two technologies have recurrently existed side by side: one authoritarian, the other democratic, the first system-centred, immensely powerful, but inherently unstable, the other man-centred 13 relatively weak, but resourceful and durable. If I am right, we are now rapidly approaching a point at which, unless we radically alter our present course, our surviving democratic technics will be completely suppressed or supplanted, so that every residual autonomy will be wiped out, or will be permitted only as a playful device of government, like national balloting for already chosen leaders in totalitarian countries.

The data on which this thesis is based are familiar; but their significance has, I believe, been overlooked. What I would call democratic technics is the small scale method of production, resting mainly on human skill and animal energy but always, even when employing machines, remaining under the active direction of the craftsman or the farmer, each group developing its own gifts, through appropriate arts and social ceremonies, as well as making discreet use of the gifts of nature. This technology had limited horizons of achievement, but, just because of its wide diffusion and its modest demands, it had great powers of adaptation and recuperation. This democratic technics has underpinned and firmly supported every historic culture until our own day, and redeemed the constant tendency of authoritarian technics to misapply its powers. Even when paying tribute to the most oppressive authoritarian regimes, there yet remained within the workshop or the farmyard some degree of autonomy, selectivity, creativity. No royal mace, no slave-driver's whip, no bureaucratic directive left its imprint on the textiles of Damascus or the pottery of fifth century Athens.

If this democratic technics goes back to the earliest use of tools, authoritarian technics is a much more recent achievement: it begins around the fourth millennium B.C. in a new configuration of technical invention, scientific observation, and centralized political control that gave rise to the peculiar mode of life we may now identify, without eulogy, as civilization. Under the new institution of kingship, activities that had been scattered, diversified, cut to the human measure, were united on a monumental scale into an entirely new kind of theological-technological mass organization. In the person of an absolute ruler, whose word was law, cosmic powers came down to earth, mobilizing and unifying the efforts of thousands of men, hitherto all-too-autonomous and too decentralized to act voluntarily in unison for purposes that lay beyond the village horizon.

The new authoritarian technology was not limited by village custom or human sentiment: its herculean feats of mechanical organization rested on ruthless physical coercion, forced labor and slavery, which brought into existence machines that were capable of exerting thousands of horsepower centuries before horses were harnessed or wheels invented. This centralized technics drew on inventions and scientific discoveries of a high order: the written record, mathematics and astronomy, irrigation and canalization: above all, it created complex human machines composed of specialized, standardized, replaceable, interdependent parts — the work army, the military army, the bureaucracy. These work armies and military armies raised the ceiling of human achievement: the first in mass construction, the second in mass destruction, both on a scale hitherto inconceivable. Despite its constant drive to destruction, this totalitarian technics was tolerated, perhaps even welcomed, in home territory, for it created the first economy of controlled abundance: notably, immense food crops that not merely supported a big urban population but released a large trained minority for purely religious, scientific, bureaucratic, or military activity. But the efficiency of the system was impaired by weaknesses that were never overcome until our own day.

To begin with, the democratic economy of the agricultural village resisted incorporation into the new authoritarian system. So even the Roman Empire found it expedient, once resistance was broken and taxes were collected, to consent to a large degree of local autonomy in religion and government. Moreover as long as agriculture absorbed the labor of some 90 per cent of the population, mass technics were confined largely to the populous urban centres. Since authoritarian technics first took form in an age when metals were scarce and human raw material, captured in war, was easily convertible into machines, its directors never bothered to invent inorganic mechanical substitutes. But there were even greater weaknesses: the system had no inner coherence: a break in communication, a missing link in the chain of command, and the great human machines fell apart. Finally, the myths upon which the whole system was based — particularly the essential myth of kingship — were irrational, with their paranoid suspicions and animosities and their paranoid claims to unconditional obedience and absolute power. For all its redoubtable constructive achievements, authoritarian technics expressed a deep hostility to life.

By now you doubtless see the point of this brief historic excursus. That authoritarian technics has come back today in an immensely magnified and adroitly perfected form. Up to now, following the optimistic premises of nineteenth century thinkers like Auguste Comte and Herbert Spencer, we have regarded the spread of experimental science and mechanical invention as the soundest guarantee of a peaceful, productive, above all democratic, industrial society. Many have even comfortably supposed that the revolt against arbitrary political power in the seventeenth century was causally connected with the industrial revolution that accompanied it. But what we have interpreted as the new freedom now turns out to be a much more sophisticated version of the old slavery: for the rise of political democracy during the last few centuries has been increasingly nullified by the successful resurrection of a centralized authoritarian technics — a technics that had in fact for long lapsed in many parts of the world.

Let us fool ourselves no longer. At the very moment Western nations, threw off the ancient regime of absolute government, operating under a once-divine king, they were restoring this same system in a far more effective form in their technology, reintroducing coercions of a military character no less strict in the organization of a factory than in that of the new drilled, uniformed, and regimented army. During the transitional stages of the last two centuries, the ultimate tendency of this system might b e in doubt, for in many areas there were strong democratic reactions; but with the knitting together of a scientific ideology, itself liberated from theological restrictions or humanistic purposes, authoritarian technics found an instrument at hand that h as now given it absolute command of physical energies of cosmic dimensions. The inventors of nuclear bombs, space rockets, and computers are the pyramid builders of our own age: psychologically inflated by a similar myth of unqualified power, boasting through their science of their increasing omnipotence, if not omniscience, moved by obsessions and compulsions no less irrational than those of earlier absolute systems: particularly the notion that the system itself must be expanded, at whatever eventual cost to life.

Through mechanization, automation, cybernetic direction, this authoritarian technics has at last successfully overcome its most serious weakness: its original dependence upon resistant, sometimes actively disobedient servomechanisms, still human enough to harbour purposes that do not always coincide with those of the system.

Like the earliest form of authoritarian technics, this new technology is marvellously dynamic and productive: its power in every form tends to increase without limits, in quantities that defy assimilation and defeat control, whether we are thinking of the output of scientific knowledge or of industrial assembly lines. To maximize energy, speed, or automation, without reference to the complex conditions that sustain organic life, have become ends in themselves. As with the earliest forms of authoritarian technics, the weight of effort, if one is to judge by national budgets, is toward absolute instruments of destruction, designed for absolutely irrational purposes whose chief by-product would be the mutilation or extermination of the human race. Even Ashurbanipal and Genghis Khan performed their gory operations under normal human limits.

The centre of authority in this new system is no longer a visible personality, an all-powerful king: even in totalitarian dictatorships the centre now lies in the system itself, invisible but omnipresent: all its human components, even the technical and managerial elite, even the sacred priesthood of science, who alone have access to the secret knowledge by means of which total control is now swiftly being effected, are themselves trapped by the very perfection of the organization they have invented. Like the Pharoahs of the Pyramid Age, these servants of the system identify its goods with their own kind of well-being: as with the divine king, their praise of the system is an act of self-worship; and again like the king, they are in the grip of an irrational compulsion to extend their means of control and expand the scope of their authority. In this new systems-centred collective, this Pentagon of power, there is no visible presence who issues commands: unlike job's God, the new deities cannot be confronted, still less defied. Under the pretext of saving labor, the ultimate end of this technics is to displace life, or rather, to transfer the attributes of life to the machine and the mechanical collective, allowing only so much of the organism to remain as may be controlled and manipulated.

Do not misunderstand this analysis. The danger to democracy does not spring from any specific scientific discoveries or electronic inventions. The human compulsions that dominate the authoritarian technics of our own day date back to a period before eve n the wheel had been invented. The danger springs from the fact that, since Francis Bacon and Galileo defined the new methods and objectives of technics, our great physical transformations have been effected by a system that deliberately eliminates the whole human personality, ignores the historic process, overplays the role of the abstract intelligence, and — makes control over physical nature, ultimately control over man himself, the chief purpose of existence. This system has made its way so insidiously into Western society, that my analysis of its derivation and its intentions may well seem more questionable — indeed more shocking — than the facts themselves.

Why has our age surrendered so easily to the controllers, the manipulators, the conditioners of an authoritarian technics? The answer to this question is both paradoxical and ironic. Present day technics differs from that of the overtly brutal, half-baked authoritarian systems of the past in one highly favourable particular: it has accepted the basic principle of democracy, that every member of society should have a share in its goods. By progressively fulfilling this part of the democratic promise, our system has achieved a hold over the whole community that threatens to wipe out every other vestige of democracy.

The bargain we are being asked to ratify takes the form of a magnificent bribe. Under the democratic-authoritarian social contract, each member of the community may claim every material advantage, every intellectual and emotional stimulus he may desire, in quantities hardly available hitherto even for a restricted minority: food, housing, swift transportation, instantaneous communication, medical care, entertainment, education. But on one condition: that one must not merely ask for nothing that the system does not provide, but likewise agree to take everything offered, duly processed and fabricated, homogenized and equalized, in the precise quantities that the system, rather than the person, requires. Once one opts for the system no further choice remains. In a word, if one surrenders one's life at source, authoritarian technics will give back as much of it as can be mechanically graded, quantitatively multiplied, collectively manipulated and magnified.

"Is this not a fair bargain?" those who speak for the system will ask. "Are not the goods authoritarian technics promises real goods? Is this not the horn of plenty that mankind has long dreamed of, and that every ruling class has tried to secure, at whatever cost of brutality and injustice, for itself?" I would not belittle, still less deny, the many admirable products this technology has brought forth, products that a self-regulating economy would make good use of. I would only suggest that it is time to reckon up the human disadvantages and costs, to say nothing of the dangers, of our unqualified acceptance of the system itself. Even the immediate price is heavy; for the system is so far from being under effective human direction that it may poison us wholesale to provide us with food or exterminate us to provide national security, before we can enjoy its promised goods. Is it really humanly profitable to give up the possibility of living a few years at Walden Pond, so to say, for the privilege of spending a lifetime in Walden Two? Once our authoritarian technics consolidates its powers, with, the aid of its new forms of mass control, its panoply of tranquillizers and sedatives and aphrodisiacs, could democracy in any form survive?

That question is absurd: life itself will not survive, except what is funnelled through the mechanical collective. The spread of a sterilized scientific intelligence over the planet would not, as Teilhard de Chardin so innocently imagined, be the happy consummation of divine purpose: it would rather ensure the final arrest of any further human development.

Again: do not mistake my meaning. This is not a prediction of what will happen, but a warning against what may happen.

What means must be taken to escape this fate? In characterizing the authoritarian technics that has begun to dominate us, I have not forgotten the great lesson of history: Prepare for the unexpected! Nor do I overlook the immense reserves of vitality an d creativity that a more humane democratic tradition still offers us. What I wish to do is to persuade those who are concerned with maintaining democratic institutions to see that their constructive efforts must include technology itself. There, too, we must return to the human centre. We must challenge this authoritarian system that has given to an underdimensioned ideology and technology the authority that belongs to the human personality. I repeat: life cannot be delegated.

Curiously, the first words in support of this thesis came forth, with exquisite symbolic aptness, from a willing agent-but very nearly a classic victim! — of the new authoritarian technics. They came from the astronaut, John Glenn, whose life was endangered by the malfunctioning of his automatic controls, operated from a remote centre. After he barely saved his life by personal intervention, he emerged from his space capsule with these ringing words: "Now let man take over!"

That command is easier to utter than obey. But if we are not to be driven to even more drastic measures than Samuel Butler suggested in Erewhon, we had better map out a more positive course: namely, the reconstitution of both our science and our technics in such a fashion as to insert the rejected parts of the human personality at every stage in the process.

This means gladly sacrificing mere quantity in order to restore qualitative choice, shifting the seat of authority from the mechanical collective to the human personality and the autonomous group, favouring variety and ecological complexity, instead of stressing undue uniformity and standardization, above all, reducing the insensate drive to extend the system it elf, instead of containing it within definite human limits and thus releasing man himself for other purposes.

We must ask, not what is good for science or technology, still less what is good for General Motors or Union Carbide or IBM or the Pentagon, but what is good for man: not machine-conditioned, system-regulated, mass-man, but man in person, moving freely over every area of life.

There are large areas of technology that can be redeemed by the democratic process, once we have overcome the infantile compulsions and automatisms that now threaten to cancel out our real gains. The very leisure that the machine now gives in advanced countries can be profitably used, not for further commitment to still other kinds of machine, furnishing automatic recreation, but by doing significant forms of work, unprofitable or technically impossible under mass production: work dependent upon special skill, knowledge, aesthetic sense.

The do-it-yourself movement prematurely got bogged down in an attempt to sell still more machines; but its slogan pointed in the right direction, provided we still have a self to do it with. The glut of motor cars that is now destroying our cities can be coped with only if we redesign our cities to make fuller use of a more efficient human agent: the walker. Even in childbirth, the emphasis is already happily shifting from an officious, often lethal, authoritarian procedure, centred in hospital routine, to a more human mode, which restores initiative to the mother and to the body's natural rhythms.

Unitary State

A unitary state is a sovereign state governed as one single unit in which the central government is supreme and any administrative divisions (subnational units) exercise only powers that the central government chooses to delegate. Many states in the world have a unitary system of government.

Unitary states are contrasted with federal states (federations):

- In a unitary state, subnational units are created and abolished and their powers may be broadened and narrowed, by the central government. Although political power in unitary states may be delegated through devolution to local government by statute, the central government remains supreme; it may abrogate the acts of devolved governments or çurtail their powers.
    - o The United Kingdom is an example of a unitary state. Scotland, Wales, and Northern Ireland, which along with England are the constituent countries of the United Kingdom, have a degree of autonomous devolved power-the Scottish Government and Scottish Parliament in Scotland, the Welsh Assembly Government and National Assembly for Wales in Wales, and the Northern Ireland Executive and Northern Ireland Assembly in Northern Ireland. But such devolved power is only delegated by Britain's central government, more specifically by the Parliament of the United Kingdom, which is supreme under the doctrine of parliamentary supremacy. Further, the devolved governments cannot challenge the constitutionality of acts of Parliament, and the powers of the devolved governments can be revoked or reduced by the central government (the Parliament with a government comprising the Cabinet, headed by the Prime Minister). For example, the Northern Ireland Assembly has been suspended four times, with its powers reverting to the central government's Northern Ireland Office.
- In federal states, by contrast, states or other subnational units share sovereignty with the central government, and

the states comprising the federation have an existence and power functions that cannot be unilaterally changed by the central government. In some cases, such as in the United States, it is the federal government that has only those powers expressly delegated to it.

- An example of a federal state is the United States; under the United States Constitution, power is shared between the federal government of the United States and the U.S. states. Many federal states also have unitary lower levels of government; while the United States is federal, the states themselves are unitary under Dillon's Rule-counties and municipalities have only the authority granted to them by the state governments by the state constitution or legislative act.

Most countries with the Westminster system of government are unitary states except Australia, Canada and Malaysia, which have federal systems. These nations may be considered hybrids of both systems, employing the centrality of the unitary system at the federal level, and the sharing of power with states, provinces and territories found in federal systems.

Devolution (like federation) may be symmetrical, with all subnational units having the same powers and status, or asymmetric, with regions varying in their powers and status.

Federation

A federation (Latin: *foedus, foederis*, 'covenant'), also known as a federal state, is a type of sovereign state characterized by a union of partially self-governing states or regions united by a central (federal) government. In a federation, the self-governing status of the component states is typically constitutionally entrenched and may not be altered by a unilateral decision of the central government.

The form of government or constitutional structure found in a federation is known as federalism. It can be considered the opposite of another system, the unitary state. The government of Germany with sixteen federated *Länder* is an example of a federation, whereas neighbouring Austria and its *Bundesländer* was a unitary state with administrative divisions that became federated, and neighbouring France by contrast has always been unitary.

Federations may be multi-ethnic, or cover a large area of territory, although neither is necessarily the case. Federations are most often founded on an original agreement between a number of sovereign states based on mutual concerns or interests. The initial agreements create a stability that encourages other common interests, brings the disparate territories closer, and gives them all even more common ground. At some time this is recognized and a movement is organized to merge more closely. Other times, especially when common cultural factors are at play such as ethnicity and language, some of these steps in this pattern are expedited and compressed.

The international council for federal countries, the Forum of Federations, is based in Ottawa, Ontario. It helps share best practices amongst countries with federal systems of government, and currently includes nine countries as partner governments.

Federations and Other Forms of State

In a federation the component states are regarded as in some sense sovereign, insofar as certain powers are reserved to them that may not be exercised by the central government. However, a federation is more than a mere loose alliance of independent states. The component states of a federation usually possess no powers in relation to foreign policy and so they enjoy no independent status under international law.

Some federations are called asymmetric because some states have more autonomy than others. An example of such a federation is Malaysia, in which Sarawak and Sabah entered the federation on different terms and conditions to the states of Peninsular Malaysia.

A federation often emerges from an initial agreement between a number of separate states. The purpose can be the will to solve mutual problems or to provide for mutual defence, or to create a nation state for an ethnicity spread over several states. The former was the case with the United States and Switzerland, the latter with Germany. However, as the history of countries and nations varies, the federalism system of a state can be quite different from these models. Australia, for instance, is unique in that it came into existence as a nation by the democratic vote of the citizens of each State who voted "yes" in referendums to adopt the Australian Constitution. Brazil, otherwise, has experienced both the federal and the unitary state through its history; some present day States of the Federation retain the borders set during Portuguese colonization (i.e. previous to the very existence of Brazilian state), whereas the latest State (Tocantins) was created by the 1988 Constitution, chiefly for administrative reasons.

Eight of ten of the World's largest countries by area are governed as Federations.

Unitary States

A unitary state is sometimes one with only a single, centralised, national tier of government. However, unitary states often also include one or more self-governing regions. The difference between a federation and this kind of unitary state is that in a unitary state the autonomous status of self-governing regions exists by the sufferance of the central government, and may be unilaterally revoked. While it is common for a federation to be brought into being by agreement between a number of formally independent states, in a unitary state self-governing regions are often created through a process of devolution, where a formerly centralised state agrees to grant autonomy to a region that was previously entirely subordinate. Thus federations are often established voluntarily from 'below' whereas devolution grants self-government from 'above'.

It is often part of the philosophy of a unitary state that, regardless of the actual status of any of its parts, its entire territory constitutes a single sovereign entity or nation-state, and that by virtue of this the central government exercises sovereignty over the whole territory *as of right*. In a federation, on the other hand, sovereignty is often regarded as residing notionally in the component states, or as being shared between these states and the central government.

De facto *Federations*

The distinction between a federation and a unitary state is often quite ambiguous. A unitary state may closely resemble a federation in structure and, while a central government may possess the theoretical right to revoke the autonomy of a self-governing region, it may be politically difficult for it to do so in practice. The self-governing regions of some unitary states also often enjoy greater autonomy than those of some federations. For these reasons, it is sometimes argued that some modern unitary states are *de facto* federations.

Spain

Spain is suggested as one possible de facto federation as it grants more self-government to its autonomous communities than most federations allow their constituent parts. For the Spanish parliament to revoke the autonomy of regions such as Galicia, Catalonia or the Basque Country would be a political near-impossibility, though nothing bars it legally. Additionally, some regions such as Navarra or the Basque Country have full control over taxation and spending, transferring a small payment to the central government for the common services (army, foreign relations, macroeconomic policy).

People's Republic of China

In the People's Republic of China, a form of de facto federation has evolved without formal legislation. This has occurred as largely informal grants of power to the provinces, to handle economic affairs and implement national policies. This has resulted in a system some have termed "de facto federalism with Chinese characteristics" (in reference to Deng Xiaoping's policy of socialism with Chinese characteristics). Constitutionally, the power vested in the special administrative regions of the People's Republic is granted from the Central People's Government, through decision by the National People's Congress.

European Union

The European Union (EU) is based on supranational principles which are neither confederal or federal. Robert Schuman the initiator of the European Community system wrote that a supranational Community like the Europe's founding European Coal and Steel Community lay midway between an association of States where they retained complete independence and a federation leading to a fusion of States in a super-state. The European Founding Fathers made a Europe Declaration at the time of the signing of the Treaty of Paris on 18 April 1951 saying that the Europe should be organized on a supranational foundation. They envisaged a structure quite different from a federation called the European Political Community.

The EU is a three pillar structure of the original supranational European Economic Community and the nuclear non-poliferation treaty, Euratom plus two largely intergovernmental pillars dealing with External Affairs and Justice and Home Affairs. The EU is therefore not a *de jure* federation, although some academic observers conclude that after 50 years of institutional evolution since the Treaties of Rome it is *becoming* one. The European Union possesses attributes of a federal state. However, its central government is far weaker than that of most federations and the individual members are sovereign states under international law, so it is usually characterized as an unprecedented form of supernational union. The EU possesses all the elements of a federal system, but each of the EU states is far more sovereign than in any other federal system. The EU has responsibility for important areas such as trade, monetary union, agriculture, fisheries. Nonetheless, EU member states retain the right to act independently in matters of foreign policy and defence, and also enjoy a near monopoly over other major policy areas such as criminal justice and taxation. Since the Treaty of Lisbon, Member States' right to leave the Union is codified, and the Union operates with more qualified majority voting (rather than unanimity) in many areas.

By the signature of this Treaty, the participating Parties give proof of their determination to create the first supranational institution and that thus they are laying the true foundation of an organized Europe. This Europe remains open to all nations. We profoundly hope that other nations will join us in our common endeavour.

– Europe Declaration signed by Konrad Adenauer (West Germany), Paul van Zeeland, Joseph Meurice (Belgium) Robert Schuman (France) Count Sforza (Italy) Joseph Bech (Luxembourg) and Dirk Stikker, J. R. M. van den Brink (The Netherlands).

Europe has charted its own brand of constitutional federalism.

– Joseph H. H. Weiler

Those uncomfortable using the "F" word in the EU context should feel free to refer to it as a quasi-federal or federal-like system. Nevertheless, for the purposes of the analysis here, the EU has the necessary attributes of a federal system. It is striking that while many scholars of the EU continue to resist analysing it as a federation, most contemporary students of federalism view the EU as a federal system. – *R. Daniel Kelemen*

A more announced view has been given by the German Constitutional Court. Here the EU is defined as 'an association of sovereign national states (*Staatenverbund*)'. With this view, the European Union resembles more of a confederation.

Capitalist vs. Socialist System

Recently, in our world of political ideas, words like Socialist and Fascist have made a resurgent comeback. Some people hurl them at domestic opponents and foreign enemies alike in order to rouse emotional responses. Others seek to redefine them to make them more avoidable or even acceptable, and still others seek to make them taboo in order to avoid discussion altogether. Many everyday voters believe such terms to be either cloudy artifacts of intellectual philosophy or simple labels for people they don't like.

The fact is that modern socioeconomic systems are very definite and can be explained in a way that is very understandable. That is the goal of this article. In it, I will explore what the terms Capitalism and Socialism actually mean. I will try to be as objective as possible, because both systems have strengths and weakness, but I hope you will agree with me in the end that one is preferable to the other. These socioeconomic systems can be explained simply and accurately, but we need to define a few terms.

The Nature of Wealth

The production of each worker in a society can be enumerated in the basic wealth unit of that society; US dollars in modern America, precious metals like gold and silver in ages past, or even agricultural units such as the koku of feudal Japan, which was the amount of rice one warrior consumed in one year. The full sum of this production is an individual's Wealth. This Wealth can be divided into two portions. Each worker uses one portion of his (or her) produced Wealth to provide the necessities of survival and basic comfort for himself and his dependents. This portion is called Maintenance. The other portion is called Capital, and it is this portion that enables civilization. Capital is the excess wealth an individual produces beyond his own needs and is distributed to the greater economy for a variety of purposes to include purchasing luxuries or status symbols, investing to create new sources of Wealth, providing for the common defence, and supporting public services, charity and savings. The division between these two portions is called the Subsistence Line.

Every socioeconomic system can be defined by who decides where the Subsistence Line is located and how Capital is distributed. In order to do this, we must define the possible decision authorities. There are only two in the systems discussed here. As has already been described, the worker is anyone who produces Wealth. The term 'worker' in this context should not be confused with the often described 'working class'. Classes are artificial constructs based on how much Capital groups of individuals produce. For example, the working class describes individuals who typically produce just enough Wealth to get them slightly over the Subsistence Line. The poor reside below the Line, the middle class well above and the Wealth production of the rich is almost all Capital. All of them are workers in this definition. The other possible decision authority is the State, which is synonymous with the political elite. This can include any individual or group that has that capacity to make policy at a national level. A dictator, a hereditary or selected oligarchy, or elected officials are among the persons who can embody the State. How such persons come into power defines the political system of a society which also plays into the definition of its socioeconomic system.

The relationship between the workers and the State, how Wealth is distributed in a society and how the political elite are empowered can describe any socioeconomic system. For example, one of the oldest socioeconomic systems is Despotism. Despotism is a system that arises in a society with no understanding or respect for the Rule of Law, and in which one person, the Despot, is able to make policy by the exertion or threat of force on which he has a monopoly. In this way, the Despot is free to choose the location of the Subsistence Line for his subjects and distribute their Capital as he sees fit. If he sets the Subsistence Line way too low, his subjects will starve and either die off or rebel. If he sets it just a little too low, they will suffer from malnutrition and squalor and become less productive and more restive. However, if he sets it too high he will have less Capital to invest in his own security. Additionally, his subjects may choose to voluntarily lower their own Subsistence Line, thereby creating a source of Capital under their control which they may invest in things that weaken the Despot's power, such as weapons or foreign assistance. Luckily, Despotism has long since fallen out of style in the modern developed world. Democratic traditions and a respect for the Rule of Law (which took modern civilization centuries to develop) have elevated two socioeconomic systems to the forefront of modern ideas: Capitalism and Socialism.

The Case for Capitalism

In a Capitalist society, the Subsistence Line is set by popular opinion and each individual is free to define it as he sees fit. If an individual feels that a large enough residence to provide private living space for each member of his family, a fulfilling quantity of quality food and entertainment and one car for each adult are the necessities of life, than the Wealth necessary to procure these things lie below his Subsistence Line. All additional Wealth is Capital that the individual chooses how to reinvest. He may choose to purchase unnecessary luxuries, invest in status symbols or education to advance his career, save for retirement or to start a business, or give it to his favorite charity. In a Capitalist society each individual is considered to own the Wealth they produce, and the State exists to guarantee their Rights. The central Right that all others derive from in a Capitalist society is the Right to property.

A Capitalist society generally requires a Constitutional Republic to operate, and it is essentially inseparable from the concept of the Free Market. A basic definition of the Free Market is that prices for goods and services are determined solely by supply and demand. Because individuals are responsible for reinvesting their Capital they will generally purchase goods and services at the best possible price. A Capitalist believes that the complex and unpredictable nature of a full economic system will grow and remain stable due to this bottom up style of planning.

Major changes to Capital distribution will only take place when a large number of people believe it to be in their best interest and will only last as long as they remain profitable. The Constitutional Republic is necessary because the State will naturally attempt to increase its own influence. The Constitution serves to chain the State down within the limits of the Law and checks and balances must be used to prevent the political elite from circumventing the Constitution.

Criticisms of Capitalism

There are two primary criticisms of the Capitalist system. The first is based on the extremes of the economic classes. The critics point out that the wealthiest classes, who have much more Capital than most, are able to influence society disproportionately by the way they choose to distribute that Capital. They conclude that since each individual acts to advance their own interests, these actions are probably detrimental to some other individual or group in society, and therefore the rich shall abuse the poor and the working classes whom no one has a motivation to protect. The poor, who reside below the Subsistence Line, will never have Capital to invest in their own interest and will therefore never have the opportunity to advance.

The second criticism of Capitalism states that faith in the Free Market is erroneous. While generally accepting the theory of supply and demand, the critics believe that the people as a mass are capable of being panicked or defrauded by a variety of nefarious entities, including foreign governments, plotting corporations, scapegoat populations and demagogues. These critics believe that a central governing body, the State, must be entrusted with the responsibility and empowered with the resources to guide and protect the population from these corrupting influences, which brings us the other dominant modern socioeconomic system – Socialism.

The Socialist State

In a Socialist society, the State, embodied by the political elite, determines how much of an individual's produced Wealth is Capital. It then takes this Capital from the workers and decides how to distribute it in order to meet the needs of the nation and of the interests that maintain the State's power. What differentiates a Socialist system from the Despotic system earlier used as an example is the source of the State's power. It is true that the State's ultimate power still lies in the application of force. If a worker fails to deliver his Capital to the state, he will be fined and eventually arrested. If he resists arrest, he will be captured or killed. However, a Socialist State rarely requires the full use of this force when compared to a Despotic system, because the State relies on its society's respect for the Rule of Law. The State uses the Law, as it was intended or not, to justify the use of force. Due to their respect for the Rule of Law, the people cooperate as long as the powers and actions of the State remain tolerable.

The typical political systems that support a Socialist socioeconomic system are Democracy and Selected Oligarchy. While Democracy is not completely necessary, it is often the political system of a Socialist society because Democratic traditions and the Rule of Law usually develop together in a symbiotic relationship, and as stated previously, the Rule of Law is necessary for a Socialist society. Democracy, or majority rule, also serves to promote Socialism as it is much simpler to convince large groups to vote away theirs' and others' property rights than to freely invest their Capital in a cause.

Divisions in Socialism

There are two broad styles of Socialism – Popular (Marxism) and National (Fascism) – that are defined by the priorities the State follows when distributing Capital. If the State's primary goal is to provide for the economic and social security of the workers it is a Popular Socialist State. In a Democracy, the Popular Socialist State derives its power mainly by promising the distribution of Wealth to several large, dissatisfied political or social minority groups which together make a majority. A National Socialist State invests the majority of its Capital in the security and aggrandizement of the State itself. In a Democracy, the National Socialist State derives much of its power by encouraging the population to identify as part of the State so that individuals take pride in the State's accomplishments (scientific, cultural or political) whatever their own economic status. In this way, dissent against the State becomes dissent against the Nation. Other common elements of National Socialism are continuous war and conquest as well as the identification of a scapegoat population.

Criticisms of Socialism

There are three primary criticisms levelled against Socialism. The first and simplest is that the State is incapable of effectively managing large and complex structures like a national economy. After all, the State is made up of error-prone individuals. Critics believe that any action the State takes (price fixing, tampering with the monetary unit, foreign intervention, etc.) will inevitably cause unintended side effects or "blowback". To correct this blowback, the State will intervene further creating additional unexpected blowback, and in this way the problem will eventually become unmanageable.

The second criticism asserts that because individuals are deprived of their Capital and because they believe the State will care for them if they fail, individuals have no incentive to produce more than they need for their own Maintenance. The State's source of Capital will therefore dry up, and it will be forced to lower the Subsistence Line to artificially produce more Capital. Eventually, it will not be able to fulfil the promises it has made to the populous or the commitments of its Empire.

The critics' final point is that as the State develops more power to distribute Wealth, it becomes a greater target of manipulation. Powerful individuals, special interest groups and even foreign governments will lobby for their share of the loot. The critics believe that the more loot that is at stake the more determined these interests will be to influence the State.

The Current Condition of the American System and the Way Forward

Most Americans recognize that a battle of socioeconomic philosophies exists in our nation today. However, most also mistakenly believe that this battle is between Capitalism and Socialism, using whatever words they choose for the concepts I have previously elucidated. This is not the case. Free Market Capitalism has been swiftly eroded by manipulations and outright negligence of our Nation's Laws and Constitution over the last century. The 16th Amendment of 1913 which paved the way for the Federal Income Tax determined that the State had the right to deprive individuals of their property – their Capital. The establishment of the Fed and of dozens of other "regulatory" institutions and the redistribution of vast sums of Wealth have made the State extremely powerful. The United States of America is ruled today by a Socialist State.

The debate now in our two-party system is between Popular Socialism – the Democrats – and National Socialism – the Republicans. Both systems are doomed to failure as is made obvious by the failures of Socialism in the past. It is vital that the citizens of this nation seek to educate themselves on the founding principles of our Constitution and be wary of lessons they are taught on broadcast television or mass newspapers. The State's interest lies in convincing the citizenry that the Free Market is the cause of internal failures and not its own misguided attempts at intervention. The State's interest also lies in convincing the citizenry that foreign enemies exist for no avoidable reason rather than due to its own misguided attempts at intervention overseas.

No system is perfect. The criticisms of Capitalism are valid. However, a Capitalist system lays the onus of morality on the individual by how he chooses to invest his Capital. A Socialist system deprives the individual of all responsibility. Moreover, it is intrinsically immoral because it is based on the forced deprivation of individuals' property. The way forward for America lies in the Founding Fathers wise faith in Free Market Capitalism and the way to destruction lies in the dangerous lure of Socialism.

3

Political Traditions and Revolutionary Legacies

Secretariat: United Nations

In the light of the international community's increasing awareness of slow economic growth in many developing countries and countries in transition from a centrally planned economy to a free-market economy (transitional economy countries) and of the related negative global implications, it is essential that the United Nations should promote and implement action-oriented responses aimed at helping those countries to reduce poverty and achieve sustainable economic growth. In the long run, the eradication of poverty throughout the world will serve the interests of economically developed countries as well as those of other countries.

Approximately one third of the total population of developing countries-over 1 billion people-live in poverty according to the yardstick currently applied, namely annual per capita consumption of less than $370. They are the "forgotten people" in the development process, having received little or no benefits from economic growth over the past decades. The poor are unable to achieve a minimum level of living and cannot afford adequate food, clothing or housing. Their life expectancies are low, the death rates of their children are high and about 10 million children receive absolutely no basic education. In fact, some 15 million children under 5 years of age die annually in circumstances that would not normally result in death in economically developed countries.

Generally speaking, poverty is more acute in rural areas, although urban poverty has been on the rise. The poor tend to live on marginal rural lands or in shanty towns on the outskirts of cities. The rural poor have little or nor access to government services, technical assistance or sources of credit. The rural poor include large numbers of the landless as well as tenants or sharecroppers with precarious land tenure arrangements. This group of poor has greatly expanded in recent decades; it forms the largest group of potential migrants to urban areas.

The most effective means of reducing poverty is the adoption of national development strategies, including sound macroeconomic and structural policies, which encourage sustainable growth that increases income-earning opportunities for the poor and develop the human resources of the poor, particularly through broad access to education, health and family planning services. In a working paper entitled "Approach to overcoming poverty through self-help and target-group-oriented financing instruments" prepared for the Ministry for Economic Cooperation of the Federal Republic of Germany in 1994, it was observed that "the poor in the third world do help themselves:

"they achieve individually and as groups, a considerable output in terms of savings and labour;"-

they may become creditworthy, obtain, put to good use and repay credit: the poorest people have proved to be particularly reliable clients of banks; they work productively in many different ways and are able to increase their productivity;

"they form groups, often on a voluntary basis and informally, which arrange their activities: neighbourhood help, labour, amount, purpose and sequence of credits, group security, settlement of conflicts;"-they contribute to the balanced development of all members of the group without curbing the dynamism of the individual;

"all these activities help to form the nucleus and points of crystallization for democratic processes of development."

The use of public financial resources to improve the health and education of the poor has proved to be an investment that benefits the economy as a whole, for a healthy, well-educated workforce means higher productivity and more rapid economic growth. However, welfare programmes which include no measures aimed at bringing about corresponding increases in the productivity of the recipients are bound to be short-lived and even counterproductive.

Generally speaking, the capitalist revolution (free-market reforms and well-conceived and prudently implemented privatization in the post cold war period) has increased foreign investment, streamlined the public sector and reduced inflation, bringing about a significant level of stability and prosperity. However, in countries where objectively justifiable reforms have been marred by cronyism and nepotism and undertaken without a concomitant commitment to justice, solid money, competitive markets and democracy, the result has been unbridled mercantilism, with the vast majority of the population being denied the opportunities and benefits of economic growth. In some cases, populist opposition has emerged in protest against dishonestly implemented privatizations which have simply replaced public monopolies with private monopolies. The inadequacies of the self-offs are being used by enemies of free-market reforms, who claim that such reforms are simply a subterfuge for giving more advantages to the rich while neglecting the poor. Improperly implemented free-market reforms have also sometimes given rise to populist opposition to structural adjustments backed by the International Monetary Fund (IMF), which, while often necessary, are perceived as being harmful to the poor.

It is against this background that developing and transitional economy countries must grapple with the problem of maximizing the mobilization of financial resources from both domestic and foreign sources while at the same time ensuring that those resources are used in the most efficient and productive way so as to benefit all classes of the population, including the poor, and that public financial operations are reliably accounted for so as to inspire confidence among both citizens and foreign donors and investors.

To that end, the Governments of developing and transitional economy countries, with the cooperation of the international community, in particular the United Nations, should seek to strengthen their capacity in the following areas:

I. Enhanced resource mobilization:

A. Enhanced mobilization of domestic financial resources:

1. Enhanced mobilization of government revenue;

- Enhanced mobilization of private (business and personal) savings;
- Enhanced mobilizations of private foreign investment;

II. Improved government financial management (public expenditure planning, budgeting, performance evaluation and accountability);

III. Public enterprise reform and private enterprise development:

A. Public enterprise reform;

B. Private enterprise development.

Enhanced Resource Mobilization

Although governmentalism is not the solution, inducing economic and social progress within the free market system, that is through private persuasion, depends to a very significant extent on the efforts of Governments. Government policies should reflect a sustained commitment to improving the lot of the poor. International factors-notably world trade, foreign direct investment, foreign loans and foreign aid-can play an important part in a strategy for reducing poverty. Foreign aid can provide investment capital, foreign technology and skilled personnel. It has sometimes been an effective instrument for alleviating poverty, but it has not always fulfilled its potential, for various reasons. Bilateral donors have many different motives (political, strategic, commercial and humanitarian), the reduction of poverty usually being far from the most important. Furthermore, a number of recipient countries seem to have fallen into what has been referred to as "aid dependency" and many poverty-oriented projects funded by aid have failed to benefit the poor. A solid case for greater amounts of aid could, however, be made if more recipient countries were to concentrate seriously on combating poverty and if donors profited from the lessons of experience. Projection by the Development Assistance Committee (DAC) of the Organisation for Economic Cooperation and Development (OECD) have indicated that aid could increase to $108 billion or $144 billion by the year 2000 if aid/GNP ratios of 0.5 or 0.7 per cent respectively were attained by those donors which are currently below these ratios while donors above them maintain their current levels. However, foreign aid could increase to only $64 billion in the year 2000 if it grows at 2 per cent a year. Foreign aid fosters a prospering and peaceful international environment. When properly used, it is a catalyst for development.

Despite the encouraging trend in the international flow of foreign direct investment, net resource flows, particularly to low-income countries and severely indebted lower-middle-income countries, have remained stagnant or declined, highlighting the need for the international community to continue mobilizing adequate financing in support of developing countries' efforts to move towards external viability combined with sustainable growth. International efforts in the form of increased foreign aid and open trade policies can support and complement the actions of recipient countries, but it is the Governments of the latter countries which bear the primary responsibility for their own economic and social progress.

Revitalizing the vision of development requires expanded capital formation through enhanced efforts to mobilize financial resources. This means intensified efforts to mobilize an increased volume of domestic financial resources and attain more private foreign capital.

Enhanced Mobilization of Domestic Financial Resources

No matter how great the contribution of foreign capital, it must essentially serve as a supplement to domestic financial resources if a country is to embark on a self-sustaining development process. Thus the investment requirements of a country have to be met increasingly from the savings of the three major sectors of its national economy: (a) the government sector, whose savings are represented by the excess of tax revenue (including customs duties) and non-tax resources (i.e. grants, property income, sales proceeds of public assets, fines and other government receipts) over current government expenditures; (b) the business sector, whether corporate or unincorporated, which derives its savings from the retained profits of enterprises; and (c) the household sector, which derives its savings from salaries, wages and professional fees in the case of individuals and from profits in the case of family businesses. The savings of the household sector include the savings of property owners or rentiers who do not operate business enterprises and the strictly personal savings of individual households. In most, if not all countries, the household sector currently accounts for the greater part of savings.

Enhanced Mobilization of Government Revenue

Governments have a broad responsibility for providing services of vital importance for development, including notably education, health, water and sewerage, roads, public transport and essential housing. Certain elements of government current expenditures, notably for such purposes as education and health, are as important to development as capital expenditures on roads and buildings. In addition, the Government may either engage directly in productive activity, if the private sector is unwilling to fill any gap that may exist in the provision of essential services or seek to channel resources to the private sector for the promotion or expansion of enterprises. The ability of the Government to provide necessary services depends on the amount of tax revenue that it is in a position to collect. Failure to raise adequate revenue tends to reduce the amount of services that can be provided or to cause inflationary pressures, which in turn, by generating additional import demand, spill over to the external sector intensifying pressures on the balance of payments.

A critical bottleneck in the process of poverty eradication is weak fiscal discipline, which in an unstable economic environment may give rise to large fiscal imbalances that are financed through inflation. Many countries run fiscal deficits to finance their expenditures because their tax bases are too limited to allow a high tax burden. Even when broader tax bases are available, tax administrations are too inefficient to collect the taxes legally due and political realities often make it difficult to increase the tax burden. Owing to the lack of developed capital markets and the non-availability of external borrowing, fiscal deficits are often financed wholly or partly by central banks, that is, through money creation, which increases the general price level, thus reducing the real value of the monetary unit. Greater efficiency in the collection of taxes can reduce deficit financing and the inflationary process. High inflation has critical allocative and distributional implications that impede growth, inter alia by encouraging capital flight.

Fiscal policy plays a major role in promoting and sustaining stabilization and growth, given the close interdependence between fiscal, monetary and external sector policies. Specific fiscal instruments affect savings, capital flight, foreign investment and so on.

Tax evasion and avoidance at both the national and international levels have serious implications for fiscal policy. They violate the principle of fiscal equity and undermine the concept of voluntary compliance with tax laws. They can greatly diminish the value of codified incentives and thereby affect allocative behaviour to thwart redistributional programmes, create artificial biases in macroeconomic indicators and increase the tax burden when tax rates must be increased in order to offset the revenue losses incurred, thereby imposing an unfair burden on taxpayers who cannot shift their tax liabilities. The greater the extent of tax evasion and avoidance, the more difficult it is to finance government expenditure without inflation or in other words to increase tax revenue adequately, with the result that the excess of expenditure over taxation is positively correlated with the tax burden. Tax paying has, in fact, come to be regarded as unfair, since public expenditure has been increasingly perceived as failing to yield commensurate benefits either to taxpayers personally or to their communities.

Tax administrators have adopted various measures to reduce opportunities for tax evasion and avoidance. The scope of these measures varies according to the characteristics of the country concerned, including its legal structure, its political system, its traditions and the psychology of its people. These measures have included reliance on indirect taxes, reliance on declarations and withholding of taxes by third parties, the operation of an efficient system and cross-checking of information, auditing and the unilateral determination of taxable income, the bilateral determination of taxable income (forfeit method) and the use of legislative provision administrative rulings and judicial decisions, as well as the enactment and enforcement of penalties. International tax evasion and avoidance can be combated by the conclusion of bilateral tax treaties providing for mutual assistance and the exchange of information.

The proper implementation of the aforementioned measures requires an efficient and effective revenue administration. The need to introduce higher tax rates and/or new taxes can often be reduced or eliminated by strengthening the revenue administration. Similarly, the result of attempts to generate additional revenue through higher tax rates or more taxes may prove disappointing unless determined and coordinated efforts are made to enhance the efficiency and effectiveness of the revenue administration. The weaker the revenue administration, the more limited the choice of taxes, and unless the administration is capable of enforcing any new taxes, they may not have a significant impact on tax revenue. Efforts to gear a country's tax structure to the capability of the revenue administration can lead to an increase in revenue by reducing tax evasion and avoidance. Revenue administration constraints tend to determine a country's actual tax structure. Revenue administration performance may lead to the amendment of existing tax laws or the adoption of new laws, so as to introduce more broadly based income and consumption taxes, thus reducing dependence on foreign trade taxes.

Action aimed at enhancing the efficiency and effectiveness of revenue administrations has focused on such factors as the institutional framework, management, compliance (including registration) assessment, collection, investigation and audit, revenue accounting, information systems and taxpayer education information and assistance. Furthermore, steps have been taken to make taxes easier to administer, thus permitting more effective application of the tax laws with a more economical use of resources. A revenue administration capable of applying the tax laws efficiently and effectively constitutes a major means of securing additional government revenue without raising taxes and/or introducing new taxes, an unpopular course which many Governments would prefer to avoid. As the Roman Emperor Tiberius observed when advised to raise taxes, "a good shepherd shears his sheep, he does not flay them". In a world environment characterized by disillusionment with governmentalism or state interventionism, a revenue administration of high quality will bolster economic restructuring through entrepreneurial development, with positive effects on both the pattern and the rate of growth.

Enhanced Mobilization of Private (Business and Personal) Savings

In the business sector, savings are an essential component of successful business operations. Business profits furnish by far the most readily available source of financing for capital expenditure, and this is especially so in the developing countries, where highly developed capital markets do not generally exist to permit external financing. Business enterprises, both corporate and unincorporate, tend to save and invest a large proportion of their savings-a proportion which is invariably much higher than the corresponding share of wage and salary income savings. Thus, the higher the share of business profits in total income, the larger will the aggregate savings ratio tend to be.

Personal savings out of wages and salary incomes largely represent the postponement of consumption, more importantly from the working age to the retirement age. To the extent that the retirement motive predominates, the net contributions of this source will depend on the excess of the income earned by the current generation of working age over the income earned by the generation currently in retirement. It will, therefore, depend on the rate of growth of real incomes, and particularly on the rate of growth of the number of wage and salary earners and on earnings per head.

In some cases a large part of the monetized agricultural output is turned over as payment of rent to owners who are economically passive, for example to absentee landlords. The propensity to save out of such rentier income is likely to be low, since such rentiers normally have little motive for saving. They have no business motive, and since income derived from the ownership of land may be regarded as safe and permanent, there may be little retirement motive for saving either.

Personal savings take the form of cash, sight deposits (whether in current accounts or savings accounts), time-deposits, securities, life insurance policies and contributions to pension schemes. Relatively substantial savings in developing countries are held in the form of cash, the most obvious reason for this situation being the inadequacy of the financial intermediation framework. The hoarding of cash and the preference of savers for other highly liquid types of savings may be attributed to a number of factors, including the desire to have cash on hand for use in emergencies or in speculative transactions as a hedge against the gradual depreciation of the real value of savings, indifference to, or ignorance of, the interest that could be earned if the savings were deposited with a savings institution, and even mistrust of financial intermediaries. The development of banking services towards more advanced customer-oriented concepts including payment of wages and salaries, pensions etc. via bank accounts, might increasingly counteract these types of behaviour.

Efforts to increase the aggregate volume of personal savings deposited with financial institutions have involved the use of various incentives adapted to the social and economic conditions in the countries concerned. These incentives may be classified into three main categories:

(a) Incentives involving the protection of savings;

(b) Incentives involving higher rates of return on savings;

(c) Incentives involving the offer of credit facilities to savers.

The protection of savings may relate to their nominal value, their real value or both. Protection of the nominal value of savings depends on a combination of factors, namely: efficient and prudent internal management of savings mobilization institutions supplemented by efficient government supervisory action; availability of adequate risk-bearing resources, supplemented by the existence of lenders of last resort; and availability of a formal guarantee of all or part of the funds deposited with savings mobilization institutions.

With regard to the maintenance of the real value of savings, it is well known that persistent inflation results in a redistribution of real income and wealth which benefits those whose income and wealth increase more rapidly than prices and is prejudicial to those whose income and wealth lag behind the rise in prices. The latter group includes fixed-income groups and pensioners, holders of bank deposits and holders of fixed-interest securities and insurance policies. Inflationary pressures tend to curb the propensity to save, thus diminishing the volume of voluntary savings available for productive investment. The continuous erosion of the purchase power of money undermines the ability and willingness of households to save in monetary forms and induces a shift to domestic nonmonetary assets such as land, housing, precious metal and jewellery, or else to foreign assets. Various techniques have been used to counteract the effects of inflation. They include techniques which do not adjust the value of financial transactions to the actual rate of inflation and the techniques which do. The techniques in the first category involve increasing interest rates on both savings and loans to a level commensurate with the expected rate of inflation. The techniques which adjust savings transactions and loan transactions so as to maintain their real value are known by various names such as indexing techniques, value-linking techniques, monetary correction techniques and purchasing power guarantees.

The incentives involving higher rates of return on savings include attractive rates of interest, tax privileges and premiums and bonuses. Concerning incentives involving the use of credit facilities to savers, the promise of liens as a means of encouraging personal saving goes back to the origin of cooperative and mutualist credit, although its use has spread since the end of the Second World War, both geographically and in range of purposes.

Enhanced Mobilization of Private Foreign Investment

In 1995, private capital flows to developing countries exceeded $170 billion. However, 75 per cent of those flows went to just 12 countries. About 50 countries-most of them very poor-received virtually no private flows. Addressing the Board of Governors of the World Bank Group in October 1996, the President of the Bank observed "Our new world of open markets raises the stakes for developing countries. Investment is linked to good policies and good governance, liberal trade regimes and high savings rate, combined with sound legal and judicial systems. Simply put, capital goes to those countries that get the fundamentals right".

The internal rate of capital formation in many developing countries and transitional economy countries is far below that necessary for satisfactory development performance. If such a rate is to be achieved, there must be a very large increase in the rate at which capital flows into those countries from outside sources. Private foreign investment may give a great impetus to economic development, as it provides capital-importing countries not only with much-needed capital, but also with managerial and technological know-how. In particular, it may help to diversify the economy and to strengthen exports through improved technology. The attraction of private foreign investment requires a sound understanding of the rights and obligations of capital-importing countries, investors and Governments of capital exporting countries.

Joint ventures ideally provide a highly desirable arrangement for bringing together foreign private capital, Governments of capital-importing countries and local entrepreneurs. However, the extent of participation of local capital in individual projects depends on such factors as public policy, local conditions and the availability of domestic capital and entrepreneurship. There may be a need to reform the tax systems in both capital-exporting and capital-importing countries so as to encourage investment in the latter. Bilateral tax treaties provide an important medium for defining the scope of tax liability in both categories of countries eliminating double taxation and avoiding the negation of incentives afforded by capital-importing countries. International double taxation has a detrimental effect on the movement of capital, technology and persons, as well as on the exchange of goods and services. The removal of this obstacle is highly important for the development of economic relations between countries. In particular, it is most desirable to clarify, standardize and guarantee the tax situation of individuals or enterprises deriving income from, or owning capital in, other countries. Bilateral tax agreements constitute by their very existence a proof of active encouragement of foreign investment. They allay legitimate tax concerns of private foreign entrepreneurs about policy reversals and sudden unexpected decisions prompted by domestic political considerations. They are viewed as placing on an equal tax reciprocity footing countries possessing equal tax sovereignty, but unequal economic and financial status. The constantly evolving nature of fiscal circumstances makes it necessary at the current juncture to revise the 1979 United Nations Model Double Taxation Convention between Developed and Developing Countries to take into account the growing globalization and liberalization of the world economy, the broadening of international fiscal relations, the emergence of new technologies and new methods of effecting cross-border transactions and the increased sophistication of transfer pricing techniques and tax evasion and avoidance practices.

Domestic financial institutions have served as a catalyst in attracting foreign capital and the development of capital markets so as to increase the rate at which domestic private capital is generated. Such institutions as the national development banks combine specialist knowledge of finance and industry with an awareness of local conditions and problems. They are, therefore, well placed to deal with questions involving relations with local partners, transfer of technology and the scale of investment required for particular projects. They can also assist in the promotion and organization of other financial bodies such as local stock exchanges and may introduce new forms of investment media.

Improved Government Financial Management

Developing countries and transitional economy countries must constantly bear in mind that government financial management plays a major role in the implementation of policies aimed at promoting national economic social and other developmental goals. Government financial management encompasses all or part of the processes and functions of planning and programming budgeting, budget execution and accounting audit and evaluation. It is aimed at ensuring that to the maximum practical extent, a government's financial resources are used lawfully, efficiently and effectively and with transparency and accountability to the legislature and the people.

Financial management reform typically incorporates the following components:

(a) Use of structured planning and programming as a means of evaluating and selecting ways of achieving desired objectives;

(b) Taking resource allocation decisions within the framework of a unified budget;

(c) Integration of budgeting and accounting;

(d) Use of accounting principles that match service delivery with service costs;

(e) Encouragement of financial accountability;

(f) Measurement of outputs as well as inputs;

(g) Preparation of consolidated reports.

As the Group of Experts on Public Administration and Finance noted in the report on its twelfth meeting (A/50/525-E/1995/122, paras. 113-114): "In many countries, financial management capabilities have been eroded by the pursuit of financial populism, ineffective and distorted budgetary mechanisms and the breakdown of existing financial management institutions. "A central concern for all countries is how to harmonize methods of strategic management and control of aggregate financial variables with processes for changing expenditure priorities and enabling effective and innovative management of service delivery institutions".

In view of the limited buoyancy of revenue mobilizations, the financial resources obtained, whether from foreign or domestic sources, must be used rationally if development goals or planned fiscal adjustments are to be attained. Accordingly, an increasing number of countries have been re-examining their expenditure priorities with the dual aim of curtailing their fiscal deficits and ensuring that the available financial resources are put to the most effective use.

Budget administration and expenditure monitoring and control procedures must be improved. Reduction in the overall budget deficit tends often to be achieved by expenditure-containment measures rather than revenue-increasing measures. Indeed, in the short term, the possibility for substantial increases in term, the possibility for substantial increases in revenue is limited. More emphasis should be placed on controlling expenditure growth, given that the expenditure base is generally larger than the revenue base. Good budgeting is a prerequisite.

Budgeting ideally involves:

(a) The appraisal of various governmental activities in terms of their contribution to national objectives;

(b) The projection of government activities over an adequate time period;

(c) The determination of how these objectives can be attained with minimum resources;

(d) The revision of the budget, in the light of changing circumstances and experiences.

All budgets are plans, but not all plans are budgets. Generally speaking, a plan is aimed at identifying and defining the policies best calculated to achieve objectives; it provides guidelines for policies through the translation of these guidelines into physical targets and specific tasks.

Numerous countries have adopted the planning-programming-budgeting system, which specifies programme objectives in quantitative terms, measures benefits and evaluates the cost of each programme in the light of the expected results and the results actually achieved. Indeed, the scope of a government budget should not be limited to a statement of the receipts and expenditures of government, but should reflect the overall concerns of development. In order to give a comprehensive picture of government strategy, a central government budget should cover consolidated transactions of the levels of government and of government entities. Similarly, to ensure consistency and balance in the mobilization and use of real resources, the main budget should be accompanied by budgets for foreign exchange, credit manpower and other real and material resources. Multi-year budgeting stimulates the formulation and pursuance of long-term and consistent policies for the mobilization of resources. It brings into focus issues of demand management and real resource balance and enables coordinated and uninterrupted implementation of long-term projects.

Programming budgeting is an effective management tool in developing countries and transitional economy countries, it must take into account uncertainties of both external and internal origins, which are likely to increase in the foreseeable future. In order to avoid major economic collapses and setbacks, such countries have to establish reserves not only of foreign exchange, but also of other material resources; they should exert a substantially greater control over income distributions and national flow of funds. Increasing external vulnerability exerts a strong influence on budgeting. Coping with uncertainties calls for considerable innovation and flexibility in budget policies and techniques. Success in the preparation of comprehensive budgets in the formulation of sound budget policies and in the monitoring of budget implementation depends on the availability of required data and information. Measures must, therefore, be implemented for improving the collection and compilation of needed data.

In the monitoring of the development process, agencies and officials responsible for budgets and programmes need continuous information on the structure of the economy, the mobilization and use of resources and their costs, the outputs generated and the contribution of outputs to national objectives and goals. Moreover, data is required, not only on the financial aspects of transactions, but also on their economic and physical aspects and performance. In order to achieve consistency and allocative efficiency in the management and implementation of programmes and projects, such data is needed at the national, sectoral, programme and project levels. It may be difficult to generate such information in many countries because of the weakness of the accounting system. The reforms needed in these systems should include the reconciliation of budget and accounting structures training of accountants, decentralization of accounting responsibilities, proper record-keeping and production of timely and accurate data.

The scope of public accounting systems may need to be extended to define and introduce new accounting concepts and to establish multiple accounting structures to generate the various kinds of data required for managing public affairs and measuring the cost, performance and productivity of government programmes and projects. The strengthening of accounting at the project level can improve management of the project and also throw considerable light on the efficient use of resources and on optimal resource mixes.

In many countries, there is little liaison among planning, budget, accounting and audit agencies. If accounting is to serve the overall needs of financial management, coordination among all these agencies must be ensured.

With regard to public enterprise accounting, management accounting needs must be formulated in terms of sources and use of finance, draft on real resources, value-added in production, outputs generated, rate of consumption, fulfilment of objectives etc. As a first step, it is essential to establish uniform, but practicable definition of concepts. Clarity in concepts is a prerequisite for the development of a methodology and a coherent framework for evaluation. Practical approaches in accounting are flow-of-funds accounting, cost accounting, cash management accounting and depreciation accounting. The principal problem in cost accounting is to strengthen its use and extend its application to various facets of operations.

Quite often, the function of traditional audit, which is to verify the legality and financial accuracy of transactions, is not effectively performed, owing to the weakness of the accounting systems that provide the basis for audit, the lack of trained auditors, the insufficiency of the resources allocated to audit, the absence of clearly defined audit standards and, in some cases, the less than full independence enjoyed by audit authorities. Several measures are essential to enable audit systems to participate with other relevant agencies in the task of evaluating the efficiency and effectiveness of government programmes and projects. In the first place, budgeting has to provide a foundation for audit of performance. Planning and budgeting have to formulate clear targets and specific efficiency goals against which performance can be measured. A comprehensive methodology of evaluation incorporating targets efficiency goals, and target efficiency-related reporting and analysis needs to be developed to facilitate the audit of performance and to link it more closely with programme and project implementation. Agencies involved in planning, budgeting, accounting and audit have to collaborate in jointly defining the underlying concepts and units of measurement. They have to agree on their respective roles in performance audit and on the linkages between internal and external audits.

A sound public financial management system must be supported by an appropriate audit system which will determine how public resources have been used, evaluate the results achieved with those resources and verify compliance with legal accounting and administrative provisions and procedures. An adequate integrated public finance management and auditing system is essential to sustainable economic growth and the strengthening of democracy. It ensures that the Government will obtain the necessary resources while satisfying the collective needs of the population through the efficient, economical and effective use of those resources. It strengthens democracy by fostering accountability of government officials and promoting the credibility of the Government through transparency. To facilitate measurement of the efficiency of public commercial and industrial enterprises, there should be clear guidelines on the objectives to be attained at both the sectoral and plant levels. Productive efficiency is a prerequisite for profitability. Precise guidelines should be provided at the plant level and should indicate clearly the goods and services in respect of which subsidies are warranted on grounds of social welfare considerations. Such guidelines should be consistent and apply equally to both public and private enterprises producing the same goods and services. Pricing policies should cover the costs (operating costs, depreciation, interest etc.) and, where feasible, aim at maximizing profits. Instead of concentrating the ownership of assets of non-privatized public enterprises entirely in government hands, workers, farmers, artisans, cooperative societies etc. can be induced to subscribe to the equity and loan capital of such enterprises. Through linkages, public enterprise involvement may induce private sector initiative and investment and an accelerated growth of backward areas.

Public Enterprise Reform and Private Enterprise Development

Public Enterprise Reform

Public enterprises have played an important role in many countries, both developed and developing, notwithstanding differences of political regime and philosophy. In many cases, they were established because private entrepreneurs did not have sufficient capital or incentive to undertake investments of benefit to the economy as a whole or to avoid the establishment of a private monopoly. Other reasons included distributional and allocative considerations, a desire to provide essential consumption goods and intermediate inputs at low prices, and the need to raise government revenue in the face of an ineffective tax system. Constituted as corporations, companies, holding companies, boards, statutory authorities, special accounts and autonomous agencies, they have encompassed not only public utilities and public transport (sectors in which they usually originated), but also other sectors including banking and finance, trading, tourism, agriculture and high-risk sectors such as aerospace. Their functions have included the manufacturing of capital and consumer goods, and mining and extractive industries. In a number of countries, strategic sectors such as energy, transportation, communications and iron, steel and coal productions have been completely operated by State-owned enterprises.

In recent decades, however, there has been increasing concern about the financial performance of the latter. Their dependence on the Government for subsidies and other forms of assistance has contributed to deficits in government budgets and has aggravated inflationary pressures and difficulties in controlling aggregate spending in national economies. As the growing operating deficits of inefficient public enterprises compounded the decline in real fiscal revenues during the recession of the early 1990s in many developing countries, disillusionment with their performance became increasingly common. The World Bank and several members of the Development Assistance Committee of OECD suggested efficiency measures which included closure investment, reduction of functions and private contact management. Western aid agencies generally refrained from financing State industrial enterprises, except where large economies of scale could be achieved only through public corporations, as in the case of certain fertilizers and metal plants in low-income countries.

A notable feature of the late 1980s and early 1990s was the ability of some developing countries to accelerate growth or maintain relatively high growth rates in the face of recession in the industrial world. However, in Central and Eastern Europe (including the former Union of Soviet Socialist Republics) the difficulties inherent in introducing viable market and State mechanisms ab initio to replace the defunct system of control and command took a severe toll, with sharp declines in industrial output, shortfalls in agricultural production, disruption of trade flows, external financial strains and fiscal imbalances.

The 1990s have seen the public sector in developing countries and transitional economy countries in severe crises, and radical reforms have often been needed. Three major options for reform emerged: restructuring, liquidation and privatization. No single option has been applicable everywhere and much depends on the performance record of a given public enterprise as judged against the objectives set for it. Privatization of enterprises partly or wholly owned by the Government and the restructuring of key strategic entities may be considered the most desirable options, particularly when a public enterprise is plagued by bad management owing to the lack of an effective system of ownership, control and budgeting, or to political pressures and corruption. Often, public enterprises have been pursuing goals having little or no connection with the original rationale for their establishment and some have been allowed to continue operating even when the reason for their existence no longer obtains. Privatization should not be equated with abandonment of all government intervention.

In most developing countries, government intervention through the provision of training, collaborative research and sometimes temporary budget support for expanded operations has not been detrimental to private initiative. Governments must, of course, assume their responsibilities by acting to foster financial stability and stimulate the level of economic activity.

A healthy dose of public prudence, scepticism and pragmatism is essential in order to achieve a smooth transition from communism to capitalism without reaching too far and going too fast. Public enterprise reform should be introduced thoughtfully on the basis of facts, not fiction. It should aim (a) at improving non-privatized public enterprise performance through the strengthening of management capabilities in corporate planning, performance contracting, financial accounting and information systems and (b) at strengthening the capacity of the overseeing institutions to manage the performance contracting, financial accounting analysis and public enterprise information systems and assist in the public enterprise reform process.

Private Enterprise Development

Private enterprise development can bring about a more widely based and dynamic development process. In developing countries and transitional economy countries there are actual or latent entrepreneurial resources which can be mobilized: there are many individuals who want to engage in activities of their own in which they see a direct relationship between their own efforts and the results achieved and from which they can derive profits and a personal sense of accomplishment. Broader mobilization of entrepreneurial talent can play an important role in exploiting widely scattered raw materials and in providing goods and services catering to local, as distinct from national, market requirements.

Entrepreneurship development must be thought of in the foreseeable future as a process in which small capital is allocated in various industrial and commercial fields. Capital is in very short supply and often unavailable through the ordinary channels. Banks are reluctant to incur the risks involved in the financing of indigenous businesses and will ration credit to entrepreneurs despite the desire of the latter to expand their business rapidly. New entrepreneurs may have to start with scarce capital funds and expand only to the extent to which they can generate and reinvest profits. Sometimes the intrusion of political considerations may force banks to provide loans to individuals with little or no capital of their own, who lack the business and technical know-how needed to use the loans wisely. Inadequate pre-investment investigations and the lack of any post-investment supervision will inhibit entrepreneurial development. The establishment of some sort of business extension service and of a proper system for guaranteeing bank loans wholly or partially in cases whose financing institutions do not want to assume the entire risk might promote entrepreneurial initiative and development. The guarantee scheme should stimulate that claims will be honoured within a specified time-limit after defaults are duly certified.

Entrepreneurship development can help to mobilize savings which otherwise would not be available for development. At the outset, small enterprises are almost invariably self-financed and can grow only through the reinvestment of internally generated profits. Because of the low capital-output ratios which generally characterize small and medium-sized enterprises, their development tends to bring about more employment in relation to investment than is the case with large enterprises. Practical constraints on the capacity of State and cooperative institutions call for the development of private initiative. The more that is privatized, the more crucial is the role of Government in ensuring that the enlarged private sector, in following its private interests, is also meeting the requirements of society as a whole. While the private sector is the "engine of development", the Government has to lay and maintain the "tracks" that is, create and maintain the legal and regulatory environment for private ownership and fair competition, correct appropriately for market failures, protect the disadvantaged and maintain economic stability, law and order. Similarly, only the Government can lead in envisioning and planning, in consultation with the business community, the key support institutions and infrastructure-physical and human resources-for business to thrive in an enabling environment conducive to private sector growth and investment support institutions include specialized agencies in fields such as finance, research and development acquisition of technology, export promotion, market intelligence and human resource development. All areas of policy impact on business so their business consequences need to be explored with relevant private sector representatives in a spirit of partnership. Particularly important are policies on trade and liberalization, deregulation, privatization competition, human resource development, labour investment promotion, anti-corruption and bribery action and environmental protection.

At the Microcredit Summit held in Washington, D.C. on 2 February 1997, Presidents of the world's poorest nations, development bankers and global corporate chiefs promised that they would work to steer $10 billion in commercial credit to small-business owners worldwide living below the poverty line. Microcredit supporters hope to reach their goal of nurturing prosperity from the ground up by tapping about $10 billion of "private capital flows" from commercial banks and investors. An equal amount of aid money would come from charities and Governments in the next seven years. The conference organizers said that by 2005, they intend to steer some $21 billion into 100 million micro-loans. The organizers of the Summit observed that what is needed for small lending to grow are small institutions through which the credit can be processed and that building them was the goal of the Summit organizers. It was noted that since market-friendly South-East Asian and Latin American countries have posted growth rates outpacing developed country rates in recent years, the idea of shifting into private hands the industries and services formerly run by the State has become popular in development circles. As a result, entrepreneurship is a new buzzword among aid providers. Sheikh Hasina, the Prime Minister of Bangladesh declared that loans as small as $100, often called microloans or microcredit "have the potential to strike a serious blow to poverty, in my country and in countries all around the world".

The Ambiguous Legacy of the French Revolution

At its core, the French Revolution was a political movement devoted to liberty. But what that liberty actually was and what was required to realize it remained open questions during the Revolution, as they have ever since. Some historians have suggested that what the revolutionaries' liberty meant in practice was violence and a loss of personal security that pointed to the totalitarian regimes of the 20th century. This negative view had its roots in the ideas of many counter-revolutionaries, who criticized the Revolution from its beginning. These ideas gained new popularity during the period of reaction that set in after Napoleon's final defeat in 1815, when the monarchy and its counter-revolutionary allies were restored to power.

However, the majority of Europeans and non-Europeans came to see the Revolution as much more than a bloody tragedy. These people were more impressed by what the Revolution accomplished than by what it failed to do. They recalled the Revolution's abolition of serfdom, slavery, inherited privilege, and judicial torture; its experiments with democracy; and its opening of opportunities to those who, for reasons of social status or religion, had been traditionally excluded.

One of the most important contributions of the French Revolution was to make revolution part of the world's political tradition. The French Revolution continued to provide instruction for revolutionaries in the 19th and 20th centuries, as peoples in Europe and around the world sought to realize their different versions of freedom. Karl Marx would, at least at the outset, pattern his notion of a proletarian revolution on the French Revolution of 1789. And 200 years later Chinese students, who weeks before had fought their government in Tiananmen Square, confirmed the contemporary relevance of the French Revolution when they led the revolutionary bicentennial parade in Paris on July 14, 1989.

Along with offering lessons about liberty and democracy, the Revolution also promoted nationalism. Napoleon's occupation provoked nationalist groups to organize in Italy and Germany. Also influential was the revolutionaries' belief that a nation was not a group of royal subjects but a society of equal citizens. The fact that most European countries are or are becoming parliamentary democracies, along the lines set out by the French Revolution, suggests its enduring influence.

Socially, the Revolution was also important. Clearly, society in France and to a lesser extent in other parts of Europe would never be the same. Once the ancient structure of privilege was smashed, it could not be pieced together again. The Revolution did not fundamentally alter the distribution of wealth, but that had not been the intention of most of the revolutionaries. Insofar as legal equality gradually became the norm in France and Europe, the revolutionaries succeeded.

The cultural impact is harder to assess. The Revolution did not succeed in establishing the national school system it envisioned, but it did found some of France's elite educational institutions that have produced some of that nation's greatest leaders. Its attack on the church had profound repercussions, making the status of the church a central political issue, which even today divides France politically and culturally.

As for economic development, the Revolution probably hurt more than it helped. In the long term, the liberation of the economy from royal controls, the standardization of weights and measures, and the development of a uniform civil law code helped pave the way for the Industrial Revolution. But the disruptive effects of war on the French economy offset the positive effects of these changes. In terms of total output, the economy was probably set back a generation.

The Legacy of the Russian Revolution

In 1997, on the 80th anniversary of the Russian revolution, PETER TAAFFE reviewed Orlando Figes's book, A People's Tragedy, acclaimed as an authoritative history but, in reality, an attempt to obscure the real significance of the momentous events of 1917. (Socialism Today No.23, November 1997) As the 90th anniversary approaches we reprint this defence of the October revolution.

From the outset of the Russian revolution the representatives of the possessing classes, in Russia and worldwide, predicted the early collapse of what they called the 'Bolshevik dictatorship'.

On 9 November 1917, *The Times* approvingly quoted Naklukoff, the ambassador to Paris of the recently overthrown Kerensky government: "The situation must be regarded seriously but not tragically. Even if the facts be true there is no occasion for undue alarm... It is better that it should have taken place and be disposed of once and for all. The maximalist (Bolshevik) movement, by its arbitrary action, is already doomed. I have no doubt that the movement will be stopped by the first Cossack regiment that appears on the scene". The leader of the Social Revolutionary party gave the Bolsheviks 'no more than a few days', while the famous writer, Maxim Gorky, expected them to stay in power for two weeks. However, once it became clear that the soviet regime of the Bolsheviks would be more enduring than their earlier prophecies, the capitalists resorted to lies and slander. This was insufficient, so a more powerful 'argument' was used: arms, tanks, aeroplanes and interventionist armies to attack and destroy the revolution.

In the years since, no effort has been spared to distort what happened in 1917 and to falsify the ideas of the great leaders of the revolution, particularly Lenin and Trotsky. If the capitalists' fear of the contagious effects of the Russian revolution was justified in 1917 and subsequently, why today do historians like Orlando Figes still go to such lengths (over 900 pages) to carry out, in essence, the same role as earlier calumniators of the Russian revolution? After all, with the collapse of the Stalinist regimes of Eastern Europe and the Soviet Union in 1989-90, the heritage of the Russian revolution, particularly the planned economy, has apparently been eradicated 'forever'.

Yet the fact that those, like Figes or the even more reactionary historian, Richard Pipes, have devoted so much attention to the revolution's anniversary, shows its enduring attraction to workers today. This will be even more so in the future given the economic, political, social and ecological disasters which loom for world capitalism. Everything must be done to obscure the lessons of 1917 for today.

Could capitalism have Developed Russia?

THE REVOLUTION, AND the introduction of a planned economy, laid the basis for the transformation of Russia from the 'India' of Europe to, at one stage, the second most powerful economy and country on the globe. In the detail which Figes gives about the conditions in the Russian cities, he confirms the backwardness of Russia at the time of the revolution: "The death rate in this city of the Tsars (St Petersburg) was the highest of any European capital, including Constantinople, with a cholera epidemic on average once in every three years". The same primitiveness and economic backwardness in the countryside is also elaborated by Figes. However, his mission is to demonstrate that it was 'by no means inevitable' that the revolution should have ended in the Bolshevik 'dictatorship'. He argues that a 'democratic' path for Russia was possible and that the October revolution was a 'coup d'état' organised by the 'cowardly' and 'dictatorial' Lenin and his Bolshevik Party.

Others, particularly bourgeois economists, have complemented Figes to demonstrate that left to itself, without the intervention of the October revolution, Russia would have developed at a much greater economic pace than it did through the planned economy. On the contrary, despite the monstrous, one-party, totalitarian regime which developed under Stalinism, the planned economy which issued from the Russian revolution led to a colossal development of industry and society and also the living standards of the mass of the population, unrivalled by any other comparable country.

'Not so', argue the bourgeois opponents of Marxism, 'what about the phenomenal growth rates of the Southeast Asian Tigers and Japan post 1945?' But these economies developed at a phenomenal rate because of their unique circumstances and the special measures of US imperialism and its puppets in the post-war situation. Faced by the challenge of Stalinism, which rested on the gains of the October revolution including the planned economy, US imperialism in Korea and Japan carried through a major part of the bourgeois democratic revolution, by expropriating the landlords and giving land to the peasants. The same task was undertaken by the Kuomintang who took the land of the native Taiwanese landlords when they were driven from the Chinese mainland. They cleared out of the way the remnants of feudal and semi-feudal land relations, paving the way for the development of capitalism. It was this and access to the US market, together with sweated, slave labour (in Korea and Taiwan) which laid the basis for the development of the 'Tigers'. This was not the pattern for the majority of the countries in the colonial or former colonial world where the bourgeois democratic revolution remained, and remains, uncompleted.

Even the Scientific American, in December 1968, after a study of comparative growth rates of Japan and the USSR between 1928-66, concluded: "Taking into account the fact that the USSR's growth was set back severely by World War II, its average annual rate for the 38-year period since 1928 nevertheless ranges between 5.4-6.7%: the Soviet accomplishment appears to be essentially unprecedented". The rate of growth of the USSR only slowed down, its potential vitiated by the one-party, totalitarian Stalinist regime, in the 1970s and 1980s. The maintenance of Stalinism actually led to a regression in the economy and society in the immediate period prior to its collapse in 1989-90.

The tasks which confronted Russia in 1917 were those of the bourgeois democratic revolution, which entailed a thoroughgoing land reform, with land to the peasants, the solution of the national question, with the right of self-determination to the oppressed nationalities, democracy and the development of a modern economy. Basing himself upon the 1905 revolution, Lenin argued that the liberal capitalists were incapable of carrying through the capitalist democratic revolution. Trotsky in his famous theory of the Permanent Revolution, and Lenin in his April Theses, showed that the industrialists and bankers were bound with iron hoops to the semi-feudal landlords. The capitalists invested in land and the landlords invested in industry. Four thousand million roubles were owed by the landlords to the bankers and the expropriation of the landlords would endanger the investments of the bankers and the industrialists.

This, in broad outline, is the situation which still obtains in much of the former colonial or semi-colonial world, in Africa, Asia and Latin America. In India, for instance, the landlord and the capitalist is often one and the same figure, united through bank capital. A thoroughgoing land reform, giving land to the peasants, would come up against the opposition of not just the landlords and their armed detachments but also the capitalists.

1917-Accident or Necessity?

IN RUSSIA, THE landlords and the capitalists were linked to the bureaucracy and the system was crowned by the tsarist regime which was used to alternately stupefy the masses and crush opposition. Figes argues that perhaps timely land reform and democratic concessions from tsarism may have saved the regime. However, in much of the detail he supplies he shows how utopian is this idea. It is true that the capitalists had wanted the monarchy to give limited democratic reforms. But this would not have fundamentally altered the course of the revolution as the experience of the Spanish revolution between 1931-37 showed. King Alfonso replaced the dictator Primo de Rivera only to follow him later into exile.

Milyukov, the leader of the capitalist Cadet party, in urging concessions from the tsar in 1915, declared: "We are treading the volcano... tension has reached its extreme limit... a carelessly dropped match will be enough to start a terrible conflagration". Concession or repression, this was the dilemma for the possessing classes in 1917. Either road risked igniting a revolution.

The fear of Milyukov in 1915 was well founded. Russian peasants were groaning under the burdens placed upon them by the war. Figes and bourgeois historians, even when the material they furnish contradicts their conclusions, have essentially a conspiratorial view of history and particularly of revolution. This is certainly their view in relation to the October revolution. But revolution, as Trotsky points out, "breaks out when all the antagonisms of a society have reached their highest tension".

It is not a product of agitation and propaganda alone but arises when society cannot further progress without a sharp break. In general, four conditions have to be present before mass opposition to a regime overflows the bounds of normal protests and develops into a revolutionary movement. The ruling class has to be divided, which was quite evident even to Figes prior to February. There was growing opposition both to the war and the regime in the period leading up to February 1917. Amongst the working class, the idea gradually developed that 'we cannot live like this any longer'. This is another vital condition for revolution, the preparedness of the working class to go the whole way. This mood developed in the months prior to the February revolution. It is possible that in 1916, if the tsarist regime had made concessions, events could have developed differently in the first period of the revolution. But the process would not have been fundamentally different.

A widespread strike developed in January 1916 in St Petersburg on the anniversary of 'Bloody Sunday' when workers were massacred in the 1905 revolution. The number of strikes doubled during the following year, going from economic strikes to political strikes, from partial and sectional struggles to the idea of a general strike. The intermediary layers, particularly in the countryside, were in ferment, a process enormously speeded up by the slaughter of the first world war.

But, according to Figes, these were not the reasons why the Russian workers eagerly embraced the ideas of Marxism. The acceptance of "this dogmatism has much to do with the relative scarcity of alternative political ideas, which might at least have caused the workers to regard the Marxist doctrine with a little more reserve and scepticism. But it also had its roots in the way most of the workers had been educated in philosophy. When people learn as adults what children are normally taught in schools, they often find it difficult to progress beyond the simplest abstract ideas. These tend to lodge deep in their minds, making them resistant to the subsequent absorption of knowledge on a more sophisticated level. They see the world in black-and-white terms because their narrow learning obscures any other coloration".

So the fact that Russian workers absorbed Marxist ideas was not because these ideas accurately described their condition under the Russian landlord/capitalist regime. If only they had passed through a university, preferably one where Figes was the principal tutor, the consciousness of the Russian working class would have been different. When it comes to the social sciences and, in particular, when dealing with revolution the universities are, in general, institutions for obscurantism and dust-blowing on a gigantic scale. Bourgeois academics are utterly incapable of perceiving and understanding the working class, in particular, its guiding advanced layer, as anything other than putty in the hands of leaders' and intellectuals. Lenin, Trotsky and the Bolshevik Party prepared for the Russian revolution by an assiduous study of the French revolution, the Paris Commune and the first 1905 revolution. They saw their task as making conscious the unconscious will of the working class to change society. The agitation and propaganda of the Bolsheviks expressed the clear class interests of the workers and poor peasants in 1917. As Trotsky explained: "Not only in the soldiers' Soviets but also in the 'workers' Soviets, the Bolshevik faction generally constituted one to two per cent, at best five per cent. The leading parties of the petit bourgeois democracy (Mensheviks and so-called Social Revolutionaries) had the following of at least 95% of the workers, soldiers and peasants participating in the struggle" at the beginning of 1917.

The Bolsheviks were denounced as sectarians and then as agents of the German Kaiser. But "all their attention was directed to the masses and, moreover, not to their top layer but to the deepest and most oppressed millions and tens of millions, who parliamentary babblers usually forget". The whole of the press, including the papers of the Mensheviks and Social Revolutionaries, carried on a vicious campaign against the Bolsheviks. Even in the first months after February, this torrent of abuse, the suggestion that carloads of gold had been delivered to the Bolsheviks from Germany, etc., led the sailors and soldiers to threaten to bayonet Lenin and the other leaders of Bolshevism.

But the experience of the masses led to their disillusionment in the other parties, who betrayed the interests of the workers and peasants, in a bloc with the bourgeois Cadets. It pushed them into adopting a more sympathetic attitude to the speeches of the Bolsheviks. As Trotsky comments: "To the worker in the shop, the soldier in the trench, the starving peasant, it became clear that the capitalists and their lackeys were slandering the Bolsheviks precisely because the Bolsheviks were firmly devoted to the interests of the oppressed.

Yesterday's indignation of the soldier and sailor against the Bolsheviks became remoulded into passionate devotion to them, an unselfish readiness to follow them to the very end. And, on the other hand, the hatred of the masses for the Cadet Party was inevitably transferred to their allies, the Mensheviks and Social Revolutionaries".

These words, directed to an audience of workers in the 1930s, are far too 'simplistic' for our lofty historians. Yet they are more accurate than the heavy tomes of Figes and his like in explaining the triumph of the Bolshevik Party, the soviets and the October revolution of 1917.

Coup d'état or Mass Uprising?

Following The February revolution, the Mensheviks and Social Revolutionaries handed power to the capitalists. Even the Bolshevik leaders in Petrograd, led by Stalin and Kamenev, gave 'critical support' to the capitalist coalition. Only Lenin in Switzerland and Trotsky in New York understood the significance of the February events as the beginning not only of the Russian revolution but of the international revolution.

Lenin demanded that the workers place no trust in the Provisional Government. However, the Bolsheviks were only 8,000 strong after the February revolution. Lenin explained that it was necessary for the Bolsheviks to base themselves on the consciousness of the masses. In the first stage, inevitably, the masses take the line of least resistance. In Russia they gave massive support to the Mensheviks and Social Revolutionaries as explained above. Only big events would teach them the correctness of the perspectives, strategy and tactics of the Bolsheviks.

The working class learns rapidly in a revolution. The Bolsheviks grew quickly. They numbered 2,000 members in Petrograd in February 1917 (Figes puts the figure at 3,000), 16,000 by April (with 79,000 nationally). By July, says Figes, the membership of the Bolshevik Party stood at 200,000. This had risen, according to him, to 350,000 on the eve of the October revolution, "the vast majority of these blue-collar workers". (Most accounts give the membership of the Bolsheviks as 240,000 in October).

But the revolution did not develop in a straight line. Between February and October there were many sharp turns in the situation. In April, with the continuation of the war, the workers of Petrograd were already becoming disillusioned with the Provisional Government. The masses, particularly the ten million soldiers exhausted by the war, yearned for an end to the slaughter. But even the workers' and peasants' councils, the soviets, which the masses themselves had improvised based on the experience of the

1905 revolution, supported the continuation of the war. The national soviet congress in April, dominated by the Mensheviks and Social Revolutionaries, refused to ratify the eight-hour day. The disappointment and anger of the masses were reflected in the 'July days', which both Pipes and Figes are incapable of understanding. Against all the evidence of the participants at the time, from Trotsky to the leaders of the Petrograd Bolsheviks, Pipes argues that the Bolshevik leaders attempted a 'power seizure'. Only when it failed did the Bolsheviks then argue, according to this 'historian', that it was a spontaneous demonstration which they sought to direct into peaceful channels. Figes adopts a more vacillating view. On the one side, he quotes Sukhanov in support of Pipes but then implies that the Bolsheviks were of 'two minds' as to whether to use the July demonstrations to seek power or not. Moreover, Lenin is described as a hopeless vacillator unable to make up his mind.

On the contrary, the massive 400,000-strong demonstration of workers and soldiers in July was a stage which has been seen in all revolutions. Bitterly disappointed at the results of the revolution so far they called for the eviction of the ten capitalist ministers from the coalition government: 'Down with the offensive and all power to the soviets'. As with the 'June days' of 1848, the 'Spartacist uprising' in January 1919 and the 'May days' in Barcelona in 1937, the July days represented the consciousness of the masses that the gains of their revolution were being snatched out of their hands. The mass manifestation in Petrograd was an attempt to prevent the derailment of the revolution.

The Bolshevik leadership, contrary to Figes's account, opposed the July demonstration but were compelled to go along with it. Already the workers of Petrograd were ready to overthrow the government but the Bolshevik leadership opposed this. Lenin and Trotsky warned that the rest of the country, and particularly the peasants and soldiers at the front, needed time to see through the coalition of Mensheviks and Social Revolutionaries. The masses could only learn this through bitter experience.

Figes's description of Lenin as a 'coward', both before and during the July days, is itself sufficient to discredit the whole book as a serious scientific and objective appraisal of 1917 (p385). In July, he has Lenin running away from St Petersburg to Finland to save his own skin! He writes: "Lenin was always prone to overestimate the physical danger to himself; in this respect he was something of a coward. It cannot be said that his life was ever at direct risk during his summer on the run". Yet, barely a paragraph later, he writes of "the frenzied anti-Bolshevik atmosphere... a time of lynch law with the tabloid press full of cartoons showing Lenin on the scaffold".

Lenin's refusal to appear before a court, which would have been composed of the bitterest class enemies of the Bolsheviks, was entirely correct. As Trotsky comments: "It is sufficient to remember the fate of Karl Liebknecht and Rosa Luxemburg". Lenin went into hiding not out of concern for himself as an individual but for what was at stake for the revolution. With Trotsky, Lenin was the 'brain' of the Bolshevik Party and, therefore, of the revolution. It was the interests of the revolution that were paramount in Lenin's attitude during the July days. If neither Lenin nor Trotsky had survived, then the Russian revolution itself would have been shipwrecked. The murder of Luxemburg and Liebknecht was a major factor in the derailment of the German revolution.

The July days led to reaction, with repression against the Bolsheviks and the imprisonment of Trotsky, while Lenin was driven underground. The counter-revolution, in the figure of General Kornilov, attempted a coup in August, which was defeated by the working class with the Bolsheviks playing the most prominent role. The troops of Kornilov refused to take action once the real situation was explained to them by delegates and agitators from the Soviets. The railway workers completely disintegrated the army of Kornilov by stranding them in railway sidings, etc.

Revolution sometimes needs the whip of the counter-revolution. The August events gave an enormous access of support to the Bolsheviks. In the two months that followed, the majority of the workers' and soldiers' soviets were won over to the Bolsheviks. Using the Military Revolutionary Committee, set up by the soviets in Petrograd under the leadership of Trotsky, the working class took power on 25 October.

Figes's verdict on the October revolution, which Marxists consider as the single greatest event in human history, is that it was "in reality such a small-scale event, being in effect no more than a military coup, that it passed unnoticed by the vast majority of the inhabitants of Petrograd". Incredibly, he then goes on to comment: "The whole insurrection, as Trotsky himself acknowledged, was carried out as a coup d'état". In support of this claim he quotes Trotsky's comment that the insurrection was, "a series of small operations, calculated and prepared in advance".

These claims are made by Figes despite the fact that Trotsky, in a brilliant chapter in his History of the Russian Revolution, The Art of Insurrection, goes to considerable lengths to show that the October revolution and insurrection was entirely different to the classical idea of a 'coup d'état'. The latter, pursued by conspirators from a group or section of the ruling class or army, usually results in the replacement of one clique of the same ruling class by another. But, says Trotsky, "only mass insurrection has ever brought the victory of one social regime over another".

The Importance of the Bolshevik Party

There was a fundamental difference between the February and October revolutions. The February revolution was a mass insurrection which overthrew the old power but did not result in the working class and peasantry taking power into their own hands. The objective prerequisites have to be there before a successful socialist revolution and insurrection is possible. But something more than this is needed for the working class to take power. In October, as opposed to February, there was the presence of the 'subjective factor', a mass revolutionary party with a far-sighted leadership, capable of leading the masses to power.

A revolutionary situation is not long lived: the fate of a revolution can be determined in a two-or three-day struggle. In Russia, the conditions probably existed for a successful revolution between September and November, a three-month period. Failure to take power then would have led Russia back into the noose of a capitalist dictator like Kornilov.

The active support for the revolution is reflected in the victory of the Bolsheviks in the soviets and the dramatic swing towards the left in the peasants' soviets prior to October. Figes has the revolution being carried through by a minority. It is true that the technical military aspect of the seizure of power in October was carried out by a minority. This is the case in all revolutions; a minority acts but with the support of the mass. To be successful in October, as opposed to July, meant that the actions of the Bolsheviks under the banner of the soviets needed the mass support of the proletariat and the peasantry. The relatively 'bloodless' character of the October overturn, recognised by Figes, would not have been possible without the mass of the Petrograd proletariat supporting the insurrection. Conversely, the virtually nonexistent forces at the disposal of Kerensky's Provisional Government reflected the demoralisation of those opposed to the revolution. The "series of small operations, calculated and prepared in advance", mentioned by Trotsky, merely dealt with the technical military aspects of the October revolution and not with its mass support. It is, moreover, an incontestable historical fact that only in Russia, following the overturn in October, did the workers take power and establish real workers' democracy.

In the years since there have been many opportunities for the working class to follow in the path of the Russian workers of 1917. In its sweep, scope and potential for victory of the working class, the Chinese revolution of 1925-27 was equal to, if not greater, than even that of Russia. The working class in Spain attempted not once but on ten occasions between 1931-37 to carry through a revolution. In 1968 in France, the working class organised a general strike of ten million; the capitalist bonaparte, De Gaulle, fled to Germany believing that 'the game was up', and yet the French workers were not able to emulate their Russian counterparts of 50 years before. The same process developed in the Portuguese revolution in 1974 when the capitalist state disintegrated. Unlike in the Russian revolution, the great majority of the Portuguese officer caste were radicalised and were searching in the direction of 'socialism' but, unfortunately, the capitalist state machine was reassembled and was able to liquidate the gains of the Portuguese revolution. It was the false policies of the leadership of the workers' organisations-the social democracy and the mass Communist Party-which prevented the revolution from being completed.

All this stands in stark contrast to what happened in Russia in 1917. It was the policy and the tactics of the Bolshevik Party, under the leadership of Lenin and Trotsky, which led the Russian workers to victory. This initiated the 'ten days that shook the world'. Unbelievably, Figes deals with the creation of the

Communist International in passing and with only slight reference to the international ramifications of the Russian revolution. The October revolution led, as Lenin and Trotsky had anticipated, to enormous revolutionary ferment throughout Europe, America and the world. At one stage the revolution, because of the intervention of the 21 armies of imperialism, was reduced to the two major cities of Moscow and Petrograd, the old province of Muscovy. Most of Russia was in the hands of the counter-revolutionary White forces backed up by imperialist bayonets. And yet, impoverished, reduced to cannibalism in certain parts of Russia, the revolution triumphed not because of superiority of arms but through appeals to the working class in the armies of imperialism and throughout the world.

From Bolshevism to Stalinism?

Like Many Before, Figes finds the seeds of Stalinism in the policies and methods of Lenin and of the Bolshevik Party. He argues that the Bolsheviks sought to "centralise all power in the hands of the party and, by the use of terror, to wipe out all political opposition". Nothing of the kind occurred in the early part of the revolution. Indeed, the only parties and newspapers which were suppressed were the bourgeois opposition of the Cadets and the semi-fascist Black Hundreds. Only when the Mensheviks and Social Revolutionaries went over to military counter-revolutionary resistance were measures taken against their press. This is no different to what occurred in other civil wars, including in capitalist civil wars such as that of the USA. Did Abraham Lincoln and the north permit the functioning of newspapers and grant democratic rights to the southern slaveholders and their supporters in the north? Did Oliver Cromwell, in the English bourgeois revolution of the 17th century, allow the royalists to operate freely in areas controlled by the parliamentary forces? On the contrary, they resorted to military repression, which was the logic of civil war. The same was true of the Bolsheviks who took repressive measures only when it was absolutely necessary and who argued, at the time, that with the spread of the revolution to western Europe even these military measures and repression would be unnecessary.

Figes, perhaps without intending to, shows the popularity of the Bolshevik regime and the weakness of the counter-revolution in the first period when he writes about the convening of the Constituent Assembly. He gives many useful facts to show the overwhelming swing of the peasantry towards the Left Social Revolutionaries, who were then in collaboration with the Bolsheviks. He even comments about the mood in the cities: "There was no mass reaction to the closure of the Constituent Assembly". This does not, however, prevent him from arguing: "The political civilisation of the provincial towns is not much more advanced than in backward peasant Russia and outside the capital city there was no real urban middle class to sustain the democratic revolution. That was the tragedy of 1917".

But that begs the question as to why there was not a stable 'urban middle class' and, if it had existed, whether it would have prevented the Russian revolution. Firstly, the weakness of the middle class was itself a reflection of the incapacity of the Russian bourgeoisie to carry through the bourgeois democratic revolution. This meant that these tasks fell on the shoulders of the working class who, having come to power, completed the bourgeois democratic revolution, in alliance with the peasantry, and then went over to the socialist tasks. Moreover, in Germany the presence of an 'urban middle class' did not prevent the revolution of 1918-19 which was only not carried through to a conclusion because, unlike in Russia, the 'subjective factor' did not exist.

The Bolshevik Party of Lenin and Trotsky in the Russian revolution was separated by a river of blood from Stalinism. It was the most democratic party in history and, at the same time, the most determined in the pursuit of mobilising the working class for power. The revolution was conceived as the beginning of the European and world revolution. Without the victory of the revolution in the west, the Russian revolution would inevitably be defeated or degenerate. Lenin and Trotsky argued this many times in advance of the revolution.

Stalinism did not arise from Bolshevism but was rooted in the isolation of the Russian revolution and the backward cultural conditions of Russia. This, along with the slaughter of the flower of the Russian proletariat in the civil war and the disappointment of the masses in the failure of the European revolution to come to their assistance, led to the gradual crystallisation of a privileged stratum. Stalin personified this layer which gradually usurped power from the proletariat. Rather than issuing from Leninism, Stalinism rose in mortal combat with Bolshevism. A precondition for the consolidation of the power and privileges of the rising bureaucracy was the destruction of all remnants of Bolshevism. The annihilation of the Left Opposition and all those connected with the heroic period of Bolshevism culminated in the purges, described by Trotsky as a 'one-sided civil war'.

Does the degeneration of the Russian revolution and the rise of Stalinism, which ultimately led to the liquidation of the planned economy, invalidate the relevance of the Russian revolution? On the contrary, an assiduous study of the revolution, and of events since, shows that it is impossible to understand the 20th century, including the present situation, without understanding the Russian revolution and its subsequent degeneration. The achievements of the planned economy, despite Stalinism, give an example of what was possible, particularly if it had been organised on the basis of workers' control and management.

A study of the revolution today provides the advanced layers of workers with the possibility of understanding the laws of revolution. Of course, events will not develop in exactly the same fashion, nor with the same speed, as did the Russian revolution. Nevertheless, the struggles of the working class, despite the inane claims of bourgeois ideologists that we are at the 'end of history', that ideology has disappeared, etc., are similar in all capitalist countries.

The class struggle will break out with redoubled force in the period we are going into. The best representatives of the workers and youth will look for the ideological and theoretical weapons that can offer them an explanation of how to act in mobilising the working class against capitalism. They will find what they need, not in Figes's book, but in the works of Marx, Engels and, particularly for today, of Lenin and Trotsky, and in the immortal work in the Russian revolution of the Bolsheviks in 1917.

Legacies of the French Revolutions

The powerful influence of the French Revolution can be traced in the reactions of those who witnessed the event firsthand and in the strong emotions it has aroused ever since. For some, the French Revolution was a beacon of light that gave a world dominated by aristocratic privilege and monarchical tyranny a hope of freedom. Nineteenth-century revolutionaries and nationalists frequently harkened back to the days of 1789, sometimes even taking up the names, terms, colors, and rituals of the original French Revolution. Twentieth-century revolutionaries looked to 1789 as a kind of template for revolutionary events. If Robespierre could come on the heels of Lafayette and he, in turn, could give way to Napoleon, then might modern revolutions inevitably follow a similar scripted path, toward authoritarianism? Did revolutions always begin with hope and enthusiasm only to turn violently radical and then permit an authoritarian, even dictatorial figure, to seize power? Were revolutions like some sort of political fever, with distinct symptoms? Scholars and political activists continue to argue these questions. Yet no matter what their interpretation, the lessons and impact of the Revolution continue to be at the heart of several different historical and contemporary political debates.

Contemporary Reactions to the French Revolution

The events of the French Revolution alternately energized and repulsed contemporaries. Many experienced what English poet William Wordsworth immortalized in his poem *French Revolution As It Appears to Enthusiasts* (1804; also in *Prelude*): "Bliss was it in that dawn to be alive/But to be young was very heaven!" The French overthrow of the old regime and all it stood for was celebrated and commemorated in songs, engravings, poems, paintings, and music. Some, like Wordsworth, even voyaged to France to see events firsthand. Yet from the first months of the Revolution, others saw a darker side of the unfolding drama. The first major debate about the French Revolution outside of France was sparked by a lively polemical tract written by Edmund Burke just months after the fall of the Bastille. A member of the British Parliament, Burke had gained a reputation defending the Americans in their revolt against the British crown. He was much less favorably impressed by the French Revolution, however. In *Reflections on the Revolution in France* (1790), he expressed reservations about the revolutionaries' reliance on reason as the sole standard of government and predicted, quite presciently it turned out, that the French would eventually turn to violence to enforce their decisions. Burke went beyond criticizing the French revolutionaries; he offered the first systematic defence of "conservative" principles, arguing that gradual change and a kind of organic continuity in society stretching across the generations were preferable to violent, rapid upheavals in the structure of government. From its very beginning then, the French Revolution stimulated profound political controversy and equally profound rethinking of the nature of government itself. Because the revolutionaries aimed to rebuild government from the foundation upward, substituting reason for tradition and equal rights for privilege, they inevitably provoked wide-ranging reactions.

Burke's attack set off a firestorm of protest within Great Britain. His passing reference to the lower classes as "the swinish multitude" got him swift responses, with titles such as "Hog's Wash" and "Pig's Meat" and an "Address to the Hon. Edmund Burke from the Swinish Multitude." The most effective response was that of Thomas Paine, the English author of the famous defence of the American cause, *Common Sense* (1776). Paine's *Rights of Man: Being an Answer to Mr. Burke's Attack on the French Revolution* (1791 and 1792) laid out a cogent defence of the use of reason in remaking the forms of government. Paine insisted that good government depended on establishing a constitution that guaranteed the natural rights of all men. In his view, Great Britain did not have a constitution; it had only a long history of fraudulent monarchical and aristocratic claims guaranteed by force. By 1793 Paine's attack on the English social and political establishment had sold some 200,000 copies, more than any other political polemic in English history. Paine's prestige became so great that he was elected to the National Convention despite the fact that he did not speak French.

Burke's tract also provoked one of the first sustained feminist arguments in world history in Mary Wollstonecraft's *A Vindication of the Rights of Women* (1792). (Document 3) Wollstonecraft's pronouncement that women should be educated like men in order to become virtuous citizens created instant controversy. One critic declared that her works would be read "with disgust by every female who has any pretensions to delicacy; with detestation by every one attached to the interests of religion and morality". If her arguments for women's rights seem relatively tame to present-day readers, then that is probably a good measure of the impact on the modern world of French Revolutionary feminists. North Americans followed the French Revolution with special interest. Americans believed that the events of 1789 drew heavily on their own experience. The French *Declaration of the Rights of Man and Citizen* seemed to borrow strikingly from the states' bill of rights. Even more direct influence took place when Thomas Jefferson, resident in France at this time, passed along specific ideas to the legislators through the Marquis de Lafayette. Although the French Revolution took a far different path than the North American variety, this interaction was close, so it is not surprising that the initial U.S. reaction to the Revolution was positive. Virtually the only dissenting voice among the leading American politicians was that of John Adams who, like Burke, expressed his reservations early. Indeed, throughout the revolutionary decade, the Republican Party, led by Jefferson, remained generally favourable, although the Terror did inspire some wavering. Others, however, became opposed, especially the Federalists. Despite its declining influence in American politics, this party carried the day with regard to U.S. policy toward France. Conflict over land and borders between these two ostensibly friendly nations would sour many Americans on France and its revolution by the late years of the revolutionary decade.

Philosophers, poets, and novelists felt compelled to comment on the French Revolution as much as politicians. The German philosopher Immanuel Kant followed events with interest, sometimes enthusiasm, but also with worry. As his treatises show, he appreciated the deep power of the notion of right. The French aristocrat François-René Chateaubriand took a more negative view. In his *Historical, Political and Moral Essay on Revolutions, Ancient and Modern*, he denounced the Jacobins as "infuriated men" who had erected "a thousand sanguinary guillotines" in all the villages and towns of France. The German philosopher Georg Wilhelm Friedrich Hegel used the course of the French Revolution to develop his notions about the essential, inner meaning of history. Such use of the Revolution as a springboard for philosophical and political inquiry marked the degree to which contemporaries viewed this event as both a turning point and as a break with older ways of doing things.

Revolutionary Legacies in the Nineteenth and Twentieth Centuries

Since the beginning of the nineteenth century the legacy of the French Revolution has been hotly debated by politicians, revolutionaries, and political theorists. The Revolution of 1789 gave birth to what soon came to be called "ideologies," a word that was first used during the French Revolution. An ideology is a defined doctrine about the best form of social and political organization. Before 1789, most people (the Americans of the new United States were the great exception) lived with the general form of government their ancestors had known for centuries, and by and large this meant hereditary monarchy. After 1789, no form of government could be accepted as legitimate without justification. The revolutionaries had established a republic, so from the foundation of the republic in 1792 onward, at the very least, republicans would challenge monarchists. Among republicans, some preferred a government directed by the elite, whereas others, known as democratic republicans, advocated a more democratic structure. Many other self-conscious ideological alternatives arose during this era—nationalism, liberalism, socialism, and eventually communism—all as a result of, or in reaction to, the French Revolution. Only conservatism stood opposed, arguing that all of these doctrines of social or political change were dangerous innovations.

Modern nationalism began in France during the revolutionary decade and was spread by revolutionary and Napoleonic armies to the rest of Europe. Many Europeans adopted this idea because nationalism defended the right of a nation to resist French control. After the fall of Napoleon and the remaking of European boundaries at the Congress of Vienna in 1815, nationalists turned their ire on foreign rulers: the Austrians in Italy, the Russians in Poland, and so on. From Derry (Northern Ireland) to Danang (Vietnam) and from Helsinki to the Cape of Good Hope, this struggle for national liberation became one of the most important themes of nineteenth-and twentieth-century European and world politics.

Nationalists hoping for their own nation-state might favour either a monarchy or a republic. Among republicans, they might be either socialists or liberals. The Italian nationalist Giuseppe

Mazzini took the left-wing nationalist position; he believed that nationalism should be revolutionary and allied with projects to defend the interests of the poor. Others, such as the "utopian socialist" Charles Fourier, wanted to keep the revolutionary legacy of social reform but limit the violence that was increasingly associated with the "Reign of Terror" of 1793–94. This same violence repelled other generally favourable nineteenth-century commentators such as the philosopher John Stuart Mill and the historian and politician Alexis de Tocqueville, who preferred a more elitist approach to any reform of the structure of government.

Not only did the Revolution spawn many beliefs that further extended its logic, but as Hegel surmised, it also created reactions against it. Even before 1789, the "anti-philosophes" had decried Enlightenment thinking. Burke and others quickly denounced the Revolution itself, particularly the potential for violence. The next two centuries would witness the rise of a powerful and diverse group of detractors. Even Hippolyte Taine, holding a chair in the history of the French Revolution at the Sorbonne and a defender of the legacy of freedom he saw emanating from the Revolution, considered the event as a whole monstrous.

Many French who opposed the French Revolution did so because of their religious beliefs. Although the Revolution had instigated a degree of religious oppression, it also permitted an uneasy truce with the churches. The fundamental secularism of the revolutionary project offended those who preferred that state power be dependent on religious authority. Typical of these critics was Joseph de Maistre, an aristocratic writer and philosopher who condemned the Revolution as fundamentally evil and impious. In the course of the nineteenth and twentieth centuries, conservatives also linked the French Revolution to what they saw as the negative aspects of democracy and mass politics. Gustave Le Bon, an influential theorist of "crowd" behaviour, warned that the French Revolution epitomized the irrationality, savagery, and violence of the mob. Some conservatives went even further, decrying the universal principles of human rights upon which the Revolution was based. Critics saw danger in these universal appeals, especially as they promised to open first France and then the world to social equality for Jews and for immigrants. The "cosmopolitan" form of thinking, so they alleged, ate away at the fibers knitting together the French people and violated the deep roots of moral strength of France vested in its people. These two commitments—religion and nativism—had separable chronologies, but became increasingly linked as some individuals, such as Charles Maurras, leader of the right-wing organization *Action française,* insisted that France must become, or return to being, more devout and more nationalistic. For such critics, the legacy of the French Revolution was almost wholly negative.

Socialists and communists had a more positive view of the French Revolution: they considered it an important harbinger of the future. However, they wanted to go beyond its tentative promises of individual rights and legal change within a constitutional order. Socialists and communists believed that the French Revolution had not gone far enough. The founders of communism as an international movement, Karl Marx and Friedrich Engels, both commented extensively on the French Revolution, hoping to find in those events important lessons for the future course not only of communism but of history itself.

Interest in the French Revolution was especially intense at the end of the nineteenth century and the beginning of the twentieth. In 1889 France's Third Republic celebrated the centennial of the French Revolution with the building of the Eiffel Tower. Arguments about revolutionary events continued to be heated, especially because ü had broken out again in France in 1830, 1848, and 1870–71. The latter revolution, associated with the Paris Commune, was especially violent; as many as 20,000 people died in street fighting in 1871 when the new republican government sent its army to disband the revolutionary commune (city government) of Paris. Because of the continuing cycle of revolutions in France and the promise of a worldwide revolution through communism, memories of the original French Revolution of 1789 continued to haunt the writings of important socialists, anarchists, and communist revolutionaries.

The French Revolution clearly had repercussions throughout the world. For example, the Napoleonic occupation of Spain in 1808 was the spark that ignited the independence movement in Latin America. Beginning with Mexico in 1810, Central and South American local elites declared their independence from Spain and Portugal. Most countries achieved independence in the 1820s.

Others, like the revolutionary Simon Bolívar, rejected the control of these elites, preferring to follow the example of Haiti. The spread of nationalism to Latin America was accompanied by some of the other liberal ideas associated with the French Revolution, but not by all.

Twentieth-century revolutionaries in east Asia were interested not only in the potent ideology of nationalism, but also in the transformative power of revolutions on both society and the state. Exposed early to the model of the French Revolution, those espousing revolutionary change in China and Vietnam made the French Revolution of 1789 topical in a new part of the world.

Outside the realm of politics, the allure of the Revolution remained important, not only for those who wished to comment on contemporary events but also for the innate drama and pathos of many revolutionary events. Alexis de Tocqueville observed, "What remains most alive in the original spirit of the Revolution is in... literature.... [T]he only Frenchmen who today can be connected by a kind of esprit de corps to their fathers are the men of letters" (Roger Boesche, ed., *Alexis de Tocqueville: Selected Letters on Politics and Society*, trans. James Toupin and Roger Boesche [Berkeley, 1985], 329). Some of the giants of nineteenth-century European literature wrote about the French Revolution, including Honoré de Balzac, Charles Dickens, Victor Hugo, and Anatole France. These literary treatments kept the people, the events, and the ideas of the Revolution alive for generations. In the twentieth century, the powerful imagery and impact of the Revolution made it an ideal candidate for the cinema. Some of the greatest films in French cinematic history have focused on the revolutionary period. From Abel Gance's *Napoleon* in 1927 to Andrezj Wajda's *Danton* in 1984, directors have grappled with the meaning of the events of the French Revolution. The frequent twentieth-century remakes of films about the Scarlet Pimpernel demonstrate that the allure of the Revolution remains alive and well in the English-speaking world too.

Has the importance of the French Revolution now faded? In some ways, it has simply shifted. Scholars continue to be interested in the causes, course, and legacy of the French Revolution, but they have a wider view of it: not only do they seek its meaning in a broader range of events and activities, in the traditional arenas of diplomacy and high politics as well as in the newer ones of festivals, symbols, engravings, and songs. They also seek its significance in many more places, from Haiti and the other French colonies to Egypt, Russia, and wherever the French armies marched, indeed, to wherever the message of the Revolution was heard.

Even before the Revolution had ended, before the rise of Napoleon Bonaparte, enterprising artists and printers had begun to publish collections of engravings that recounted the principal events of the French Revolution for subscribers. Revolutionary governments aimed to spread their message through propaganda, and they left no item of everyday life untouched in their efforts to spread the gospel of revolution.

Memories of the French Revolution of 1789 are not only historical in nature, but also constitute a living legacy. They are found in places, images, and objects. A few liberty trees still stand today, usually large oaks on the village square. Many people kept mementos of the Revolution, whether engravings, ribbons (in the form of cockades), crockery, even bits of the stones of the Bastille prison. Songs continued in popular memory. The sheer weight of these memories can be measured by the very large number of objects and images still in existence. The Bibliothèque Nationale in Paris houses some 30,000 engravings from the time of the French Revolution. Libraries in the United States have many thousands of them too. Museums all over France have material collections of crockery, ribbons, flags, swords, and clothing, all of which could serve as emblems of revolution—or counterrevolution. The Museum of the French Revolution in Vizille, France, has the most systematic and extensive of these collections, which we can only sample here.

China: Youth and the Cultural Revolution

The revolution that brought the Chinese Communist Party (CCP) to power in 1949 marked the second great breach, after the Russian Revolution of October 1917, in the 20th century imperialist world order, and initiated a process that was to remove from the capitalist orbit the most populous nation in the world, containing over a quarter of its population. The revolution of 1949 aroused vast expectations not only among China's popular masses, but also among the peoples of the Third World as a whole, and indeed among the socialist-minded everywhere. However, by the end of the 20th century, communism had been overturned in Eastern Europe and the USSR, while in China a largely discredited, authoritarian, Stalinist regime had virtually abandoned anything more than a nominal adherence to socialist ideals. So what went wrong?

In China, one of the central events that occurred between the 1949 revolution and the crushing of the movement for socialist democracy in 1989 was the experience of the "Great Proletarian Cultural Revolution". This volcanic event lasted from 1966-1976 (ending only with the death of Mao Zedong and the fall of the "Gang of Four"), but the period of greatest upheaval was concentrated between 1966 and 1969. C.L. Chiou, in his reasonably balanced analysis of the Cultural Revolution published in the mid-1970s, divides the schools of intepretation of it into three: one holding that the event marked a crisis in legitimacy of the regime similar to those prefiguring the "end of a dynasty" in Chinese history; a second defining the events as a conscious policy move on Mao's part, and over which Mao exercised control throughout; and the third (to which Chiou himself subscribes) in which Mao is seen as only partly in control, not acting in accordance with a preordained plan, but not the victim of a crisis situation either.

Power Struggle

The Cultural Revolution can perhaps best be understood not so much in terms of the ideological labels used by the Mao faction during the course of the struggle, but more in terms of a fairly ruthless power struggle between Mao's group in the party and the army on the one hand, and his more conservative opponents on the other — leading figures among whom, such as Liu Shao-chi and Deng Xiaping, were ousted from their positions.

Looking back on the literature of the time, it is interesting to note that the lexicon of the Mao faction, and the Maoist regime's conceptual understanding of what the struggle was about, was taken over, often more or less uncritically, by Western observers situated on the left politically. Fred Halliday, an editor of the London-based *New Left Review*, saw no problem in drawing a parallel between Mao's "Red Guards" and the revolutionary May

4th student movement of 1919. The US *Monthly Review* editors, while not uncritical of the Cultural Revolution, nevertheless endorsed it as a legitimate fight against bureaucratic degeneration, a view rejected by their US Trotskyist critics. Some left-liberal commentators, such as the Committee of Concerned Asian Scholars, accepted in essence the claims of the Chinese regime that the Cultural Revolution was primarily an exercise in shifting the "ideological-cultural superstructure" more in line with the "socioeconomic base", in accordance with Mao's notion, expressed in the 1950s, that the class struggle should continue to be sharply prosecuted in the transitional period between capitalism and socialism.

Some conservative observers have attempted to explain these remarkable events, which brought China to the brink of civil war, in psychological terms. Robert Jay Lifton's studies have focused on the methods of "thought control", or "brainwashing", in China — familiar notions from Cold War discourse. The phenomena considered in the Cultural Revolution are linked with the various earlier Maoist "rectification campaigns". Lifton's book *Revolutionary Immortality*, while it is psychologistic in approach, could be making a valid point concerning Mao's desire to guarantee the future of the revolution after his death, by bringing forth a new revolutionary generation through the Cultural Revolution. Leslie Marchant's idea that Chinese communism is a millenarian, eschatological movement and ideology, similar to earlier chiliastic religious movements, is not a helpful tool in understanding the Cultural Revolution, or very much else about revolutionary China. One is always tempted, when confronted with these type of arguments, to ask: should not conservatism be defined in similar terms as an "eschatology of the present"?

Alongside and often in opposition to the above outlined perspectives is an unalloyed revolutionary Marxist tradition of writing and scholarship on the Cultural Revolution, going back in some cases to the 1960s. Isaac Deutscher saw the essential parallel of Mao's campaign not in the *Proletkult* of the 1920s in Russia, but with Zhdanov's and Stalin's cultural repression of the late 1940s. Peng Shu-tse, a founder of the Chinese Communist Party who became an important leader of the Trotskyist current in China, and who went into exile after 1949, wrote superb analytical commentaries on Chinese politics — articles that often appeared in obscure journals. More recently, Charlie Hore, a British socialist, has produced a fine overview of China's history in the 20th century which consistently argues the case for a revolutionary Marxist standpoint, as against the Stalinist and other non-Marxist orthodoxies that have distorted the picture.

Young People

Young people have always been of importance in movements for revolutionary social and political change. Post-World War II demographics have made youth, in China as elsewhere, of growing significance as a sector of the population. The international communist movement had, from its earliest history, placed stress on the creation of strong youth organisations, and the Chinese Communist Party after 1949 mainitained a large and extensive Young Communist League for people ageed 15-25. Before 1966, the YCL incorporated a sizeable proportion of China's youth, with up to 35 million members. The YCL was to be eclipsed during the Cultural Revolution by the Red Guards, mobilised from among China's youth by the Mao faction.

Education in China, in the period before the Cultural Revolution, has been described as reflecting a fundamentally "bourgeois" ethos, with a tendency for university education in particular to be dominated by students from non-proletarian or non-lower-peasant backgrounds, i.e. by the sons and daughters of CCP functionaries or of the middle class. Ronald Price has pointed out that virtually any system of university selection would tend to favour the children of educated parents. But if Chinese schools and universities were "academically stultifying" before the depredations of the Red Guards, as Luckin maintains, then it is hard to see how these institutions' ceasing to function altogether, as was often the case between 1966-1969, could have improved the situation. Freedom of thought and of adademic inquiry, always defended and promoted by genuine Marxists, were certainly never on the agenda during the Cultural Revolution.

Nothing illustrates the character of the Cultural Revolution, and its impact on the education system of China, more clearly than the fact that the education ministry was abolished in 1966, and not reopened until 1975. The rationale of Mao's program was rooted supposedly in the notion that "bourgeois intellectuals" would be re-educated through physical labour, and that young people in the urban areas would be integrated with the rural peasant population. To facilitate the latter project, it is estimated that 12 million or more youth were transferred to rural China during the Cultural Revolution. This program has been seriously assessed as having been a developmental and educational strategy for Third World countries! Other such uncritical works, reflecting the influence of Maoist ideology, have also taken seriously the regime's claims concerning education strategy.

Critics have, more realistically, seen the hand of a ruling party bureaucracy behind the rhetoric of the "mass line", while some Soviet observers for example pointed out the obvious contradiction between Lenin's real views on "cultural revolution" on the one hand, and the destructive impact of Maoist nostrums on China's educational infrastructure, on the other. The low quality of Mao's Marxism has been remarked upon, and the poverty of much of the ideology generated by the Cultural Revolution is clear from the literature circulated during its course.

The psychological effects of the Cultural Revolution on China's youth may best be discerned from a survey of the often excellent and revealing memoir literature that has come out of China, particularly since the 1980s. Some of these works, such as Jung Chang's *Wild Swans*, have become bestsellers in the West. The clearest message emerging from this literature is one of disorientation and disillusionment, and this theme contradicts the claim made by Wilfred Burchett and Rewi Alley that the "Cultural Revolution did much to restore the confidence of young people in themselves".

Accounts of Red Guard activity, including factional fighting, while they may reflect the initial euphoria felt by secondary and university students at being freed from formal study and being allowed free travel and accomodation, usually end with disappointed hopes and a sense of betrayal. Those young people whose family members suffered during the crisis, and who were often torn in loyalty between parents and party authorities, were often very bitter about their experiences.

"Class labelling" among the young, even involving pre-school children, and the immense psychological damage this must have done, was one of the more insidious features of the Cultural Revolution. The Confucian family tradition seems to have been fused with crudely conceived class critiria to damn whole groups of so-called "black" or "bad-class" categories. The real purpose behind this push, as has been pointed out above, was primarily the promotion of the interests of the Mao faction in its struggle against opponent groups in the bureaucratic ruling stratum in China.

The misdirection of youth by Mao's faction, and the cynical misuse of the idealism of an entire generation of the young in China, had devastating consequences on the psychological wellbeing of these young people, as well as on the political prospects of socialism. Of the many students who were sent out to the countryside to perform menial tasks, thousands were still there in the 1980s, "abandoned by their radical patrons at the top". The massive scale of the disillusionment among China's youth, caused by their negative experiences during the Cultural Revolution, underlines the fundamental responsibility of the regime for the spreading mood of cynicism about socialism and politics in general among that generation. The struggle for democratic freedoms in the Chinese People's Republic that was crushed in the Tienanmen Square massacre of 1989, a movement led by a fresh generation of student and worker youth, should have led to the flowering of socialist democracy, but socialism itself was further discredited as the grip of the Stalinist police state in China fastened anew on the populace, young and old.

The future of socialism in China surely lies with the rediscovery of the lost tradition of revolutionary socialism; a tradition buried with the defeat of the Second Revolution of 1925-27, but which emerged again with the student-worker upsurge of 1989. A future generation of youth in China, determined to build a humane, socially just and democratic future for their country, will hopefully find the path to genuine Marxist socialism.

The Cultural Revolution retains its significance as a defining episode in China's 20th century history, and it strikes me as useful to review the general background of this event, and to focus in particular on the issue of youth. Many revolutionary socialists in the West, including myself, come from a background in student politics, and it is worthwhile drawing attention to the connections that were made by the Western student left at the time of the Cultural Revolution in China. I admit myself to purchasing a copy in 1970 of the *Little Red Book* of Mao's "Thoughts" at a bookshop in the city where I live, and brandishing it as an act of defiance during a school assembly at which the Gideons were distributing their free copies of the New Testament and Psalms. Some of the sources mentioned make it plain that significant layers of the student left in the West in the 1960s and early 1970s saw the "Red Guards" as an authentic expression of student protest against authority.

I have tried to demonstrate from the sources that this in fact was not so, and that the youth were largely being manipulated for the purposes of intra-bureaucratic faction fighting within the party-state hierarchy.

Acts of Parliament in the United Kingdom

Both houses of the British Parliament are presided over by a speaker, the Speaker of the House for the Commons and the Lord Speaker in the House of Lords.

For the Commons, the approval of the Sovereign is theoretically required before the election of the Speaker becomes valid, but it is, by modern convention, always granted. The Speaker's place may be taken by three deputies, known as the Chairman, First Deputy Chairman and Second Deputy Chairman of Ways and Means. (They take their name from the Committee of Ways and Means, of which they were once presiding officers, but which no longer exists.)

Prior to July 2006, the House of Lords was presided over by a Lord Chancellor (a Cabinet member), whose influence as Speaker was very limited (whilst the powers belonging to the Speaker of the House of Commons are vast). However, as part of the Constitutional Reform Act 2005, the position of Speaker of the House of Lords (as it is termed in the Act) was separated from the office of Lord Chancellor, though the Lords remain largely self-governing. Decisions on points of order and on the disciplining of unruly members are made by the whole body in the Upper House, but by the Speaker alone in the Lower House. Speeches in the House of Lords are addressed to the House as a whole (using the words "My Lords"), but those in the House of Commons are addressed to the Speaker alone (using "Mr Speaker" or "Madam Speaker"). Speeches may be made to both Houses simultaneously. As of March 2008, French President Nicolas Sarkozy was the most recent person to address both Houses.

Both Houses may decide questions by voice vote; members shout out "Aye" and "No" in the Commons — or "Content" and "Not-Content" in the Lords —, and the presiding officer declares the result. The pronouncement of either Speaker may be challenged, and a recorded vote (known as a division) demanded. (The Speaker of the House of Commons may choose to overrule a frivolous request for a division, but the Lord Speaker does not have that power). In each House, a division requires members to file into one of the two lobbies alongside the Chamber; their names are recorded by clerks, and their votes are counted as they exit the lobbies to re-enter the Chamber. The Speaker of the House of Commons is expected to be non-partisan, and does not cast a vote except in the case of a tie; the Lord Speaker, however, votes along with the other Lords.

Both Houses normally conduct their business in public, and there are galleries where visitors may sit.

Term

Following a general election, a new Parliamentary session begins. Parliament is formally summoned 40 days in advance by the Sovereign, who is the source of parliamentary authority. On the day indicated by the Sovereign's proclamation, the two Houses assemble in their respective chambers. The Commons are then summoned to the House of Lords, where Lords Commissioners (representatives of the Sovereign) instruct them to elect a Speaker. The Commons perform the election; on the next day, they return to the House of Lords, where the Lords Commissioners confirm the election and grant the new Speaker the royal approval in the Sovereign's name.

The business of Parliament for the next few days of its session involves the taking of the oaths of allegiance. Once a majority of the members has taken the oath in each House, the State Opening of Parliament may occur. The Lords take their seats in the House of Lords Chamber, the Commons appear at the Bar (immediately outside the Chamber), and the Sovereign takes his or her seat on the throne. The Sovereign then reads the Speech from the Throne — the content of which is determined by the Ministers of the Crown — outlining the Government's legislative agenda for the upcoming year. Thereafter, each House proceeds to the transaction of legislative business.

By custom, before considering the Government's legislative agenda, a bill is introduced *pro forma* in each House — the Select Vestries Bill in the House of Lords and the Outlawries Bill in the House of Commons. These bills do not become laws; they are ceremonial indications of the power of each House to debate independently of the Crown. After the *pro forma* bill is introduced, each House debates the content of the Speech from the Throne for several days. Once each House formally sends its reply to the Speech, legislative business may commence, appointing committees, electing officers, passing resolutions and considering legislation.

A session of Parliament is brought to an end by a prorogation. There is a ceremony similar to the State Opening, but much less well-known. Normally, the Sovereign does not personally attend the prorogation ceremony in the House of Lords; he or she is represented by Lords Commissioners. The next session of Parliament begins under the procedures described above, but it is not necessary to conduct another election of a Speaker or take the oaths of allegiance afresh at the beginning of such subsequent sessions. Instead, the State Opening of Parliament proceeds directly. To avoid the delay of opening a new session in the event of an emergency during the long summer recess, Parliament is no longer prorogued beforehand, but only after the Houses have reconvened in the autumn; the State Opening follows a few days later.

Each Parliament comes to an end, after a number of sessions, either by the command of the Sovereign or by effluxion of time, the former being more common in modern times. The dissolution of Parliament is effected by the Sovereign, always on the advice of the Prime Minister. The Prime Minister may seek dissolution because the time is politically advantageous to his or her party. If the Prime Minister loses the support of the House of Commons, he must either resign or seek dissolution of Parliament to renew his or her mandate.

Originally there was no fixed limit on the length of a Parliament, but the Triennial Act 1694 set the maximum duration at three years. As the frequent elections were deemed inconvenient, the Septennial Act 1715 extended the maximum to seven years, but the Parliament Act 1911 reduced it to five. During the Second World War, the term was temporarily extended to ten years by Acts of Parliament. Since the end of the war the maximum has remained five years. Modern Parliaments, however, rarely continue for the maximum duration; normally, they are dissolved earlier. For instance, the 52nd, which assembled in 1997, was dissolved after four years.

Formerly, the demise of the Sovereign automatically brought a Parliament to an end, the Crown being seen as the *caput, principium, et finis* (beginning, basis and end) of the body, but this is no longer the case. The first change was during the reign of William and Mary, when it was seen to be inconvenient to have no Parliament at a time when succession to the Crown could be disputed, and an act was passed that provided that a Parliament was to continue for six months after the death of a Sovereign, unless dissolved earlier. (This provision is today contained in the Representation of the People Act 1867.)

After each Parliament concludes, the Crown issues writs to hold a general election and elect new members of the House of Commons. Membership of the House of Lords does not change due to dissolution. Each Parliament that assembles following a general election is deemed to be distinct from the one which just concluded, and is separately numbered, the present Parliament being the Fifty-Fourth Parliament of the United Kingdom since the formation of the United Kingdom of Great Britain and Ireland in 1801. (Previous Parliaments were "of Great Britain" or "of England", "of Scotland" or "of Ireland".)

Legislative Functions

Laws can be made by Acts of the United Kingdom Parliament. While Acts can apply to the whole of the United Kingdom including Scotland, due to the continuing separation of Scots law many Acts do not apply to Scotland and are either matched by equivalent Acts that apply to Scotland alone or, since 1999, by legislation set by the Scottish Parliament relating to devolved matters.

This has led to a paradox known as the West Lothian question. The existence of a devolved Scottish Parliament means that while Westminster MPs from Scotland may vote directly on matters that affect English constituencies, they may not have much power over their laws effecting their own constituency. While any Act of the Scottish Parliament may be overturned, amended or ignored by Westminster, in practice this has yet to happen. Furthermore, the existence of the Legislative Consent Motion enables English MPs to vote on issues nominally devolved to Scotland, as part of United Kingdom legislation. Since there is no devolved "English Parliament", the converse is not true.

Laws, in draft form known as bills, may be introduced by any member of either House, but usually a bill is introduced by a Minister of the Crown. A bill introduced by a Minister is known as a "Government Bill"; one introduced by another member is called a "Private Member's Bill". A different way of categorising bills involves the subject. Most bills, involving the general public, are called "Public Bills". A bill that seeks to grant special rights to an individual or small group of individuals, or a body such as a local authority, is called a "Private Bill". A Public Bill which affects private rights (in the way a Private Bill would) is called a "Hybrid Bill".

Private Members' Bills make up the majority of bills, but are far less likely to be passed than government bills. There are three methods for an MP to introduce a Private Member's Bill. The Private Members' Ballot (once per Session) put names into a ballot, and those who win are given time to propose a bill. The Ten Minute Rule is another method, where MPs are granted ten minutes to outline the case for a new piece of legislation. Standing Order 57 is the third method, which allows a bill to be introduced without debate if a day's notice is given to the Table Office. Filibustering is a danger, as an opponent to a bill can waste much of the limited time allotted to it. Private Members' Bills have no chance of success if the current government opposes them, but they are used in moral issues: the bills to decriminalise homosexuality and abortion were Private Members' Bills, for example. Governments can sometimes attempt to use Private Members' Bills to pass things it would rather not be associated with. "Handout bills" are bills which a government hands to MPs who win Private Members' Ballots. Each Bill goes through several stages in each House. The first stage, called the first reading, is a formality. At the second reading, the general principles of the bill are debated, and the House may vote to reject the bill, by not passing the motion "That the Bill be now read a second time". Defeats of Government Bills are extremely rare, the last being in 2005.

Following the second reading, the bill is sent to a committee. In the House of Lords, the Committee of the Whole House or the Grand Committee are used. Each consists of all members of the House; the latter operates under special procedures, and is used only for uncontroversial bills. In the House of Commons, the bill is usually committed to a Public Bill Committee, consisting of between 16 and 50 members, but the Committee of the Whole House is used for important legislation. Several other types of committees, including Select Committees, may be used, but rarely. A committee considers the bill clause by clause, and reports the bill as amended to the House, where further detailed consideration ("consideration stage" or "report stage") occurs. However, a practice which used to be called the *kangaroo* (Standing Order 31) allows the Speaker to select which amendments are debated. This device is also used under Standing Order 89 by the committee chairman, to restrict debate in committee.

Once the House has considered the bill, the third reading follows. In the House of Commons, no further amendments may be made, and the passage of the motion "That the Bill be now read a third time" is passage of the whole bill. In the House of Lords further amendments to the bill may be moved. After the passage of the third reading motion, the House of Lords must vote on the motion "That the Bill do now pass." Following its passage in one House, the bill is sent to the other House. If passed in identical form by both Houses, it may be presented for the Sovereign's Assent. If one House passes amendments that the other will not agree to, and the two Houses cannot resolve their disagreements, the bill fails.

However, since the passage of the Parliament Act 1911 the power of the House of Lords to reject bills passed by the House of Commons has been restricted, and further restrictions were placed by the Parliament Act 1949. If the House of Commons passes a public bill in two successive sessions, and the House of Lords rejects it both times, the Commons may direct that the bill be presented to the Sovereign for his or her Assent, disregarding the rejection of the Bill in the House of Lords. In each case, the bill must be passed by the House of Commons at least one calendar month before the end of the session. The provision does not apply to bills originated in the House of Lords, to bills seeking to extend the duration of a Parliament beyond five years, or to Private Bills. A special procedure applies in relation to bills classified by the Speaker of the House of Commons as "Money Bills". A Money Bill concerns *solely* national taxation or public funds; the Speaker's certificate is deemed conclusive under all circumstances. If the House of Lords fails to pass a Money Bill within one month of its passage in the House of Commons, the Lower House may direct that the Bill be submitted for the Sovereign's Assent immediately.

Even before the passage of the Parliament Acts, the Commons possessed pre-eminence in cases of financial matters. By ancient custom, the House of Lords may not introduce a bill relating to taxation or Supply, nor amend a bill so as to insert a provision relating to taxation or Supply, nor amend a Supply Bill in any way. The House of Commons is free to waive this privilege, and sometimes does so to allow the House of Lords to pass amendments with financial implications. The House of Lords remains free to reject bills relating to Supply and taxation, but may be overruled easily if the bills are Money Bills. (A bill relating to revenue and Supply may not be a Money Bill if, for example, it includes subjects other than national taxation and public funds). The last stage of a bill involves the granting of the Royal Assent. Theoretically, the Sovereign may either grant the Royal Assent (that is, make the bill a law) or withhold it (that is, veto the bill). Under modern conventions the Sovereign always grants the Royal Assent, in the Norman French words "La reyne le veult" (the Queen wishes it; "Le roy" instead in the case of a king). The last refusal to grant the Assent was in 1708, when Queen Anne withheld her Assent from a bill "for the settling of Militia in Scotland", in the words "La reyne s'avisera" (the Queen will think it over).

Thus, every bill obtains the assent of all three components of Parliament before it becomes law (except where the House of

Lords is overridden under the Parliament Acts 1911 and 1949). The words "BE IT ENACTED by the Queen's [King's] most Excellent Majesty, by and with the advice and consent of the Lords Spiritual and Temporal, and Commons, in this present Parliament assembled, and by the authority of the same, as follows:-", or, where the House of Lords' authority has been overridden by use of the Parliament Acts, the words "BE IT ENACTED by The Queen's [King's] most Excellent Majesty, by and with the advice and consent of the Commons in this present Parliament assembled, in accordance with the provisions of the Parliament Acts 1911 and 1949, and by the authority of the same, as follows:-" appear near the beginning of each Act of Parliament. These words are known as the enacting formula.

Judicial Functions

Prior to the creation of the Supreme Court of the United Kingdom in October 2009, Parliament also used to perform several judicial functions. The Queen-in-Parliament constituted the highest court in the realm for most purposes, but the Privy Council had jurisdiction in some cases (for instance, appeals from ecclesiastical courts). The jurisdiction of Parliament arose from the ancient custom of petitioning the Houses to redress grievances and to do justice. The House of Commons ceased considering petitions to reverse the judgements of lower courts in 1399, effectively leaving the House of Lords as the court of last resort. In modern times, the judicial functions of the House of Lords were performed not by the whole House, but by a group of "Lords of Appeal in Ordinary" (judges granted life peerage dignities under the Appellate Jurisdiction Act 1876 by the Sovereign) and by "Lords of Appeal" (other peers with experience in the judiciary). However, under the Constitutional Reform Act 2005, these judicial functions were transferred to the newly created Supreme Court in 2009, and the Lords of Appeal in Ordinary became the first Justices of the Court. Peers who hold high judicial office are no longer allowed to vote or speak in the Lords until they retire as Justices.

In the late 19th century, Acts allowed for the appointment of *Scottish Lords of Appeal in Ordinary* and ended appeal in Scottish criminal matters to the House of Lords, so that the High Court of Justiciary became the highest criminal court in Scotland.

Nowadays the House of Lords legislative committee usually has a minimum of two Scottish Judges to ensure that some experience of Scots law is brought to bear on Scottish appeals in civil cases, from the Court of Session.

Certain other judicial functions have historically been performed by the House of Lords. Until 1948, it was the body in which peers had to be tried for felonies or high treason; now, they are tried by normal juries. When the House of Commons impeaches an individual, the trial takes place in the House of Lords. Impeachments are now rare; the last one occurred in 1806. In 2006, a number of MPs attempted to revive the custom, having signed a motion for the impeachment of Tony Blair, but this was unsuccessful.

Relationship with the Government

The British Government is answerable to the House of Commons. However, neither the Prime Minister nor members of the Government are elected by the House of Commons. Instead, the Queen requests the person most likely to command the support of a majority in the House, normally the leader of the largest party in the House of Commons, to form a government. So that they may be accountable to the Lower House, the Prime Minister and most members of the Cabinet are, by convention, members of the House of Commons. The last Prime Minister to be a member of the House of Lords was Alec Douglas-Home, 14th Earl of Home, who became Prime Minister in 1963. To adhere to the convention under which he was responsible to the Lower House, he disclaimed his peerage and procured election to the House of Commons within days of becoming Prime Minister.

Governments have a tendency to dominate the legislative functions of Parliament, by using their inbuilt majority in the House of Commons, and sometimes using their patronage power to appoint supportive peers in the Lords. In practice, governments can pass any legislation (within reason) in the Commons they wish, unless there is major dissent by MPs in the governing party. But even in these situations, it is highly unlikely a bill will be defeated, though dissenting MPs may be able to extract concessions from the government. In 1976, Lord Hailsham created a now widely used name for this behaviour, in an academic paper called "elective dictatorship". Parliament controls the executive by passing or rejecting its Bills and by forcing Ministers of the Crown to answer for their actions, either at "Question Time" or during meetings of the parliamentary committees. In both cases, Ministers are asked questions by members of their Houses, and are obliged to answer.

Although the House of Lords may scrutinise the executive through Question Time and through its committees, it cannot bring down the Government. A ministry must always retain the confidence and support of the House of Commons. The Lower House may indicate its lack of support by rejecting a Motion of Confidence or by passing a Motion of No Confidence. Confidence Motions are generally originated by the Government in order to reinforce its support in the House, whilst No Confidence Motions are introduced by the Opposition. The motions sometimes take the form "That this House has [no] confidence in Her Majesty's Government" but several other varieties, many referring to specific policies supported or opposed by Parliament, are used. For instance, a Confidence Motion of 1992 used the form, "That this House expresses the support for the economic policy of Her Majesty's Government." Such a motion may theoretically be introduced in the House of Lords, but, as the Government need not enjoy the confidence of that House, would not be of the same effect as a similar motion in the House of Commons; the only modern instance of such an occurrence involves the 'No Confidence' motion that was introduced in 1993 and subsequently defeated.

Many votes are considered votes of confidence, although not including the language mentioned above. Important bills that form part of the Government's agenda (as stated in the Speech from the Throne) are generally considered matters of confidence. The defeat of such a bill by the House of Commons indicates that a Government no longer has the confidence of that House. The same effect is achieved if the House of Commons "withdraws Supply", that is, rejects the budget.

Where a Government has lost the confidence of the House of Commons, the Prime Minister is obliged either to resign, or seek the dissolution of Parliament and a new general election. Where a Prime Minister has ceased to retain a majority in that vote and requests a dissolution, the Sovereign can in theory reject his request, forcing his resignation and allowing the Leader of the Opposition to be asked to form a new government. This power is used extremely rarely. The conditions that should be met to allow such a refusal are known as the Lascelles Principles. These conditions and principles are merely informal conventions; it is possible, though highly improbable, for the Sovereign to refuse dissolution for no reason at all.

In practice, the House of Commons' scrutiny of the Government is very weak. Since the first-past-the-post electoral system is employed in elections, the governing party tends to enjoy a large majority in the Commons; there is often limited need to compromise with other parties. Modern British political parties are so tightly organised that they leave relatively little room for free action by their MPs. In many cases, MPs may be expelled from their parties for voting against the instructions of party leaders. During the 20th century, the Government has lost confidence issues only three times — twice in 1924, and once in 1979.

Sovereignty

Several different views have been taken of Parliament's sovereignty. According to the jurist Sir William Blackstone, "It has sovereign and uncontrollable authority in making, confirming, enlarging, restraining, abrogating, repealing, reviving, and expounding of laws, concerning matters of all possible denominations, ecclesiastical, or temporal, civil, military, maritime, or criminal ... it can, in short, do every thing that is not naturally impossible."

A different view has been taken by the Scottish judge Lord Cooper of Culross. When he decided the 1953 case of MacCormick v. Lord Advocate as Lord President of the Court of Session, he stated, "The principle of unlimited sovereignty of Parliament is a distinctively English principle and has no counterpart in Scottish constitutional law." He continued, "Considering that the Union legislation extinguished the Parliaments of Scotland and England and replaced them by a new Parliament, I have difficulty in seeing why the new Parliament of Great Britain must inherit all the peculiar characteristics of the English Parliament but none of the

Scottish." Nevertheless, he did not give a conclusive opinion on the subject. Thus, the question of Parliamentary sovereignty appears to remain unresolved. Parliament has not passed any Act defining its own sovereignty. A related possible limitation on Parliament relates to the Scottish legal system and Presbyterian faith, preservation of which were Scottish preconditions to the creation of the unified Parliament. Since the Parliament of the United Kingdom was set up in reliance on these promises, it may be that it has no power to make laws that break them.

Parliament's power has often been eroded by its own Acts. Acts passed in 1921 and 1925 granted the Church of Scotland complete independence in ecclesiastical matters. More recently, its power has been restricted by membership of the European Union, which has the power to make laws enforceable in each member state. In the Factortame case, the European Court of Justice ruled that British courts could have powers to overturn British legislation contravening European law. Parliament has also created national devolved assemblies with legislative authority in Scotland, Wales and Northern Ireland. Parliament still has the power over areas for which responsibility lies with the devolved institutions, but would gain the agreement of those institutions to act on their behalf. Similarly, it has granted the power to make regulations to Ministers of the Crown, and the power to enact religious legislation to the General Synod of the Church of England. (Measures of the General Synod and, in some cases proposed statutory instruments made by ministers, must be approved by both Houses before they become law.) In every case aforementioned, authority has been conceded by Act of Parliament and may be taken back in the same manner. It is entirely within the authority of Parliament, for example, to abolish the devolved governments in Scotland, Wales and Northern Ireland or to leave the EU. However, Parliament also revoked its legislative competence over Australia and Canada with the Australia and Canada Acts: although the Parliament of the United Kingdom could pass an Act reversing its action, it would not take effect in Australia or Canada as the competence of the *Imperial Parliament* is no longer recognised there in law.

One well-recognised exception to Parliament's power involves binding future Parliaments. No Act of Parliament may be made secure from amendment or repeal by a future Parliament. For example, although the Act of Union 1800 states that the Kingdoms of Great Britain and Ireland are to be united "forever", Parliament permitted southern Ireland to leave the United Kingdom in 1922.

Privileges

Each House of Parliament possesses and guards various ancient privileges. The House of Lords relies on inherent right. In the case of the House of Commons, the Speaker goes to the Lords' Chamber at the beginning of each new Parliament and requests representatives of the Sovereign to confirm the Lower House's "undoubted" privileges and rights. The ceremony observed by the House of Commons dates to the reign of King Henry VIII. Each House is the guardian of its privileges, and may punish breaches thereof. The extent of parliamentary privilege is based on law and custom. Sir William Blackstone states that these privileges are "very large and indefinite", and cannot be defined except by the Houses of Parliament themselves.

The foremost privilege claimed by both Houses is that of freedom of speech in debate; nothing said in either House may be questioned in any court or other institution outside Parliament. Another privilege claimed is that of freedom from arrest; at one time this was held to apply for any arrest except for high treason, felony or breach of the peace but it now excludes any arrest on criminal charges; it applies during a session of Parliament, and 40 days before or after such a session. Members of both Houses are no longer privileged from service on juries.

Both Houses possess the power to punish breaches of their privilege. Contempt of Parliament — for example, disobedience of a subpoena issued by a committee — may also be punished. The House of Lords may imprison an individual for any fixed period of time, but an individual imprisoned by the House of Commons is set free upon prorogation. The punishments imposed by either House may not be challenged in any court, and the Human Rights Act does not apply.

Emblem

The quasi-official emblem of the Houses of Parliament is a crowned portcullis. The portcullis was originally the badge of various English noble families from the 14th century. It went on to be adopted by the kings of the Tudor dynasty in the 1500s, under whom the Palace of Westminster became the regular meeting place of Parliament. The crown was added to make the badge a specifically royal symbol.

The portcullis probably first came to be associated with the Palace of Westminster through its use as decoration in the rebuilding of the Palace after the fire of 1512. However, at the time it was only one of many symbols. The widespread use of the portcullis throughout the Palace dates from the nineteenth century, when Charles Barry and Augustus Pugin used it extensively as a decorative feature in their designs for the new Palace built following the disastrous 1834 fire.

The crowned portcullis came to be accepted during the 20th century as the emblem of both houses of parliament. This was simply a result of custom and usage rather than a specific decision. The emblem now appears on official stationery, publications and papers, and is stamped on various items in use in the Palace of Westminster, such as cutlery, silverware and china.

Racism in the United States

Racism in the United States has been a major issue since the colonial era. Historically, the country has been dominated by a settler society of religiously and ethnically diverse Whites. The heaviest burdens of racism in the country have historically fallen upon Native Americans, Asian Americans, African Americans, Latin Americans, American Jews, Irish Americans and some other immigrant groups and their descendants.

Major racially structured institutions include slavery, Indian reservations, segregation, residential schools (for Native Americans), internment camps, and affirmative action. Racial stratification has occurred in employment, housing, education and government. Formal racial discrimination was largely banned in the mid-20th century, and it came to be perceived as socially unacceptable and/or morally repugnant as well, yet racial politics remain a major phenomenon.

Racist attitudes, or prejudice, are still held by significant portions of the U.S. population. Members of every American ethnic group have perceived racism in their dealings with other groups. Also to note the definition of "White" has changed over time; many European groups, such as Irish and Italians, were not considered "White" when they first immigrated to the United States, and were victims of racial discrimination at that time. White Americans occasionally do experience racial discrimination; it is disputed whether this is properly termed "racism," and, in general, since other groups have less economic and social power, it is uncommon that such discrimination has the power to seriously harm Whites.

History by Targeted Racial Group

Racism against Native Americans

Native Americans, who had lived on the North America continent for at least 15,000 years, had an enormously complex impact on American history and racial relations. During the colonial and independent periods, a long series of conflicts were waged, with the primary objective of obtaining resources of Native Americans. Through wars, massacres, forced displacement (such as in the Trail of Tears), and the imposition of treaties, land was taken and numerous hardships imposed. In 1540 AD, the first racial strife was with Spaniard Hernando de Soto's expedition who enslaved and murdered many New World communities. In the early 1700s, the English had enslaved nearly 800 Choctaws. After the creation of the United States, the idea of Indian removal gained momentum. However, some Native Americans choose to remain and avoided removal where they were subjected to racist institutions in their ancient homeland. The Choctaws in Mississippi described their situation in 1849, "we have had our habitations torn down and burned, our fences destroyed, cattle turned into our fields and we ourselves have been scourged, manacled, fettered and otherwise personally abused, until by such treatment some of our best men have died." Joseph B. Cobb, who moved to Mississippi from Georgia, described Choctaws as having "no nobility or virtue at all, and in some respect he found blacks, especially native Africans, more interesting and admirable, the red man's superior in every way. The Choctaw and Chickasaw, the tribes he knew best, were beneath contempt, that is, even worse than black slaves."

Ideological expansionist justification (Manifest Destiny) included stereotyped perceptions of all Native Americans as "merciless Indian savages" (as described in the United States Declaration of Independence) despite successful American efforts at civilization as proven with the Cherokee, Chickasaw, Creek, and Choctaw.

The most egregious attempt occurred with the California gold rush, the first two years of which saw the deaths of thousands of Native Americans. Under Mexican rule in California, Indians were subjected to *de facto* enslavement under a system of peonage. While in 1850, California formally entered the Union as a free state, with respect to the issue of slavery, the practice of Indian indentured servitude was not outlawed by the California Legislature until 1863.

Military and civil resistance by Native Americans has been a constant feature of American history. So too have a variety of debates around issues of sovereignty, the upholding of treaty provisions, and the civil rights of Native Americans under U.S. law.

Discrimination, Marginalization

Once their territories were incorporated into the United States, surviving Native Americans were denied equality before the law and often treated as wards of the state. Many Native Americans were relegated to reservations—constituting just 4% of U.S. territory—and the treaties signed with them violated. Tens of thousands of American Indians and Alaska Natives were forced to attend a residential school system which sought to reeducate them in white settler American values, culture and economy, to "kill the Indian, sav[ing] the man."

Further dispossession continued through concessions for industries such as oil, mining and timber and through division of land through legislation such as the Allotment Act. These concessions have raised problems of consent, exploitation of low royalty rates, environmental injustice, and gross mismanagement of funds held in trust, resulting in the loss of $10–40 billion. The Worldwatch Institute notes that 317 reservations are threatened by environmental hazards, while Western Shoshone land has been subjected to more than 1,000 nuclear explosions.

Native American Owned Slaves

Before removal, some Southern Native American tribes owned African American slaves. The Cherokee, Choctaw, and Chickasaw were known to have had slaves. Just as they adopted European American culture (Christianity, yeoman farming techniques, and educational institutions), they also adopted slavery. But unlike the United States before Emancipation, African Americans (and European Americans) were allowed to become citizens of their respective Native American nations; however, it was rare for African Americans to become citizens of Native American nations. For example, a small number of "Free People of Color" lived in many Native American nations as Cherokee, Choctaw, or Creek citizens.

Assimilation efforts into American Society

George Washington and Henry Knox believed that Native Americans were equals but that their society was inferior. The government appointed agents, like Benjamin Hawkins, to live among the Indians and to teach them, through example and instruction, how to live like whites. Washington formulated a policy to encourage the "civilizing" process. Washington had a six-point plan for civilization which included,

1. impartial justice toward Native Americans
2. regulated buying of Native American lands
3. promotion of commerce
4. promotion of experiments to civilize or improve Native American society
5. presidential authority to give presents
6. punishing those who violated Native American rights.

The Indian Citizenship Act of 1924 granted U.S. citizenship to all Native Americans. Prior to the passage of the act, nearly two-thirds of Native Americans were already U.S. citizens. The earliest recorded date of Native Americans becoming U.S. citizens was in 1831 when the Mississippi Choctaw became citizens after the United States Legislature ratified the Treaty of Dancing Rabbit Creek. Under article XIV of that treaty, any Choctaw who elected not to move to Native American Territory could become an American citizen when he registered and if he stayed on designated lands for five years after treaty ratification. Citizenship could also be obtained by:

1. Treaty Provision (as with the Mississippi Choctaw)
2. Allotment under the Act of February 8, 1887
3. Issuance of Patent in Fee Simple
4. Adopting Habits of Civilized Life
5. Minor Children
6. Citizenship by Birth
7. Becoming Soldiers and Sailors in the U.S. Armed Forces
8. Marriage
9. Special Act of Congress.

"Be it enacted by the Senate and House of Representatives of the United States of America in Congress assembled, That all noncitizen Native Americans born within the territorial limits of the United States be, and they are hereby, declared to be citizens of the United States: Provided, That the granting of such citizenship shall not in any manner impair or otherwise affect the right of any Native American to tribal or other property. " —Indian Citizenship Act of 1924

While formal equality has been legally granted, American Indians, Alaska Natives, Native Hawaiians, and Pacific Islanders remain among the most economically disadvantaged groups in the country, and according to National mental health studies, American Indians are the most affected racial group to suffer from high levels of alcoholism, depression and suicide.

Racism against African Americans

Slavery and Emancipation

In colonial America, before slavery became completely based on racial lines, thousands of African slaves served European colonists, alongside other Europeans serving a term of indentured servitude. In some cases for African slaves, a term of service meant freedom and a land grant afterward, but these were rarely awarded, and few former slaves became landowners this way. In a precursor to the American Revolution, Nathaniel Bacon led a revclt in 1676 against the Governor of Virginia and the system of exploitation he represented: exploitation of poorer colonists by the increasingly wealthy landowners where poorer people, regardless of skin color, fought side by side. However, Bacon died, probably of dysentery; hundreds of participants in the revolt were lured to disarm by a promised amnesty; and the revolt lost steam.

Slaves were primarily used for agricultural labor, notably in the production of cotton and tobacco. Black slavery in the Northeast was common until the early 19th century, when many Northeastern states abolished slavery. Slaves were used as a labor force in agricultural production, shipyards, docks, and as domestic servants. In both regions, only the wealthiest Americans owned slaves. In contrast, poor whites recognized that slavery devalued their own labor. The social rift along color lines soon became ingrained in every aspect of colonial American culture. Approximately one Southern family in four held slaves prior to war. According to the 1860 U.S. census, there were about 385,000 slaveowners out of approximately 1.5 million white families.

Although the Constitution had banned the importation of new African slaves in 1808, and in 1820 slave trade was equated with piracy, punishable by death, the practice of chattel slavery still existed for the next half century. All slaves in only the areas of the Confederate States of America that were not under direct control of the United States government were declared free by the Emancipation Proclamation, which was issued on January 1, 1863 by President Abraham Lincoln. It should be noted that the Emancipation Proclamation did not apply to areas loyal to, or controlled by, the Union, thus the document only freed slaves where the Union still had not regained the legitimacy to do so. Slavery was not actually abolished in the United States until the passage of the 13th Amendment which was declared ratified on December 6, 1865.

About 4 million black slaves were freed in 1865. Ninety-five percent of blacks lived in the South, comprising one third of the population there as opposed to one percent of the population of the North. Consequently, fears of eventual emancipation were much greater in the South than in the North. Based on 1860 census figures, 8% of all white males aged 13 to 43 died in the civil war, including 6% in the North and an extraordinary 18% in the South. Despite this, post-emancipation America was not free from racism; discriminatory practices continued in the United States with the existence of Jim Crow laws, educational disparities and widespread criminal acts against people of color.

Nadir of American Tace Relations

The new century saw a hardening of institutionalized racism and legal discrimination against citizens of African descent in the United States. Although technically able to vote, poll taxes, acts of terror (often perpetuated by groups such as the Ku Klux Klan, founded in the Reconstruction South), and discriminatory laws such as grandfather clauses kept black Americans disenfranchised particularly in the South but also nationwide following the Hayes election at the end of the Reconstruction era in 1877. In response to de jure racism, protest and lobbyist groups emerged, most notably, the NAACP (National Association for the Advancement of Colored People) in 1909.

This time period is sometimes referred to as the nadir of American race relations because racism in the United States was worse during this time than at any period before or since. Segregation, racial discrimination, and expressions of white supremacy all increased. So did anti-black violence, including lynchings and race riots.

In addition, racism which had been viewed primarily as a problem in the Southern states, burst onto the national consciousness following the Great Migration, the relocation of millions of African Americans from their roots in the Southern states to the industrial centres of the North after World War I, particularly in cities such as Boston, Chicago, and New York (Harlem). In northern cities, racial tensions exploded, most violently in Chicago, and lynchings—mob-directed hangings, usually racially motivated—increased dramatically in the 1920s.

American Civil Rights Movement

Prominent African American politicians, entertainers and activists pushed for civil rights throughout the twentieth century, quite noticeably during the 1930s and 1940s with noted allies including First Lady Eleanor Roosevelt, who facilitated singer Marian Anderson's famous 1939 Easter concert when segregated venues would not accommodate her. Activists, particularly A. Philip Randolph agitated for civil rights throughout the Great

Depression and World War II years, organizing protest marches and seeking government concessions. The efforts of civil rights activists began to bear fruit with the issuance of wartime Executive Order 8802, signed by President Franklin D. Roosevelt on June 25, 1941 to prohibit racial discrimination in the national defence industry. This was followed by Executive Order 9981 by President Harry S. Truman in July 1948, which banned racial segregation in the American armed forces, and the creation of the U.S. Commission on Civil Rights in 1957. The 1950s and 1960s saw the peaking of the American Civil Rights Movement and the desegregation of schools under the 1954 Supreme Court case Brown v. Board and the organizing of widespread protests across the nation under a younger generation of leaders.

The pastor and activist Martin Luther King, Jr. was the catalyst for many nonviolent protests in the 1960s which led to the passage of the Civil Rights Act of 1964. This signified a change in the social acceptance of legislative racism in America and a profound increase in the number of opportunities available for people of color in the United States. While substantial gains were made in the succeeding decades through middle class advancement and public employment, black poverty and lack of education deepened in the context of de-industrialization.

Many cite the 2008 United States presidential election as a step forward in race relations: White Americans played a role in electing Barack Obama, the country's first black president. However, according to exit polls, over sixty percent of white Americans voted for McCain. Barack Obama receives over thirty death threats a day, higher than Bush or Clinton, which has led some to question tolerance in white America.

Discrimination and Racism against Asian-Americans

In the Pacific States, racism was primarily directed against the resident Asian immigrants. Several immigration laws discriminated against the Asians, and at different points the ethnic Chinese or other groups were banned from entering the United States. Nonwhites were prohibited from testifying against whites, a prohibition extended to the Chinese by People v. Hall. The Chinese were often subject to harder labor on the First Transcontinental Railroad and often performed the more dangerous tasks such as using dynamite to make pathways through the mountains. The San Francisco Vigilance Movement, although ostensibly a response to crime and corruption, also systematically victimized Irish immigrants, and later this was transformed into mob violence against Chinese immigrants. Legal discrimination of Asian minorities was furthered with the passages of the Chinese Exclusion Act of 1882, which banned the entrance of virtually all ethnic Chinese immigrants into the United States until 1943.

During World War II, the United States created internment camps for Japanese American citizens in fear that they would be used as spies for the Japanese. The executive order hasn't affected any Japanese populations in the Eastern US and the large Japanese population in Hawaii.

Discrimination against Latin Americans

Americans of Latin American ancestry (often categorized as "Hispanic") come from a wide variety of racial and ethnic backgrounds. Latinos are not all distinguishable as a racial minority.

The Zoot Suit Riots were vivid incidents of racial violence against Latinos (e.g. Mexican-Americans) in Los Angeles in 1943. Naval servicemen stationed in a Latino neighborhood conflicted with youth in the dense neighborhood. Frequent confrontations between small groups and individuals had intensified into several days of non-stop rioting. Large mobs of servicemen would enter civilian quarters looking to attack Mexican American youths, some of whom were wearing zoot suits, a distinctive exaggerated fashion popular among that group. The disturbances continued unchecked, and even assisted, by the local police for several days before based commanders declared downtown Los Angeles and Mexican American neighborhoods off-limits to servicemen.

West Coast Racism

The Pacific and Western states were often portrayed to those on the East Coast as more liberal in terms of race relations in the 1960s and 1970s, but California legally allowed racial segregation of public facilities until the 1950s and other forms of racism were felt there as well.

A variety of laws were enacted to prevent African American migration to the Pacific Northwest. While slavery was criminalized in the Oregon Territory in 1844, a so-called "lash law" subjected blacks found guilty of violating the law to whippings—no less than 20 and no more than 39 strokes of the lash—every six months "until he or she shall quit the territory." An exclusion law, barring African Americans from entering the territory was passed in 1847, repealed in 1854, and added to the new Oregon state constitution in 1857. While African Americans have been present at some level since 1805, the demographic reverberations of these laws remain today.

Hate Crimes

Most hate crimes in the United States target victims on the basis of race or ethnicity (for Federal purposes, crimes targeting Hispanics based on that identity are considered based on ethnicity). Leading forms of bias cited in the FBI's Uniform Crime Reporting (UCR) Program, based on law enforcement agency filings are: anti-black, anti-Jewish, anti-white, anti-homosexual, and anti-Hispanic bias in that order in both 2004 and 2005. There are more hate crimes against whites than against Hispanics, Asians, American-Indians and multiple-race groups-a statistically expected trend given that there far more whites than other ethnic groups put together. By contrast, the National Criminal Victimization Survey, finds that per capita rates of hate crime victimization varied little by race or ethnicity, and the differences are not statistically significant. The New Century Foundation, a white nationalist organization founded by Jared Taylor, argues that blacks are more likely than whites to commit hate crimes, and that FBI figures inflate the number of hate crimes committed by whites by counting Hispanics as "white". Other analysts are sharply critical of the NCF's findings, referring to the criminological mainstream view that "Racial and ethnic data must be treated with caution.... Existing research on crime has generally shown that racial or ethnic identity is not predictive of criminal behaviour with data which has been controlled for social and economic factors." NCF's methodology and statistics are further sharply criticized as flawed and deceptive by anti-racist activists Tim Wise and the Southern Poverty Law Centre.

The first post-Jim Crow era hate crime to make sensational media attention was the beating death of Vincent Chin, an Asian

American of Chinese descent in 1982. He was attacked by a mob of white assailants who were recently laid off from a Detroit area auto factory job and blamed the Japanese for their individual unemployment. Chin was not of Japanese descent but the assailants testified at the criminal court case that he "looked like a Jap", an ethnic slur used to describe Japanese and other Asians, and that they were angry enough to beat him to death. They served no jail time and were acquitted of all charges.

Antisemitism

Antisemitism has also played a role in America. During the late 1800s and early 1900s, hundreds of thousands of Ashkenazi Jews were escaping the pogroms of Russia and Eastern Europe. They boarded boats from ports on the Baltic Sea and in Northern Germany, and largely arrived at Ellis Island, New York.

It is thought by Leo Rosten, in his book, 'The Joys of Yiddish', that as soon as they left the boat, they were subject to racism from the port immigration authorities. The derogatory term 'kike' was adopted when referring to Jews (because they often could not write so they may have signed their immigration papers with circles-or kikel in Yiddish).

From the 1910s, the Southern Jewish communities were attacked by the Ku Klux Klan, who objected to Jewish immigration, and often used 'The Jewish Banker' in their propaganda. In 1915, Texas-born, New York Jew Leo Frank was lynched by the newly re-formed Klan, after being convicted of rape and sentenced to death (his punishment was commuted to life imprisonment).

The events in Nazi Germany also attracted attention from America. Jewish lobbying for intervention in Europe drew opposition from the isolationists, amongst whom was Father Charles Coughlin, a well known radio priest, who was known to be critical of Jews, believing that they were leading America into the war. He preached in weekly, overtly anti-Semitic sermons and, from 1936, began publication of a newspaper, Social Justice, in which he printed anti-Semitic accusations such as The Protocols of the Elders of Zion.

A number of Jewish organizations, Christian organizations, Muslim organizations, and academics consider the Nation of Islam to be anti-Semitic. Specifically, they claim that the Nation of Islam has engaged in revisionist and antisemitic interpretations of the Holocaust and exaggerates the role of Jews in the African slave trade. The Jewish Anti-Defamation League (ADL) alleges that NOI Health Minister, Abdul Alim Muhammad, has accused Jewish doctors of injecting blacks with the AIDS virus, an allegation that Dr. Abdul Alim Muhammad has denied.

Anti-White Racism

In the United States, there have been crimes committed against White Americans on the basis of their ethnicity. One series of unprovoked crimes that specifically targeted White Americans is the Zebra murders that occurred in San Francisco between 1973 and 1974.

The Zebra murders were carried out by a group known as Death Angels (a radical splinter group of the Nation of Islam) that intended to kill whites to spread terror and earn favour and status within their sect. The final death count varies depending on which killings are included, but it is believed to account for more than 71 murders in addition to numerous rapes and attempted murders.

Another series of crimes that specifically targeted whites is the 2002 Beltway sniper attacks which planned to kill six whites a day for 30 days, and resulted in 10 deaths and 3 critical injuries. One of the snipers Lee Boyd Malvo testified that John Allen Muhammad was driven by hatred of America because of its "slavery, hypocrisy and foreign policy" and his belief that "the white man is the devil."

According to the Southern Poverty Law Centre, national anti-white hate groups that are currently active include Nation of Islam and New Black Panther Party.

According to FBI statistics from 1995-2002, Whites are the second most targeted group for racially motivated hate crime in New York City.

Affirmative action is sometimes called "reverse racism" by its opponents; some sociologists argue that the term "racism" can only be applied to structured systems of racial supremacy, and that opponents would more correctly call affirmative action "reverse discrimination."

Racism against Middle Easterners and Muslims

Racism against Arab Americans may rise concomittantly with tensions between the American government and the Arab world. Following the September 11, 2001 attacks in the United States, discrimination and racialized violence has markedly increased against Arab Americans and many other religious and cultural groups.

Iraqis in particular were demonized which led to hatred towards Arabs and Iranians living in the United States and elsewhere in the western world. There have been attacks against Arabs not only on the basis of their religion (Islam), but also on the basis of their ethnicity; numerous Christian Arabs have been attacked based on their appearances. In addition, non-Arabs who are mistaken for Arabs because of perceived "similarities in appearance" have been collateral victims of anti-Arabism.

Iranian people (who constitute a different ethnicity than Arabs), as well as South Asians of different ethnic/religious backgrounds (Hindus, Muslims and Sikhs) have been stereotyped as "Arabs". The case of Balbir Singh Sodhi, a Sikh who was murdered at a Phoenix gas station by a white supremacist for "looking like an Arab terrorist" (because of the turban that is a requirement of Sikhism), as well as that of Hindus being attacked for "being Muslims" have achieved prominence and criticism following the September 11 attacks.

Racism against Iranians

The November 1979 Iranian hostage crisis of the U.S. embassy in Tehran precipitated a wave of anti-Iranian sentiment in the United States, directed both against the new Islamic regime and Iranian nationals and immigrants. Even though such sentiments gradually declined after the release of the hostages at the start of 1981, they sometimes flare up. In response, some Iranian immigrants to the U.S. have distanced themselves from their nationality and instead identify primarily on the basis of their ethnic or religious affiliations. Ann Coulter called Iranians "ragheads." Brent Scowcroft called the Iranian people "rug merchants."

Since the 1980s and especially since the 1990s Hollywood's depiction of Iranians has gradually shown signs of vilifying

Iranians. Hollywood network productions such as 24, *John Doe*, *On Wings of Eagles* (1986), *Escape From Iran: The Canadian Caper* (1981), and *JAG* almost regularly host Persian speaking villains in their storylines. On May 9, 1997, CBS aired an episode of JAG in which several Hamas terrorists take a Washington hospital under siege. According to the film, they spoke in fluent "Persian", not "Arabic".

Some of Hollywood's "stereotypical" and anti-Iranian movies include: *The Peacemaker* (in which a character, apparently without any context, says "fuck Iran"), *The Hitman* (in which several mobs join together to demolish an Iranian mob operating in Canada), *MadHouse* (partially centering upon a wealthy Iranian who is in the process of divorcing his American wife. In one scene, the wife, speaking to her Iranian husband utters "you goddamn towel heads, sand rats"), *The Naked Gun, Under Siege, The Delta Force, Into the Night, Down and Out in Beverly Hills, Threads, The Final Options*, and *Silver Bears*.

4

British Parliamentary and Party System

Politics of the United Kingdom

The politics of the United Kingdom of Great Britain and Northern Ireland takes place in the framework of a constitutional monarchy, in which the Monarch is head of state and the Prime Minister of the United Kingdom is the head of government. Executive power is exercised by the UK government, the devolved governments of Scotland and Wales, and the Executive of Northern Ireland. Legislative power is vested in both the government and the two chambers of Parliament, the House of Commons and the House of Lords, as well as in the Scottish parliament and Welsh and Northern Ireland assemblies. The judiciary is independent of the executive and the legislature, though several senior judges are still members of the House of Lords. In October 2009 the judicial role of the House of Lords was removed and given to a new Supreme Court under the Constitutional Reform Act 2005.

The UK is a multi-party system and since the 1920s, the two largest political parties have been the Conservative Party and the Labour Party. Though coalition and minority governments have been an occasional feature of parliamentary politics, the first-past-the-post electoral system used for general elections tends to maintain the dominance of these two parties, though each has in the past century relied upon a third party to deliver a working majority in Parliament.

The Liberal Democrats, a party formed by the merger of the former Liberal Party and Social Democratic Party in 1988, is the third largest party in the British parliament. It seeks a reform of the electoral system to address the disproportionate dominance of the two main parties that results from the current system.

Growing support for 'Nationalist' parties in Scotland and Wales led to proposals for devolution in the 1970s though only in the 1990s did devolution actually happen. Today, Scotland, Wales and Northern Ireland each possess a legislature and government alongside that of the United Kingdom, responsible for devolved matters. However, it is a matter of dispute as to whether increased autonomy and devolution of executive and legislative powers has contributed to a reduction in support for full independence.

The principal pro-independence party, the Scottish National Party, won 20 extra MSPs at the 2007 Scottish parliament elections and now forms the Scottish Government as a minority administration, with plans to hold a referendum on negotiating for independence, before 2011. In Wales, the nationalist party, Plaid Cymru, is the junior coalition partner in the Welsh Assembly Government although unlike the Scottish National Party it does not officially advocate complete secession from the United Kingdom. In Northern Ireland, the largest Pro-Belfast Agreement party, Sinn Féin, not only advocates Northern Ireland's unification with the Republic of Ireland, but also abstains from taking their elected seats in the Westminister government, as this would entail taking a pledge of allegiance to the British monarch.

The constitution is uncodified, being made up of constitutional conventions, statutes and other elements.

This system of government, known as the *Westminster system*, has been adopted by other countries as well, such as Canada, India, Australia, New Zealand, Singapore, Malaysia and Jamaica, countries that made up part of the British Empire.

Monarch

The head of state, *theoretical* and nominal source of executive, judicial and legislative power in the UK is the British monarch, currently Queen Elizabeth II. However, sovereignty in the UK no longer rests with the monarch, since the English Bill of Rights in 1689, which established the principle of Parliamentary sovereignty. Nonetheless, the monarch is still known as the sovereign.

The British sovereign possesses many powers, including the right to choose any British citizen to be her Prime Minister and the right to call and dissolve Parliament whenever she wishes. However, in accordance with the current uncodified constitution, the Prime Minister is the leader of the largest party in the House of Commons, and Parliament is dissolved at the time suggested by the PM. For a bill to become law the monarch has to grant Royal Assent. Queen Anne was the last monarch who withheld Assent: on 11 March 1708 to a bill "for the settling of Militia in Scotland". Other royal powers called royal prerogative, such as patronage to appoint ministers and the ability to declare war, are exercised by the Prime Minister and the Cabinet, with the formal consent of the Queen.

Historically, the British monarch directly exercised all executive authority in the UK government. However, in the early 18th century, the role of Prime Minister (literally meaning the *chief* or *senior* minister in the Cabinet) emerged as a de facto executive authority, by directly implementing executive powers and collectively consulting with other members of his/her Cabinet.

Today the sovereign has an essentially ceremonial role restricted in exercise of power by convention and public opinion. However the monarch does continue to exercise three essential rights: the *right to be consulted, the right to advise and the right to warn*. As a consequence of these ideals, Prime Ministers hold weekly confidential meetings with the monarch in which the sovereign holds the right to express her opinions.

In formal terms, the *Crown in Parliament* is sovereign even though in practical terms the political head of the UK is the Prime Minister (Gordon Brown since 27 June 2007). However, the real powers of position of the monarch in the British Constitution should not be downplayed. The monarch does indeed retain some power, but it has to be used with discretion. She fulfills the necessary constitutional role as head of state, and with the absence of a distinct separation of powers as in the American model and a strong second chamber, acts as a final check on executive power. If a time came to pass, for instance, when a law threatened the freedom or security of her subjects and citizens, the Queen could decline royal assent, free as she is from the eddies of party politics. Furthermore, armed removal of her by Parliament or Government would be difficult, as the monarch remains commander-in-chief of the armed forces, who swear an oath of allegiance to her.

Executive

Executive power in the United Kingdom is exercised on behalf of the Sovereign, in whom executive power is nominally vested, by the UK government and the Scottish Government, the Welsh Assembly Government and the Northern Ireland Executive.

The United Kingdom Government

The monarch appoints a Prime Minister as the head of Her Majesty's Government in the United Kingdom, guided by the strict convention that the Prime Minister should be the member of the House of Commons most likely to be able to form a Government with the support of that House. In practice, this means that the leader of the political party with an absolute majority of seats in the House of Commons is chosen to be the Prime Minister. The Prime Minister then selects the other Ministers which make up the Government and act as political heads of the various Government Departments. About twenty of the most senior government ministers make up the Cabinet and approximately 100 ministers in total comprise the government. In accordance with constitutional convention, all ministers within the government are either Members of Parliament or peers in the House of Lords.

As in some other parliamentary systems of government (especially those based upon the Westminster System), the executive (called "the government") is drawn from and is answerable to Parliament-a successful vote of no confidence will force the government either to resign or to seek a parliamentary dissolution and a general election. In practice, members of parliament of all major parties are strictly controlled by whips who try to ensure they vote according to party policy. If the government has a large majority, then they are very unlikely to lose enough votes to be unable to pass legislation.

The Prime Minister and the Cabinet

The Prime Minister, as the label suggests, is the prime or senior minister in the Cabinet. She/he is responsible for chairing

Cabinet meetings, selecting Cabinet ministers (and all other positions in Her Majesty's government), and formulating governmental policy. The Prime Minister is the de facto source of executive authority in the UK government, since s/he exercises executive functions that are nominally vested in the sovereign (by way of the Royal Prerogatives). Historically, the British monarch was the sole source of executive powers in the government. However, following the rule of the Hanoverian monarchs, an arrangement of a "Prime Minister" chairing and leading the Cabinet began to emerge. Over time, this arrangement became the effective executive branch of government, as it assumed the day-to-day functioning of the British government away from the sovereign.

Theoretically, the Prime Minister is *primus inter pares* (,i.e. Latin for "first among equals") among his/her Cabinet colleagues. While the Prime Minister is the senior Cabinet Minister, s/he is theoretically bound to make executive decisions in a collective fashion with the other Cabinet ministers. The Cabinet, along with the PM, consists of Secretaries of State from the various government departments. Cabinet meetings are typically held weekly, while Parliament is in session.

Government Departments and the Civil Service

The Government of the United Kingdom contains a number of ministries known mainly, though not exclusively as departments, e.g. Ministry of Defence. These are politically led by a Government Minister who is often a Secretary of State and member of the Cabinet. He or she may also be supported by a number of junior Ministers. In practice, several government departments and Ministers have responsibilities that cover England alone, with devolved bodies having responsibility for Scotland, Wales and Northern Ireland, (for example-the Department of Health), or responsibilities that mainly focus on England (such as the Department for Children, Schools and Families).

Implementation of the Minister's decisions is carried out by a permanent politically neutral organization known as the civil service. Its constitutional role is to support the Government of the day regardless of which political party is in power. Unlike some other democracies, senior civil servants remain in post upon a change of Government. Administrative management of the Department is led by a head civil servant known in most Departments as a Permanent Secretary. The majority of the civil service staff in fact work in executive agencies, which are separate operational organizations reporting to Departments of State.

"Whitehall" is often used as a synonym for the central core of the Civil Service. This is because most Government Departments have headquarters in and around the former Royal Palace Whitehall.

Devolved National Administrations

Scottish Government

The Scottish Government is responsible for all issues that are not explicitly reserved to the United Kingdom Parliament at Westminster, by the Scotland Act; including NHS Scotland, education, justice, rural affairs, and transport. It manages an annual budget of more than £30 billion. The government is led by the First Minister, assisted by various Ministers with individual portfolios and remits. The Scottish Parliament nominates a Member to be appointed as First Minister by the Queen. The First Minister then appoints his Ministers (now known as Cabinet Secretaries) and junior Ministers, subject to approval by the Parliament. The First Minister, the Ministers (but not junior ministers), the Lord Advocate and Solicitor General are the Members of the 'Scottish Executive', as set out in the Scotland Act 1998. They are collectively known as "the Scottish Ministers".

Welsh Assembly Government

The Welsh Assembly Government and the National Assembly for Wales have more limited powers than those devolved to Scotland, although following the passing of the Government of Wales Act 2006, the Assembly can now legislate in some areas through Assembly Measures passed within clearly defined areas based upon, Legislative Competence Orders which can be granted on a case by case basis. The current Welsh Assembly Government was formed several weeks after the 2007 elections, following a brief period of minority administration, when Plaid Cymru joined Labour in a coalition government under the continuing leadership of First Minister Rhodri Morgan.

Northern Ireland Executive

The Northern Ireland Executive and Assembly have powers closer to those already devolved to Scotland. The Northern Ireland Executive is led by a diarchy, currently First Minister Peter Robinson (Democratic Unionist Party) and deputy First Minister Martin McGuinness (Sinn Féin).

Legislatures

The UK Parliament is the supreme legislative body in the United Kingdom (i.e., there is parliamentary sovereignty), and Government is drawn from and answerable to it. Parliament is bicameral, consisting of the House of Commons and the House of Lords. There is also a devolved Scottish Parliament and devolved Assemblies in Wales and Northern Ireland, with varying degrees of legislative authority.

UK Parliament

House of Commons

The Countries of the United Kingdom are divided into parliamentary constituencies of broadly equal population by the four Boundary Commissions. Each constituency elects a Member of Parliament (MP) to the House of Commons at General Elections and, if required, at by-elections. The number of constituencies will increase from the current 646 to 650 at the 2010 general election. Of the current 646 MPs, all but one belong to a political party. In modern times, all Prime Ministers and Leaders of the Opposition have been drawn from the Commons, not the Lords. Alec Douglas-Home resigned from his peerages days after becoming Prime Minister in 1963, and the last Prime Minister before him from the Lords left in 1902 (the Marquess of Salisbury).

One party usually has a majority in Parliament, because of the use of the First Past the Post electoral system, which has been conducive in creating the current two party system. The monarch normally asks a person commissioned to form a government simply whether it can *survive* in the House of Commons, something which majority governments are expected to be able to do. In exceptional circumstances the monarch asks someone to 'form a government' *with a parliamentary minority* which in the event of no party having a majority requires the formation of a coalition government. This option is only ever taken at a time of national emergency, such as war-time. It was given in 1916 to Andrew Bonar Law, and when he declined, to David Lloyd George and in 1940 to Winston Churchill. It is worth noting that a government is not formed by a vote of the House of Commons, merely a commission from the monarch. The House of Commons gets its first chance to indicate confidence in the new government when it votes on the Speech from the Throne (the legislative programme proposed by the new government).

House of Lords

The House of Lords was previously a largely hereditary aristocratic chamber, although including life peers,and Lords Spiritual. It is currently mid-way through extensive reforms, the most recent of these being enacted in the House of Lords Act 1999. The house still currently consists of two very different types of member, the Lords Temporal and Lords Spiritual.

Lords Temporal include appointed members (life peers with no hereditary right for their descendants to sit in the house) and ninety-two remaining hereditary peers, elected from among, and by, the holders of titles which previously gave a seat in the House of Lords. The Lords Spiritual represent the established Church of England and number 26, the Five Ancient Sees (Canterbury, York, London, Winchester and Durham) and the 21 next-most senior bishops.

The House of Lords currently acts to review legislation initiated by the House of Commons, with the power to propose amendments, and can exercise a suspensive veto. This allows it to delay legislation if it does not approve it for twelve months. However, the use of vetoes is limited by convention and by the operation of the Parliament Acts 1911 and 1949: the Lords may not veto the "money bills" or major manifesto promises. Persistent use of the veto can also be overturned by the Commons, under a provision of the Parliament Act 1911. Often governments will accept changes in legislation in order to avoid both the time delay, and the negative publicity of being seen to clash with the Lords. However the Lords still retain a full veto in acts which would extend the life of Parliament beyond the 5 year term limit introduced by the Parliament Act 1911.

The House of Lords is currently also the final court of appeal on civil cases within the United Kingdom, although in practice only a small subset of the House of Lords, known as the Law Lords, hears judicial cases. In accordance with the legal doctrine of stare decisis, the House of Lords supersedes all civil and criminal courts in England & Wales. (The House of Lords has no role in criminal case appeals in Scotland.) The Constitutional Reform Act 2005 outlines plans for a Supreme Court of the United Kingdom to replace the role of the Law Lords.

Devolved National Legislatures

Though the UK parliament remains the sovereign parliament, Scotland has a parliament and Wales and Northern Ireland have assemblies. De jure, each could have its powers broadened, narrowed or changed by an Act of the UK Parliament. However, Scotland has a tradition of popular sovereignty as opposed to parliamentary sovereignty and the fact that the Scottish parliament was established following a referendum would make it politically difficult to significantly alter its powers without popular consent. The UK is therefore a unitary state with a devolved system of government. This contrasts with a federal system, in which sub-parliaments or state parliaments and assemblies have a clearly defined constitutional *right* to exist and a *right* to exercise certain constitutionally guaranteed and defined functions and cannot be unilaterally abolished by Acts of the central parliament.

All three devolved institutions are elected by proportional representation: the Additional Member System is used in Scotland and Wales, and Single Transferable Vote is used in Northern Ireland.

England, therefore, is the only country in the UK not to have a devolved English parliament. However, senior politicians of all main parties have voiced concerns in regard to the West Lothian Question, which is raised where certain policies for England are set by MPs from all four constituent nations whereas similar policies for Scotland or Wales might be decided in the devolved assemblies by legislators from those countries alone. Alternative proposals for English regional government have stalled, following a poorly received referendum on devolved government for the North East of England, which had hitherto been considered the region most in favour of the idea, with the exception of Cornwall, where there is widespread support for a Cornish Assembly, including all five Cornish MPs. England is therefore governed according to the balance of parties across the whole of the United Kingdom.

The government has no plans to establish an English parliament or assembly although several pressure groups are calling for one. One of their main arguments is that MPs (and thus voters) from different parts of the UK have inconsistent powers. Currently an MP from Scotland can vote on legislation which affects only England but MPs from England (or indeed Scotland) cannot vote on matters devolved to the Scottish parliament. Indeed, the current Prime Minister Gordon Brown, who is an MP for a Scottish constituency, introduces some laws that only affect England and not his own constituency. This anomaly is known as the West Lothian question.

The policy of the UK Government in England was to establish elected regional assemblies with no legislative powers. The London Assembly was the first of these, established in 2000, following a referendum in 1998, but further plans were abandoned following rejection of a proposal for an elected assembly in North East England in a referendum in 2004. Unelected regional assemblies remain in place in eight regions of England.

Scottish Parliament

The Scottish Parliament is the national, unicameral legislature of Scotland, located in the Holyrood area of the capital Edinburgh. The Parliament, informally referred to as "Holyrood" (cf. "Westminster"), is a democratically elected body comprising 129 members who are known as Members of the Scottish Parliament, or MSPs. Members are elected for four-year terms under the mixed member proportional representation system. As a result, 73 MSPs represent individual geographical constituencies elected by the plurality ("first past the post") system, with a further 56 returned from eight additional member regions, each electing seven MSPs.

The current Scottish Parliament was established by the Scotland Act 1998 and its first meeting as a devolved legislature was on 12 May 1999. The parliament has the power to pass laws and has limited tax-varying capability. Another of its jobs is to hold the Scottish Government to account. The "devolved matters" over which it has responsibility include education, health, agriculture, and justice. A degree of domestic authority, and all foreign policy, remains with the UK Parliament in Westminster.

The public take part in Parliament in a way that is not the case at Westminster through Cross Party Groups on policy topics which the interested public join and attend meetings of alongside Members of the Scottish Parliament (MSPs).

The resurgence in Celtic language and identity, as well as 'regional' politics and development, has contributed to forces pulling against the unity of the state. This was clearly demonstrated when-although some argue it was influenced by general public dillusionment with Labour-the Scottish National Party became the largest party in the Scottish Parliament by one seat. Alex Salmond (leader of SNP) has since made history by becoming the first First Minister of Scotland from a party other than Labour. The SNP rule as a minority government at Holyrood. Nevertheless, recent opinion polls have suggested that nationalism (i.e. a desire to break up the UK) is rising within Scotland and England. However, the polls have been known to be inaccurate in the past (for example, in the run up to the 1992 General Election). Moreover, polls carried out in the 1970s and the 1990s showed similar results, only to be debunked at elections. While support for breaking up the UK was strongest in Scotland, there was still a clear lead for unionism over nationalism. However, an opinion poll in April 2008 suggested the result of any referendum on Scottish independence could be close as support for independence had reached 41% with just 40% supporting retention of the Union.

Welsh Assembly

The National Assembly for Wales is a devolved assembly with power to make legislation in Wales, and is also responsible for Welsh Assembly Government departments in Wales. The Assembly was formed under the Government of Wales Act 1998, by the Labour government, after a referendum in 1997 (also supported by Plaid Cymru and the Liberal Democrats) approved its creation. There is now a legal separation of the legislative and executive functions of the National Assembly, since the passing of the Government of Wales Act 2006. The Act created a separate executive called the "Welsh Assembly Government" which performs the day to day running of government affairs and contains members of the highest elected party of the Assembly chamber. The act also made the National Assembly for Wales a separate entity from the Welsh Assembly Government, and this entity scrutinizes the government in power. The "Assembly Commission" was also created to ensure the smooth running of resources and gathering of accurate facts for the Assembly to deal with.

As of the passing of the Government of Wales Act 2006, the National Assembly for Wales now has its own legislative powers known as Assembly Measures. Each Assembly Measure derives its power from a Legislative Competency Order which has to be passed by the Assembly and two Houses of Parliament. Before the 2006 Act, the Assembly did not have such legislative power and only had the right to develop Subordinate legislation off primary legislation made by the UK Parliament.

Northern Ireland Assembly

The current government of Northern Ireland was established as a result of the 1998 Good Friday Agreement. This created the Northern Ireland Assembly. The Assembly is a unicameral body consisting of 108 members elected under the Single Transferable Vote form of proportional representation. The Assembly is based on the principle of power-sharing, in order to ensure that both communities in Northern Ireland, unionist and nationalist, participate in governing the region. It has power to legislate in a wide range of areas and to elect the Northern Ireland Executive (cabinet). It sits at Parliament Buildings at Stormont in Belfast.

The Assembly has authority to legislate in a field of competencies known as "transferred matters". These matters are not explicitly enumerated in the Northern Ireland Act 1998 but instead include any competence not explicitly retained by the Parliament at Westminster. Powers reserved by Westminster are divided into "excepted matters", which it retains indefinitely, and "reserved matters", which may be transferred to the competence of the Northern Ireland Assembly at a future date. Health and education are "transferred" but criminal law and police are "reserved" and royal relations are all "excepted".

While the Assembly was in suspension, due to issues involving the main parties and the Provisional Irish Republican Army (IRA), its legislative powers were exercised by the UK government, which effectively had power to legislate by decree. Laws that would normally be within the competence of the Assembly were passed by the UK government in the form of Orders-in-Council rather than legislative acts.

There has been a significant decrease in violence over the last twenty years, though the situation remains tense, with the more hard-line parties such as Sinn Féin and the Democratic Unionists now holding the most parliamentary seats.

Judiciary

The United Kingdom does not have a single legal system due to it being created by the political union of previously independent countries with the terms of the Treaty of Union guaranteeing the continued existence of Scotland's separate legal system. Today the UK has three distinct systems of law: English law, Northern Ireland law and Scots law. Recent constitutional changes will see a new Supreme Court of the United Kingdom come into being in October 2009 that will take on the appeal functions of the Appellate Committee of the House of Lords. The Judicial Committee of the Privy Council, comprising the same members as the Appellate Committee of the House of Lords, is the highest court of appeal for several independent Commonwealth countries, the UK overseas territories, and the British crown dependencies.

England, Wales and Northern Ireland

Both English law, which applies in England and Wales, and Northern Ireland law are based on common-law principles. The essence of common-law is that law is made by judges sitting in courts, applying their common sense and knowledge of legal precedent (*stare decisis*) to the facts before them. The Courts of England and Wales are headed by the Supreme Court of Judicature of England and Wales, consisting of the Court of Appeal, the High Court of Justice (for civil cases) and the Crown Court (for criminal cases). The Appellate Committee of the House of Lords (usually just referred to, as "The House of Lords") is presently the highest court in the land for both criminal and civil cases in England,

Wales, and Northern Ireland and any decision it makes is binding on every other court in the hierarchy.

Scotland

Scots law, a hybrid system based on both common-law and civil-law principles, applies in Scotland. The chief courts are the Court of Session, for civil cases, and the High Court of Justiciary, for criminal cases. The Appellate Committee of the House of Lords (usually just referred to as "The House of Lords") presently serves as the highest court of appeal for civil cases under Scots law but only if the Court of Session grants leave to appeal or the initial judgement was by a majority decision. Sheriff courts deal with most civil and criminal cases including conducting criminal trials with a jury, known as Sheriff solemn Court, or with a Sheriff and no jury, known as (Sheriff summary Court). The Sheriff courts provide a local court service with 49 Sheriff courts organised across six Sheriffdoms.

Electoral Systems

Various electoral systems are used in the UK:

- The First Past the Post system is used for UK general elections, and also for some local government elections in England and Wales.
- The Bloc Vote system is also used for some local government elections in England and Wales.
- The Additional Member System is used for elections to the Scottish Parliament, Welsh Assembly and London Assembly.
- The Single Transferable Vote system is used in Northern Ireland to elect the Assembly, local councils, and Members of the European Parliament, and in Scotland to elect local councils.
- The Party List System is used for European Parliament elections in England, Scotland and Wales.
- The Supplementary Vote is used to elect directly-elected mayors in England, such as the Mayor of London.

Unlike many European nations, the United Kingdom uses a first-past-the-post system to elect members of Parliament.

Therefore, elections and political parties in the United Kingdom are affected by Duverger's Law, which causes the agglomeration of related political ideologies into a few large parties with many small parties rarely winning representation.

In the last few general elections, voter mandates for Westminster in the 40% ranges have been swung into 60% parliamentary majorities. No government has won a majority of the popular vote since the National Government of Stanley Baldwin in 1935. Twice since World War II (in 1951 and February 1974) the party with fewer popular votes actually came out with the larger number of seats. One reason for all the quirks is that Britain has many political parties, making it possible to win individual constituencies on less than 50% of the vote due to the opposition votes being divided.

Electoral reform has been considered for general elections many times, but after the Jenkins Commission report in October 1998, which suggested the Alternative vote top-up for general elections was effectively ignored by the government, there have been no further government proposals for reform. It is highly unlikely that electoral reform will happen unless there is a significant change in the balance of power and Labour loses its large majority, or if the Liberal Democrats, which have long campaigned for the introduction of Proportional representation, provide the keystone of a hung parliament. The broad-based Make Votes Count Coalition continues to campaign for reform.

Low turnout is a concern, as the percentage of the electorate who voted in the last general election was just 61%.

Political Parties

Historically, the United Kingdom had two major political parties, though currently three parties dominate the political landscape. Originally, the Conservatives and the Liberals dominated British politics, but the Liberal Party collapsed in the early twentieth century and was largely replaced by the Labour Party. In the 1980s, the Liberals merged with the Social Democratic Party and, as the Liberal Democrats, are viewed as the third major party. Other parties, often called minor parties (in UK terms at least) contest elections but few except those which are based in single countries of the United Kingdom win seats in Parliament.

The Scottish National Party has had MPs continuously since 1967, and Plaid Cymru, the Welsh nationalists, has had MPs continuously since 1974. All 18 MPs elected from Northern Ireland are from parties that just contest elections in Northern Ireland (or in the case of Sinn Féin, the island of Ireland.)

In the most recent general election in 2005, the Labour Party won re-election on a reduced majority, with both the Conservatives and Liberal Democrats making gains.

Labour

The Labour Party won the majority of seats in the House of Commons at the 2005 general election, with 356 MPs

The history of the Labour party goes back to 1900 when a Labour Representation Committee was established which changed its name to The Labour Party in 1906. After the First World War, this led to the demise of the Liberal Party as the main reformist force in British politics. The existence of the Labour Party on the left of British politics led to a slow waning of energy from the Liberal Party, which has consequently assumed third place in national politics. After performing poorly in the elections of 1922, 1923 and 1924, the Liberal Party was superseded by the Labour Party as the party of the left.

Following two brief spells in minority governments in 1924 and 1929–1931, the Labour Party had its first true victory after World War II in the 1945 "khaki election". Throughout the rest of the twentieth century, Labour governments alternated with Conservative governments. The Conservatives were in power for most of the time, with the Labour Party suffering the "wilderness years" of 1951-1964 (three straight General Election defeats) and 1979-1997 (four straight General Election defeats).

During this second period, Margaret Thatcher, who became leader of the Conservative party in 1975, made a fundamental change to Conservative policies, turning the Conservative Party into an economic neoliberal party. In the General Election of 1979 she defeated James Callaghan's troubled Labour government after the winter of discontent.

For most of the 1980s and the 1990s, Conservative governments under Thatcher and her successor John Major pursued policies of privatization, anti-trade-unionism, and, for a time, Monetarism, now known collectively as Thatcherism.

The Labour Party elected left-winger Michael Foot as their leader after their 1979 election defeat, and he responded to dissatisfaction with the Labour Party by pursuing a number of radical policies developed by its grass-roots members. In 1981 several right-wing Labour MPs formed a breakaway group called the Social Democratic Party (SDP), a move which split Labour and is widely believed to have made Labour unelectable for a decade. The SDP formed an alliance with the Liberal Party which contested the 1983 and 1987 general elections as a centrist alternative to Labour and the Conservatives. After some initial success, the SDP did not prosper (partly due to its unfavourable distribution of votes in the FPTP electoral system), and was accused by some of splitting the anti-Conservative vote.

The SDP eventually merged with the Liberal Party to form the Liberal Democrats in 1988. Support for the new party has increased since then, and the Liberal Democrats (often referred to as LibDems) in 1997 and 2001 gained an increased number of seats in the House of Commons.

The Labour Party was badly defeated in the Conservative landslide of the 1983 general election, and Michael Foot was replaced shortly thereafter by Neil Kinnock as leader. Kinnock expelled the far left Militant tendency group (now called the Socialist Party of England and Wales) and moderated many of the party's policies. Yet he was in turn replaced by John Smith after Labour defeats in the 1987 and 1992 general elections.

Tony Blair became leader of the Labour party after John Smith's sudden death from a heart attack in 1994. He continued to move the Labour Party back towards the 'centre' by loosening links with the unions and embracing many of Margaret Thatcher's liberal economic policies. This, coupled with the professionalising of the party machine's approach to the media, helped Labour win a historic landslide in the 1997 General Election, after 18 years of Conservative government. Some observers say the Labour Party had by then morphed from a democratic socialist party to a social democratic party, a process which delivered three general election victories but alienated some of its core base.

Conservatives (Tories)

The Conservative Party won the second largest number of seats (still under 200) at the 2005 general election and remained the official opposition, a position they have held continuously since they lost power at the 1997 general election. The crushing defeat of the 1997 election saw them lose over half their seats from 1992 and saw the party re-align with public perceptions of them.

The Conservative party can trace its origin back to 1662, with the Court Party and the Country Party being formed in the aftermath of the English Civil War. The Court Party soon became known as the Tories, a name that has stuck despite the official name being 'Conservative'. The term "Tory" originates from the Exclusion Bill crisis of 1678-1681-the Whigs were those who supported the exclusion of the Roman Catholic Duke of York from the thrones of England, Ireland and Scotland, and the Tories were those who opposed it. Both names were originally insults: a "whiggamore" was a horse drover, and a "tory" (*Tóraidhe*) was an Irish term for an outlaw, later applied to Irish Confederates and Irish Royalists, during the Wars of the Three Kingdoms.

Generally, the Tories were associated with lesser gentry and the Church of England, while Whigs were more associated with trade, money, larger land holders (or "land magnates"), expansion and tolerance.

The Rochdale Radicals were a group of more extreme reformists who were also heavily involved in the cooperative movement. They sought to bring about a more equal society, and are considered by modern standards to be left-wing.

After becoming associated with repression of popular discontent in the years after 1815, the Tories underwent a fundamental transformation under the influence of Robert Peel, himself an industrialist rather than a landowner, who in his 1834 "Tamworth Manifesto" outlined a new "Conservative" philosophy of reforming ills while conserving the good.

Though Peel's supporters subsequently split from their colleagues over the issue of free trade in 1846, ultimately joining the Whigs and the Radicals to form what would become the Liberal Party, Peel's version of the party's underlying outlook was retained by the remaining Tories, who adopted his label of

Conservative as the official name of their party. In 2008, the Conservative Party formed a pact with the Ulster Unionist Party to select joint candidates for European and House of Commons elections, this angered the DUP as by splitting the Unionist vote, republican parties will be elected in some areas.

Liberal Democrats

The Liberal Democrats won the third largest number of seats at the 2005 general election, winning 62.

The Liberal Democrats were formed in 1988 by a merger of the Liberal Party with the Social Democratic Party, but can trace their origin back to the Whigs and the Rochdale Radicals who evolved into the Liberal Party. The term 'Liberal Party' was first used officially in 1868, though it had been in use colloquially for decades beforehand. The Liberal Party formed a government in 1868 and then alternated with the Conservative Party as the party of government throughout the late 19th century and early 20th century.

Scottish and Welsh Nationalists

Members of the Scottish National Party and Plaid Cymru work together as a single parliamentary group following a formal pact signed in 1986. This group currently has 10 MPs.

The Scottish National Party has enjoyed parliamentary representation continuously since 1967 and had 6 MPs elected at the 2005 election. It has since added to this number following its by-election win in Glasgow East. Following the 2007 Scottish parliament elections, the SNP emerged as the largest party with 47 MSPs and formed a minority government with Alex Salmond the First Minister.

Plaid Cymru has enjoyed parliamentary representation continuously since 1974 and had 3 MPs elected at the 2005 election. Following the 2007 Welsh Assembly elections, they joined Labour as the junior partner in a coalition government.

Northern Ireland Parties

The Democratic Unionist Party had 9 MPs elected at the 2005 election. Founded in 1971 by Ian Paisley, it has grown to become the larger of the two main unionist political parties in Northern

Ireland. Other Northern Ireland parties represented at Westminster include the Social Democratic and Labour Party (3 MPs), the Ulster Unionist Party (1 MP) and Sinn Féin (5 MPs), though the Sinn Féin MPs are barred from taking their seats as they refuse to swear the oath to the Queen.

Other Parliamentary Parties

The Respect party, a left-wing group that came out of the anti-war movement has one MP, George Galloway, and a small number of seats on local councils across the country.

United Kingdom Independence Party has as of yet not won a single House of Commons seat at an election, but on 22 April 2008 welcomed the defection of Bob Spink MP for Castle Point, to date its only MP. However, Bob Spink later claimed to have never joined UKIP and does not sit as a UKIP MP. The party also has two Lords in the House of Lords who defected from the Conservative Party and has the joint third largest British block of MEPs in the European Parliament. Two UKIP members were elected to the London Assembly in 2000, but they quit the party in February 2005 to join Veritas which they quit in September 2005 to sit as One London members. They were not re-elected in 2008.

There are also a small number of Independent politicians in parliament with no party allegiance. In modern times, this has usually occurred when a sitting member leaves his party, and some such MPs have been re-elected as independents. However, since 1950 only two new members have been elected as independents without having ever stood for a major party:

- Martin Bell represented the Tatton constituency in Cheshire between 1997 and 2001. He was elected following a "sleaze" scandal involving the sitting Conservative MP, Neil Hamilton — Bell, a BBC journalist, stood as an anticorruption independent candidate, and the Labour and Liberal Democrat parties withdrew their candidates from the election.
- Dr. Richard Taylor MP was elected for the Wyre Forest constituency in the 2001 on a platform opposing the closure of Kidderminster hospital. He later established Health Concern, the party under which he ran in 2005.

Non-Parliamentary Political Parties

Other UK political parties exist, but generally do not succeed in returning MPs to Parliament.

The United Kingdom Independence Party (UKIP) has 13 seats in the European Parliament as well as seats in the House of Lords and a number of local councillors.

The Green Party of England and Wales has seats in the European Parliament as well as two seats on the London Assembly and around 120 local councillors.

The Scottish Green Party has 2 MSPs in the Scottish Parliament and a number of local councillors.

The Alliance Party of Northern Ireland has several MLAs in the Northern Ireland Assembly and a number of local councillors.

The British National Party (BNP) has two seats in the European Parliament, a seat on the London Assembly as well as a number of councillors.

The English Democrats, which wants a parliament for England, has some local councillors and had its candidate elected mayor of Doncaster in 2009. Other parties include: the Free England Party, the Communist Party of Britain, the Socialist Workers Party, the Scottish Socialist Party, the Liberal Party, Mebyon Kernow (a Cornish nationalist party) in Cornwall, Veritas, and the Communist Left Alliance (in Fife).

Several local parties contest only within a specific area, a single county, borough or district. Examples include the Better Bedford Independent Party, which was one of the dominant parties in Bedford Borough Council and led by Bedford's former Mayor, Frank Branston. The most notable local party is Health Concern, which controls a single seat in the UK Parliament.

The Jury Team, launched in March 2009 and described as a "non-party party", is an umbrella organisation seeking to increase the number of Independent members of both domestic and European members of Parliament in Great Britain.

Current Political Landscape

Since the 2005 General Election, each of the main political parties has changed party leader: David Cameron was elected leader of the Conservatives in 2005, Gordon Brown was elected unopposed to lead the Labour Party (and therefore become Prime Minister) in June 2007, and Nick Clegg was elected leader of the Liberal Democrats in December 2007.

The Conservatives under David Cameron have seen their popularity grow, as shown by their success at the Local Elections in May 2008, the London Mayoral Election and opinion polls which show a strong lead over Labour. They also won a by election in Crewe and Nantwich with a swing of 17.6%.

In Scotland, the Scottish National Party made some strong advances, winning the Scottish parliamentary election in May 2007 and gaining support in most national opinion polls since then. In July 2008, the SNP achieved a remarkable by-election victory in Glasgow East, winning the third safest Labour seat in Scotland with a swing of 22.54%. However,in October of the same year, despite confident public predictions by the SNP's leader Alex Salmond that they would win another by-election in Glenrothes, the seat was comfortably won by Labour with a majority of 6,737 and an increased share of the vote. Given that the SNP won the equivalent Scottish Parliament seat of Central Fife in 2007 this was viewed as a significant step back for the SNP. More recently, the SNP significantly out-polled the Labour Party in the 2009 European election.

Local Government

The UK is divided into a variety of different types of Local Authorities, with different functions and responsibilities.

England has a mix of two-tier and single-tier councils in different parts of the country. In Greater London, a unique two-tier system exists, with power shared between the London borough councils, and the Greater London Authority which is headed by an elected mayor.

Unitary Authorities are used throughout Scotland, Wales and Northern Ireland.

European Union

The United Kingdom is a member of the European Union (EU). As such, UK citizens elect 78 Members of the European Parliament to represent them in the European Parliament in

Brussels and Strasbourg. In recent years, there have been divisions in both major parties as to whether the UK should form greater ties within the EU, or reduce the EU's supranational powers. Opponents of greater European integration are known as Eurosceptics, supporters Europhiles. Division over Europe is prevalent in both major parties. The Conservative Party is seen as most split over this issue, whilst in Government up to 1997, and today in opposition. However the Labour Party is also split, with conflicting views within Cabinet over UK adoption of the euro, although the party is on the whole in favour of further integration where in the interest of the UK.

UK nationalists have long campaigned against European integration. The strong showing of the eurosceptic United Kingdom Independence Party (UKIP) in the 2004 European Parliament elections has shifted the debate over UK relations with the EU.

Parliament decided in March 2008 not to hold a referendum on the ratification of the Treaty of Lisbon, signed in December 2007. This was despite the Labour government promising in 2004 to hold a referendum on the previously proposed Constitution for Europe.

The Party System

Members of the House of Lords are organised on a party basis in much the same way as the House of Commons but with important differences: Members of the Lords do not represent constituencies and many are not members of a political party.

Lords who do not support one of the three main parties are known as Crossbenchers or Independent Peers. There is also a small number who are not affiliated to any of the main groups.

History of the Party System

The system of political parties, which has existed in one form or another since at least the 18th century, is an essential element in the working of the constitution. Since the Second World War, all the Governments in the UK have been formed by either the Labour Party or the Conservative Party.

Opposition Parties

The effectiveness of the party system in Parliament depends

on the relationship between the Government and the Opposition parties. In general, Opposition parties aim to:

- contribute to the creation of policy and legislation through constructive criticism
- oppose government proposals they disagree with
- put forward their own policies in order to improve their chances of winning the next general election.

Where do MPs sit in the Commons?

MPs from the same party tend to sit together in the House of Commons Chamber. Because the Chamber is a rectangular shape, the Government and the Opposition can face each other. The Government sits on the benches to the right of the Speaker. The official Opposition and MPs from other parties sit on the benches to the left of the Speaker.

Where do Members of the Lords sit in the Lords?

As in the Commons, the Government and the Opposition face each other. The Government and the Bishops sit on the right of the Lord Speaker. The Opposition parties sit on the benches to the left of the Lord Speaker while the Crossbench Peers sit mostly on benches that cross the Chamber of the House of Lords behind the clerks' table.

Frontbenchers and backbenchers

In both the Commons and the Lords, Government ministers and Opposition shadow ministers sit on the front benches and are known as 'frontbenchers'. MPs and Members of the Lords who do not hold ministerial positions sit towards the back of the Chamber and are known as 'backbenchers'.

Independent MPs and Crossbench and Independent Lords

MPs and Members of the Lords do not have to belong to a political party. Instead, MPs can sit as Independents and Lords can sit as Crossbenchers or Independents.

Bishops in the Lords

The Anglican Archbishops of Canterbury and York, the Bishops of Durham, London and Winchester and the 21 other senior diocesan bishops of the Church of England have seats in the Lords. This is for historical reasons. When they retire as bishops their membership of the House ends.

Crossing the Floor

Members of either the House of Commons or House of Lords can change political party at any time-known as 'crossing the floor'. The term comes from the fact that, traditionally, Members of Parliament from opposing parties sit on opposite sides of the Chamber.

Therefore, a Member who changes party usually has to cross the floor of the House to sit on the other side of the Chamber. The term is used to signify the changing of allegiance.

Party Systems

Party systems dominate politics in Britain. In "Party and Party Systems", G. Sartori describes a party system as:

"the system of interactions resulting from inter-party competition".

To develop this idea, within Britain the party system essentially means the way the political parties of the day interact with one another within the politically competitive nature of Westminster and beyond.

A number of different types of party systems have been identified:

One-party system: a one-party system cannot produce a political system as we would identify it in Britain. One party cannot produce any other system other than autocratic/dictatorial power. A state where one party rules would include the remaining communist states of the world (Cuba, North Korea and China), and Iraq (where the ruling party is the Ba'ath Party). The old Soviet union was a one party state. One of the more common features of a one-party state is that the posifion of the ruling party is guaranteed in a constitution and all forms of political opposition are banned by law. The ruling party controls all aspects of life within that state. The belief that a ruling party is all important to a state came from Lenin who believed that only one party-the Communists-could take the workers to their ultimate destiny and that the involvement of other parties would hinder this progress.

Two-party system: as the title indicates, this is a state in which just two parties dominate. Other parties might exist but they have no political importance. America has the most obvious two-party political system with the Republicans and Democrats dominating the political scene. For the system to work, one of the parties must obtain a sufficient working majority after an election and it must be in a position to be able to govern without the support from the other party. A rotation of power is expected in this system. The victory of George W Bush in the November 2000 election, fulfils this aspect of the definition.

The two-party system presents the voter with a simple choice and it is believed that the system promotes political moderation as the incumbent party must be able to appeal to the 'floating voters' within that country. Those who do not support the system claim that it leads to unnecessary policy reversals if a party loses a election as the newly elected government seeks to impose its 'mark' on the country that has just elected it to power. Such sweeping reversals, it is claimed, cannot benefit the state in the short and long term.

The multi-party system: as the title suggests, this is a system where more than two parties have some impact in a state's political life. Though the Labour Party has a very healthy majority in Westminster, its power in Scotland is reasonably well balanced by the power of the SNP (Scots Nationalist Party); in Wales within the devolutionary structure, it is balanced by Plaid Cymru; in Northern Ireland by the various Unionists groups and Sein Fein.

Within Westminster, the Tories and the Liberal Democrats provide a healthy political rivalry. Sartori defines a multi-party system as one where no party can guarantee an absolute majority. In theory, the Labour Party, regardless of its current parliamentary majority, could lose the next general election in Britain in 2006. Even its current majority of 167 cannot guarantee electoral victory in the future.

A multi-party system can lead to a coalition government as Germany and Italy have experienced. In Germany these have provided reasonably stable governments and a successful coalition can introduce an effective system of checks and balances on the government that can promote political moderation. Also many policy decisions take into account all views and interests. In Italy, coalition governments have not been a success; many have lasted less than one year. In Israel, recent governments have relied on the support of extreme minority groups to form a coalition government and this has created its own problems with such support being withdrawn on a whim or if those extreme parties feel that their own specific views are not being given enough support.

Dominant-party system: this is different from a one-party system. A party is quite capable within the political structure of a state, to become dominant to such an extent that victory at elections is considered a formality. This was the case under the Conservative governments of Margaret Thatcher and John Major. For 18 years (1979 to 1997), one party dominated politics in Britain.

In theory, the Conservatives could have lost any election during these 18 years. But such was the disarray of the opposition parties-especially Labour-that electoral victory was all but guaranteed.

The elections of the 1980's and 1990's were fought with competition from other parties-hence there can be no comparison with a one-party state. During an extended stay in power, a dominant party can shape society through its policies. During the Thatcher era, health, education, the state ownership of industry etc. were all massively changed and re-shaped. Society changed as a result of these political changes and this can only be done by a party having an extended stay in office.

Other features of a dominant system are: the party in power becomes complacent and sees that its position in power is 'guaranteed'. Such political arrogance is seen as one of the reasons for the public's overwhelming rejection of the Conservatives in 1997.

The difference between the party in power and the state loses its distinction. When both appear to merge, an unhealthy relationship develops whereby the state's machinery of carrying out government policy is seen as being done automatically and where senior state officials are rewarded by the party in power. This scenario overshadowed the Thatcher governments when the Civil Service was seen as a mere rubber stamp of government policy to do as it was told and senior Civil Servants were suitably rewarded in the Honours lists.

An era of a dominant party is also an era when opposition parties are in total disarray. This was true during the Conservatives domination of Britain in the 1980's. Once the Labour Party started to strengthen in the 1990's and internal problems were resolved, the whole issue of a dominant party was threatened leading to the defeat of the Conservatives in 1997.

It would be fair to conclude that Britain has a dominant-party system now. Within certain criteria, the Labour government with its near 180 majority in Westminster, has the freedom to do politically what it likes. The powers devolved to the regions were restrained by the simple fact that Westminster is still the major purse-holder of Scotland, Wales and Northern Ireland, thereby not giving these three regions the freedom they believe they need to be truly devolved governments.

5

Political System of the United States of America

Political Parties in the United States

Two-party System Dominating U.S. Politics since the 1860s

Washington — When America's founders wrote the U.S. Constitution in 1787, they did not envision political parties playing a role in the government. Rather, they expected constitutional provisions such as separation of powers, checks and balances, federalism and indirect election of the president by an electoral college would deter the formation of parties.

Despite these provisions, the United States in 1800 became the first nation to develop political parties organized on a national level and to transfer executive power from one party to another via an election. By the 1830s, political parties were an established part of the U.S. political environment.

Today, the Republican and Democratic parties are the two main political parties in the United States. Most elected officials serving as president, congressional representative, state governor or state legislator are members of one of these parties. The Republicans and Democrats have dominated American politics since the 1860s, and every president since 1852 has been either a Republican or Democrat.

In the 110th Congress, which convened January 4, the House of Representatives has 233 Democrats and 202 Republicans. The Senate has 49 Democrats, 49 Republicans and two independents, both of whom will meet to determine and implement policy (caucus) with the Democrats. In a November 2006 Gallup Poll (a leading barometer of public opinion operated by the Gallop Organization), approximately 59 percent of Americans identified themselves as either Republicans or Democrats. Those who say they are independents normally have partisan leanings and often are more loyal to one of these two political parties than to the other.

The most common method for electing national and state legislators in the United States is the "single-member" district system. This means that whoever receives a plurality of the vote (that is, the greatest number of votes in any given voting district) is elected. Unlike proportional systems, the single-member district arrangement permits only one party to win in any given district. The single-member system thus creates incentives to form two broadly based parties with sufficient popular appeal to win legislative district pluralities.

Support for American parties is multiclass and broadly based. With the exception of African-American voters — about 88 percent of whom voted for the Democratic candidate in the 2004 presidential election — both the Republican and Democratic parties draw significant levels of support from virtually every major U.S. socioeconomic and ethnic group.

Diversity Within Party Ranks the Norm in U.S. System

Compared to political parties in other democratic nations, political parties in the United States tend to have relatively low internal unity and lack strict adherence to an ideology or set of policy goals. Generally, Republicans have tended to support limiting federal powers and protecting the authority of state and local governments, to take a conservative approach to taxation and spending, and to oppose government interference with free enterprise. In contrast, Democrats have tended to take a more expansive view of the powers of the federal government, to support raising and spending money to address social ills on a national basis, and to favour federal regulation as a tool to improve business practices. But these are broad generalizations: In U.S. politics, "conservative" Democrats and "moderate" or even "liberal" Republicans are not unusual. The major focus for both political parties is winning elections and controlling the personnel of government. Given their broad sources of support in the electorate and their need to operate within an ideologically moderate society, American parties tend to adopt centrist policy positions and demonstrate a high level of policy flexibility. This enables the Republicans and the Democrats to tolerate great diversity within their ranks.

U.S. presidents cannot assume that their party's members in Congress will be loyal supporters of presidential programs, nor can party leaders in Congress expect all member of their party to vote along party lines. In addition, national party organizations do not involve themselves routinely in party affairs at the state level. Although American parties tend to be less ideologically cohesive and programmatic than parties in many democracies, they do play a major and often decisive role in shaping public policy.

Role of "Third" Parties

Despite broad political influence of the Democratic and Republican parties, so-called "third" parties and independent candidates remain a feature of American politics. Most third parties have tended to flourish for a single election and then die, fade, or be absorbed into one of the major parties.

There is evidence that third parties can have a major impact on election outcomes. For example, a third-party candidate might draw votes more votes away from the candidate of the party more closely aligned with to the position of the third-party candidate, thus enabling the other party to win the election – often without receiving a majority of the vote.

Public opinion surveys since the 1990s consistently have shown a high level of popular support for the concept of a third party. But in spite of such support for a third party, these parties face many obstacles. The most significant is the fear among voters that if they vote for a third-party candidate, they, in effect, will be "wasting" their votes. Voters have been shown to engage in strategic voting by casting ballots for their second choice when they sense that a third-party candidate has no chance of winning.

The preceding article was adapted from the publication article "Political Parties in the United States" by John F. Bibby in the electronic journal, *United States Elections 2004*.

Failure of the Two-Party System in America

Neither the Republicans nor the Democrats are in a position to satisfy the will of a majority of the American people. According to an NBC News/Wall Street Journal Poll (December 2007), 47% of those surveyed felt that the two-party system "has real problems," while another 29% felt that the system was "seriously broken." For many disillusioned voters, the 2008 elections will be a choice between the lesser of two evils, rather than an affirmation of support for the platform of either candidate.

The Liberal vs. Conservative Debate Has Lost its Meaning

The terms "liberal" and "conservative," which have traditionally defined the two major parties in the United States, have lost much of their meaning. Instead, the parties are now largely defined by the industries who compete for their favour through lobbyists. As a result, most of the differences between the parties have become superficial. Traditionally, liberals have supported a large government that was actively involved in society on every level. They placed the benefit of the people as a whole over the interests of the individual, by promoting social welfare programs for the poor and higher taxes on the rich to cover the cost. The conservatives were exactly the opposite. They supported a smaller, centralized government that strictly enforced the law, but otherwise tended to refrain from intervening in affairs of the individual or in the economy. They strongly supported Adam Smith's concept of capitalism, which suggested that the economy should be primarily regulated by the laws of supply and demand.

Each side has its merits, but in recent years these concepts have less and less to do with the agendas of either party. For example, the Clinton administration expanded the scope of the death penalty, and also generating the first Federal budget surplus since the 1960's. The Bush administration, on the other hand, has spent the taxpayers' money so freely that it has run up the largest deficit in the nation's history. Moreover, Bush radically expanded the bureaucratic structure of the government with the creation of the Homeland Security Administration, while at the same time invading foreign countries in name of spreading democracy around the world.

6

Decline of the Former Soviet Union

History of the Soviet Union (1985–1991)

The Soviet Union's collapse into independent nations began early in 1985. After years of Soviet military buildup at the expense of domestic development, economic growth was at a standstill. Failed attempts at reform, a stagnant economy, and war in Afghanistan led to a general feeling of discontent, especially in the Baltic republics and Eastern Europe. Greater political and social freedoms, instituted by the last Soviet leader, Mikhail Gorbachev, created an atmosphere of open criticism of the Moscow regime. The dramatic drop of the price of oil in 1985 and 1986, and consequent lack of foreign exchange reserves in following years to purchase grain profoundly influenced actions of the Soviet leadership.

Several Soviet Socialist Republics began resisting central control, and increasing democratization led to a weakening of the central government. The USSR's trade gap progressively emptied the coffers of the union, leading to eventual bankruptcy. The Soviet Union finally collapsed in 1991 when Boris Yeltsin seized power in the aftermath of a failed coup that had attempted to topple reform-minded Gorbachev.

The Rise of Gorbachev

Although reform in the Soviet Union became more and more powerful between 1969 and 1987, a generational shift gave new momentum for reform. The war in Afghanistan, often referred to as the Soviet Union's "Vietnam War," led to increased public dissatisfaction with the Moscow regime. Also, the Chernobyl disaster in 1986 added impetus to Gorbachev's glasnost and perestroika reforms, which eventually spiraled out of control and caused the Soviet system to collapse.

After years of stagnation, the "new thinking" of younger Communist apparatchiks began to emerge. Following the death of terminally ill Konstantin Chernenko, the Politburo elected Mikhail Gorbachev to the position of General Secretary of the Soviet Union in March 1985, marking the rise of a new generation of leadership. Under Gorbachev, relatively young, reform-oriented technocrats, who had begun their careers in the heyday of "de"Stalinization" under Nikita Khrushchev (1953-1964), rapidly consolidated power within the CPSU, providing new momentum for political and economic liberalization, and the impetus for cultivating warmer relations and trade with the West.

Jimmy Carter had officially ended the policy of Détente, by militarily aiding President of Pakistan Muhammad Zia-ul-Haq, who in turn funded the anti-Soviet Mujahideen movement in neighbouring Afghanistan, which served as a pretext for the Soviet intervention in Afghanistan six months later, with the aims of supporting the Afghan government, controlled by the People's Democratic Party of Afghanistan. Tensions between the superpowers increased during this time, when Carter placed trade embargoes on the Soviet Union and stated that the Soviet invasion of Afghanistan was "the most serious threat to the peace since the Second World War."

East-West tensions increased during the first term of U.S. President Ronald Reagan (1981-1985), reaching levels not seen since the 1962 Cuban missile crisis as Reagan increased US military spending to 7% of the GDP. To match the USA's military buildup, the Soviet Union increased its own military spending to 27% of its GDP and froze production of civilian goods at 1980 levels. Reagan furthermore supplied Afghan warriors with Stinger missiles which cost the US only $1 billion annually, but which cost the Soviet Union as much as $8 billion annually in military losses. Finally, Reagan also actively hindered the Soviet Union's ability to sell natural gas to Europe whilst simultaneously actively working to keep gas prices low which served to keep the price of Soviet oil low and further starved the Soviet Union of foreign capital. This "long-term strategic offensive" which "contrasts with the essentially reactive and defensive strategy of containment" accelerated the fall of the Soviet Union by encouraging it to overextend its economic base.

By the time Gorbachev ushered in the process that would lead to the dismantling of the Soviet administrative command economy through his programs of *glasnost* (political openness), *uskoreniye* (speed-up of economic development) and *perestroika* (political and economic restructuring) announced in 1986, the Soviet economy suffered from both hidden inflation and pervasive supply shortages aggravated by an increasingly open black market that undermined the official economy. Additionally, the costs of superpower status—the military, space program, subsidies to client states—were out of proportion to the Soviet economy. The new wave of industrialization based upon information technology had left the Soviet Union desperate for Western technology and credits in order to counter its increasing backwardness.

Reforms

The Law on Cooperatives enacted in May 1988 was perhaps the most radical of the economic reforms during the early part of the Gorbachev era. For the first time since Vladimir Lenin's New Economic Policy, the law permitted private ownership of businesses in the services, manufacturing, and foreign-trade sectors. Under this provision, cooperative restaurants, shops, and manufacturers became part of the Soviet scene.

Glasnost resulted in greater freedom of speech and the press becoming far less controlled. It is likely that Gorbachev's primary goal in undertaking *glasnost* was to pressure conservatives who opposed his policies of economic restructuring, although he also hoped that through different ranges of openness, debate and participation, the Soviet people as a whole would support his reform initiatives.

Thousands of political prisoners and many dissidents were also released. Soviet social science became free to explore and publish on many subjects that had previously been off limits, including conducting public opinion polls. The All"Union Centre for Public Opinion Research (VCIOM) — the most prominent of several polling organizations that were started then — was opened. State archives became more accessible, and some social statistics that had been kept secret became open for research and publication on sensitive subjects such as income disparities, crime, suicide, abortion, and infant mortality. The first centre for gender studies was opened within a newly formed Institute for the Socioeconomic Study of Human Population.

In January 1987, Gorbachev called for democratization: the infusion of democratic elements such as multi-candidate elections into the Soviet political process. A 1987 conference convened by Soviet economist and Gorbachev adviser Leonid Abalkin, concluded: "Deep transformations in the management of the economy cannot be realised without corresponding changes in the political system."

In June 1988, at the CPSU's Nineteenth Party Conference, Gorbachev launched radical reforms meant to reduce party control of the government apparatus. In December 1988, the Supreme Soviet approved the establishment of a Congress of People's Deputies, which constitutional amendments had established as the Soviet Union's new legislative body.

Elections to the new Congress of People's Deputies were held throughout the USSR in March and April 1989. Gorbachev, as General Secretary of the Communist Party, could be forced to resign at any moment if the communist elite became dissatisfied with him. In order to proceed with reforms opposed by the majority of the communist party, Gorbachev aimed to consolidate power in a new position, President of the Soviet Union, which was independent from the CPSU and the soviets (councils) and whose holder could be impeached only in case of direct violation of the law. On March 15, 1990, Gorbachev was elected as the first executive president. At the same time, the constitution was changed to deprive the CPSU of political power.

Unintended Consequences

Gorbachev's efforts to streamline the Communist system offered promise, but ultimately proved uncontrollable and resulted in a cascade of events that eventually concluded with the dissolution of the Soviet Union. Initially intended as tools to bolster the Soviet economy, the policies of *perestroika* and *glasnost* soon led to unintended consequences. Relaxation under *glasnost* resulted in the Communist Party losing its absolute grip on the media. Before long, and much to the embarrassment of the authorities, the media began to expose severe social and economic problems the Soviet government had long denied and actively concealed. Problems receiving increased attention included poor housing, alcoholism, drug abuse, pollution, outdated Stalin-era factories, and petty to large scale corruption, all of which the official media had ignored. Media reports also exposed crimes committed by Stalin and the Soviet regime, such as the gulags, his treaty with Adolf Hitler, and the Great Purges, which had been ignored by the official media. Moreover, the ongoing war in Afghanistan, and the mishandling of the 1986 Chernobyl disaster, which Gorbachev tried to cover up, further damaged the credibility of the Soviet government at a time when dissatisfaction was increasing.

In all, the very positive view of Soviet life which had long been presented to the public by the official media was being rapidly dismantled, and the negative aspects of life in the Soviet Union were brought into the spotlight. This undermined the faith of the public in the Soviet system and eroded the Communist Party's social power base, threatening the identity and integrity of the Soviet Union itself.

Fraying amongst the members of the Warsaw Pact nations and instability of its western allies, first indicated by Lech Waêsa's 1980 rise to leadership of the trade union Solidarity, accelerated, leaving the Soviet Union unable to depend upon its Eastern European satellite states for protection as a buffer zone. By 1989, Moscow had repudiated the Brezhnev Doctrine in favour of nonintervention in the internal affairs of its Warsaw Pact allies. Gradually, each of the Warsaw Pact nations saw their communist governments fall to popular elections and, in the case of Romania, a violent uprising. By 1991 the communist governments of Bulgaria, Czechoslovakia, East Germany, Hungary, Poland and Romania, all of which had been imposed after World War II, were brought down as revolution swept Eastern Europe.

The Soviet Union also began experiencing upheaval as the political consequences of *glasnost* reverberated throughout the country. Despite efforts at containment, the upheaval in Eastern Europe inevitably spread to nationalities within the USSR. In elections to the regional assemblies of the Soviet Union's constituent republics, nationalists as well as radical reformers swept the board. As Gorbachev had weakened the system of internal political repression, the ability of the USSR's central Moscow government to impose its will on the USSR's constituent republics had been largely undermined. Massive peaceful protests in the Baltic Republics such as The Baltic Way and the Singing Revolution drew international attention and bolstered independence movements in various other regions.

The rise of nationalism under *freedom of speech* soon reawakened simmering ethnic tensions in various Soviet republics, further discrediting the ideal of a unified Soviet people. One instance occurred in February 1988, when the government in Nagorno-Karabakh, a predominantly ethnic Armenian region in the Azerbaijan SSR, passed a resolution calling for unification with the Armenian SSR. Violence against local Azerbaijanis was reported on Soviet television, provoking massacres of Armenians in the Azerbaijani city of Sumgait.

Emboldened by the liberalized atmosphere of *glasnost*, public dissatisfaction with economic conditions was much more overt than ever before in the Soviet period. Although *perestroika* was considered bold in the context of Soviet history, Gorbachev's attempts at economic reform were not radical enough to restart the country's chronically sluggish economy in the late 1980s. The reforms made some inroads in decentralization, but Gorbachev and his team left intact most of the fundamental elements of the Stalinist system, including price controls, inconvertibility of the ruble, exclusion of private property ownership, and the government monopoly over most means of production.

By 1990 the Soviet government had lost control over economic conditions. Government spending increased sharply as an increasing number of unprofitable enterprises required state support and consumer price subsidies to continue. Tax revenues declined as republic and local governments withheld tax revenues from the central government under the growing spirit of regional autonomy. The anti-alcohol campaign reduced tax revenues as well, which in 1982 accounted for about 12 percent of all state revenue. The elimination of central control over production decisions, especially in the consumer goods sector, led to the breakdown in traditional supplier-producer relationships without contributing to the formation of new ones. Thus, instead of streamlining the system, Gorbachev's decentralization caused new production bottlenecks.

Dissolution of the USSR

On February, 1990, the Central Committee of the Communist Party of the Soviet Union agreed to give up its monopoly of power. Over the next several weeks, the 15 constituent republics of the USSR held their first competitive elections. Reformers and ethnic nationalists won many of the seats.

The constituent republics began to assert their national sovereignty over Moscow and started a "war of laws" with the central government, wherein the governments of the constituent republics repudiated union-wide legislation where it conflicted with local laws, asserting control over their local economies and refusing to pay tax revenue to the central Moscow government. This strife caused economic dislocation as supply lines in the economy were severed, and caused the Soviet economy to decline further.

The pro-independence movement in the Lithuanian SSR, Sàjûdis, established on June 3, 1988, caused a visit by Gorbachev in January 1990 to the Lithuanian capital, Vilnius, which provoked a pro-independence rally of around 250,000 people.

On March 11, 1990, the Lithuanian SSR, led by Chairman of the Supreme Council Vytautas Landsbergis, declared restoration of independence. However, the Soviet Army attempted to suppress the movement. The Soviet Union initiated an economic blockade of Lithuania and kept troops there "to secure the rights of ethnic Russians."

On March 30, 1990, the Estonian Supreme Council declared Soviet power in Estonian SSR since 1940 to have been illegal, and started a process to reestablish Estonia as an independent state. The process of restoration of independence of the Latvian SSR began on May 4, 1990, with a Latvian Supreme Council vote stipulating a transitional period to complete independence.

On January 13, 1991, Soviet troops, along with KGB Spetsnaz Alpha Group, stormed the Vilnius TV Tower in Vilnius, Lithuania to suppress the nationalist media. This ended with 14 unarmed civilians dead and hundreds more injured. Later that month in Georgian SSR, anti-Soviet protesters at Tbilisi demonstrated support for Lithuanian independence.

On March 17, 1991, in a Union-wide referendum 76.4% of all voters voted for the retention of the Soviet Union in a reformed form. The Baltics, Armenia, Georgia and Moldova boycotted the referendum. In each of the other nine republics, a majority of the voters supported the retention of the renewed Soviet Union. Following the results, Armenia indicated it wanted to rejoin in Union discussion.

On June 12, 1991, Yeltsin won 57% of the popular vote in the democratic elections for the post of president of the Russian SFSR, defeating Gorbachev's preferred candidate, Nikolai Ryzhkov, who won 16% of the vote. In his election campaign, Yeltsin criticized the "dictatorship of the centre", but did not suggest the introduction of a market economy. Instead, he said that he would put his head on the railtrack in the event of increased prices. Yeltsin took office on July 10.

On the night of July 31, 1991, Russian OMON from Riga, the Soviet military headquarters in the Baltics, assaulted the Lithuanian border post in Medininkai and killed seven Lithuanian servicemen. This further weakened the Soviet Union's position, internationally and domestically.

The August Coup

Faced with growing republic separatism, Gorbachev attempted to restructure the Soviet Union into a less centralized state. On August 20, 1991, the Russian SFSR was scheduled to sign the New Union Treaty, which was to convert the Soviet Union into a federation of independent republics with a common president, foreign policy and military. The new treaty was strongly supported by the Central Asian republics, which needed the economic power and common markets of the other Soviet republics to prosper. However, this meant the preservation of the Communist Party's control over economic and social life. The more radical reformists were increasingly convinced that a rapid transition to a market economy was required, even if the eventual outcome included the disintegration of the Soviet Union into several independent nation-states. Disintegration of the USSR also accorded with the desires of Yeltsin's presidency of the Russian Federation as well as regional and local authorities, to establish full power over their territories and get rid of pervasive Moscow ideological control. In contrast to the reformers' lukewarm approach to the new treaty, the conservatives and remaining 'patriots' and Russian nationalists of the USSR, still strong within the CPSU and military establishment, were completely opposed to anything which might contribute to the weakening of the Soviet state and its centralized power base.

On August 19, 1991, Gorbachev's vice president Gennadi Yanayev, prime minister Valentin Pavlov, defence minister Dmitriy Yazov, KGB chief Vladimir Kryuchkov, and other senior officials acted to prevent the signing of the union treaty by forming the "General Committee on the State Emergency." The "Committee" put Gorbachev (vacationing in Foros, Crimea) under house arrest, reintroduced political censorship, and attempted to stop the perestroika. The coup leaders quickly issued an emergency decree suspending political activity and banning most newspapers.

While coup organizers expected some popular support for their actions, the public sympathy in large cities and in republics was largely against them. Russian SFSR President Boris Yeltsin was quick to condemn the coup and grab popular support for himself.

Thousands of people in Moscow came out to defend the "White House" (the Russian Federation's parliament and Yeltsin's office), then the symbolic seat of Russian sovereignty. The organizers tried but ultimately failed to arrest Yeltsin, who rallied mass opposition to the coup. The special forces dispatched by the coup leaders took up positions near the White House, but would not storm the barricaded building.

After three days, on August 21, the coup collapsed, the organizers were detained, and Gorbachev returned as president of the Soviet Union. However, Gorbachev's powers were now fatally compromised, as neither the Union nor Russian power structures heeded his commands.

Aftermath of the Failed Coup

Through the autumn of 1991, the Russian government took over the union government, ministry by ministry. In November 1991, Yeltsin issued a decree banning the CPSU throughout the

Russian republic. As a result, many former apparatchiks abandoned the Communist Party in favour of positions in new government structures.

After the coup, the Soviet republics accelerated their process towards independence, declaring their sovereignty one by one. Their local authorities started to seize property located on their territory. On September 6, 1991, the Soviet government recognized the independence of the three Baltic states, which the western powers had always held to be sovereign. Yet, in the battle of power, on October 18 Gorbachev and the representatives of 8 republics (excluding Azerbaijan, Georgia, Moldova, Ukraine, and the Baltic States) signed an agreement on forming a new economic community.

Meanwhile, the Soviet economic situation continued to deteriorate. By December 1991, food shortages in central Russia had prompted food rationing in the Moscow area for the first time since World War II. Amid steady collapse, Soviet President Gorbachev and his government continued to oppose rapid market reforms like Yavlinsky's "500 Days" program. To break Gorbachev's opposition, Yeltsin decided to disband the USSR in accordance with the Treaty of the Union of 1922 and thereby remove Gorbachev and the Soviet government from power. The step was also enthusiastically supported by the governments of Ukraine and Belarus, which were parties of the Treaty of 1922 along with Russia.

Formation of the CIS and Official end of the USSR

The final round of the Soviet Union collapse took place following the Ukrainian popular referendum on December 1, 1991, wherein 90% of voters opted for independence. The leaders of Slavic republics agreed to meet for a discussion of possible forms of relationship, alternative to Gorbachev's struggle for a union.

On December 8, 1991, the leaders of the Russian, Ukrainian, and Belarusian republics met in Belavezhskaya Pushcha and signed the Belavezha Accords declaring the Soviet Union dissolved and replacing it with the Commonwealth of Independent States (CIS). Gorbachev described this as an unconstitutional coup, but it soon became clear that the development could not be halted.

On December 12, 1991, Russia's secession from the Union was sealed, with the Congress of People's Deputies of the Russian SFSR formally ratifying the Belavezha Accords and denouncing the 1922 Treaty on the creation of the Soviet Union.

On December 17, 1991, alongside 28 European countries, the European Community, and four non-European countries, twelve of the fifteen soviet republics signed the European Energy Charter in the Hague as sovereign states.

Doubts remained over the authority of the Belavezha Accords to affect the dissolution of the Soviet Union, since they were signed by only five of the Soviet Republics. However, on December 21, 1991, representatives of all member republics except Georgia signed the Alma-Ata Protocol, in which they confirmed the dissolution of the Union.

That same day, all former-Soviet republics agreed to join the CIS, with the exception of the three Baltic States. The documents signed at Alma-Ata also addressed several issues raised by the Union's extinction. Notably, Russia was authorized to assume the role of the USSR in the United Nations, which meant inheriting its permanent membership on the Security Council. On December 24, 1991, the Soviet Ambassador to the UN delivered to the Secretary General a letter by Russia's president, Boris Yeltsin, informing him that, in virtue of that agreement, Russia was the successor state to the USSR for the purposes of UN membership. After being circulated among the other UN member states with no objection raised, the statement was declared accepted on December 31.

On December 25, 1991, Gorbachev resigned as president of the USSR, declaring the office extinct and ceding all the powers still vested in it to the president of Russia: Yeltsin. On the night of that same day, the Soviet flag was lowered for the last time over the Kremlin. Finally, a day later on December 26, 1991, the Council of Republics (a chamber) of the Supreme Soviet of the USSR recognized the dissolution of the Soviet Union and dissolved itself (another chamber of the Supreme Soviet had been unable to work during some months before this, due to absence of a quorum). By December 31, 1991, all official Soviet institutions had ceased operations as individual republics assumed the central government's role.

Summary

The four principal elements of the old Soviet system were the hierarchy of soviets, ethnic federalism, state socialism, and Communist Party dominance. Gorbachev's programs of *perestroika* and *glasnost* produced radical unforeseen effects that brought that system down. As a means of reviving the Soviet state, Gorbachev repeatedly attempted to build a coalition of political leaders supportive of reform and created new arenas and bases of power. He implemented these measures because he wanted to resolve serious economic problems and political inertia that clearly threatened to put the Soviet Union into a state of long-term stagnation.

But by using structural reforms to widen opportunities for leaders and popular movements in the union republics to gain influence, Gorbachev also made it possible for nationalist, orthodox communist, and populist forces to oppose his attempts to liberalize and revitalize Soviet communism. Although some of the new movements aspired to replace the Soviet system altogether with a liberal democratic one, others demanded independence for the national republics. Still others insisted on the restoration of the old Soviet ways. Ultimately, Gorbachev could not forge a compromise among these forces and the consequence was the collapse of the Soviet Union.

Post-Soviet restructuring

In order to restructure the Soviet administrative command system and implement transition to a market-based economy, Yeltsin's shock program was employed within days of the dissolution of the Soviet Union. The subsidies to money-losing farms and industries were cut, price controls abolished, and the ruble moved toward convertibility. New opportunities for Yeltsin's circle and other entrepreneurs to seize the former state property were created thus restructuring old state-owned economy within a few months. After obtaining power, the vast majority of "idealistic" reformers gained huge possessions of state property using their positions in the government and became business oligarchs in a manner that appeared antithetical to an emerging democracy. Existing institutions were conspicuously abandoned prior to the establishment of new legal structures of the market economy such as those governing private property, overseeing financial markets, and enforcing taxation.

Market economists believed that the dismantling of the administrative command system in Russia would raise GDP and living standards by allocating resources more efficiently. They also thought the collapse would create new production possibilities by eliminating central planning, substituting a decentralized market system, eliminating huge macroeconomic and structural distortions through liberalization, and providing incentives through privatization.

Since the USSR's collapse, Russia faced many problems that free market proponents in 1992 did not expect. Among other things, 25% of the population lived below the poverty line, life expectancy had fallen, birthrates were low, and the GDP was halved. These problems led to a series of crises in the 1990s, which nearly led to election of Yeltsin's Communist challenger, Gennady Zyuganov, in the 1996 presidential election. In the recent years, the economy of Russia has begun to improve greatly, due to major investments and business development and also due to high prices of natural resources.

Fall of the Soviet Union

In December of 1991, as the world watched in amazement, the Soviet Union disintegrated into fifteen separate countries. Its collapse was hailed by the west as a victory for freedom, a triumph of democracy over totalitarianism, and evidence of the superiority of capitalism over socialism. The United States rejoiced as its formidable enemy was brought to its knees, thereby ending the Cold War which had hovered over these two superpowers since the end of World War II. Indeed, the breakup of the Soviet Union transformed the entire world political situation, leading to a complete reformulation of political, economic and military alliances all over the globe.

What led to this monumental historical event? In fact, the answer is a very complex one, and can only be arrived at with an understanding of the peculiar composition and history of the Soviet Union. The Soviet Union was built on approximately the same territory as the Russian Empire which it succeeded. After the Bolshevik Revolution of 1917, the newly-formed government developed a philosophy of socialism with the eventual and gradual transition to Communism. The state which the Bolsheviks created was intended to overcome national differences, and rather to create one monolithic state based on a centralized economical and political system. This state, which was built on a Communist ideology, was eventually transformed into a totalitarian state, in which the Communist leadership had complete control over the country.

However, this project of creating a unified, centralized socialist state proved problematic for several reasons. First, the Soviets underestimated the degree to which the non-Russian ethnic groups in the country (which comprised more than fifty percent of the total population of the Soviet Union) would resist assimilation into a Russianized State. Second, their economic planning failed to meet the needs of the State, which was caught up in a vicious arms race with the United States. This led to gradual economic decline, eventually necessitating the need for reform. Finally, the ideology of Communism, which the Soviet Government worked to instill in the hearts and minds of its population, never took firm root, and eventually lost whatever influence it had originally carried.

By the time of the 1985 rise to power of Mikhail Gorbachev, the Soviet Union's last leader, the country was in a situation of severe stagnation, with deep economic and political problems which sorely needed to be addressed and overcome. Recognizing this, Gorbachev introduced a two-tiered policy of reform. On one level, he initiated a policy of glasnost, or freedom of speech. On the other level, he began a program of economic reform known as perestroika, or rebuilding. What Gorbachev did not realize was that by giving people complete freedom of expression, he was unwittingly unleashing emotions and political feelings that had been pent up for decades, and which proved to be extremely powerful when brought out into the open. Moreover, his policy of economic reform did not have the immediate results he had hoped for and had publicly predicted. The Soviet people consequently used their newly allotted freedom of speech to criticize Gorbachev for his failure to improve the economy.

The disintegration of the Soviet Union began on the peripheries, in the non-Russian areas. The first region to produce mass, organized dissent was the Baltic region, where, in 1987, the government of Estonia demanded autonomy. This move was later followed by similar moves in Lithuania and Latvia, the other two Baltic republics. The nationalist movements in the Baltics constituted a strong challenge to Gorbachev's policy of glasnost. He did not want to crack down too severely on the participants in these movements, yet at the same time, it became increasingly evident that allowing them to run their course would spell disaster for the Soviet Union, which would completely collapse if all of the periphery republics were to demand independence.

After the initiative from Estonia, similar movements sprang up all over the former Soviet Union. In the Transcaucasus region (in the South of the Soviet Union), a movement developed inside the Armenian-populated autonomous region of Nagorno-Karabagh, in the Republic of Azerbaijan. The Armenian population of this region demanded that they be granted the right to secede and join the Republic of Armenia, with whose population they were ethnically linked. Massive demonstrations were held in Armenia in solidarity with the secessionists in Nagorno-Karabagh. The Gorbachev government refused to allow the population of Nagorno-Karabagh to secede, and the situation developed into a violent territorial dispute, eventually degenerating into an all-out war which continues unabated until the present day.

Once this "Pandora's box" had been opened, nationalist movements emerged in Georgia, Ukraine, Moldova, Byelorussia, and the Central Asian republics. The power of the Central Government was considerably weakened by these movements; they could no longer rely on the cooperation of Government figures in the republics.

Finally, the situation came to a head in August of 1991. In a last-ditch effort to save the Soviet Union, which was floundering under the impact of the political movements which had emerged since the implementation of Gorbachev's glasnost, a group of "hard-line" Communists organized a coup d'etat. They kidnapped Gorbachev, and then, on August 19 of 1991, they announced on state television that Gorbachev was very ill and would no longer be able to govern. The country went into an uproar. Massive protests were staged in Moscow, Leningrad, and many of the other major cities of the Soviet Union. When the coup organizers tried to bring in the military to quell the protestors, the soldiers themselves rebelled, saying that they could not fire on their fellow countrymen. After three days of massive protest, the coup organizers surrendered, realizing that without the cooperation of the military, they did not have the power to overcome the power of the entire population of the country.

After the failed coup attempt, it was only a few months until the Soviet Union completely collapsed. Both the government and the people realized that there was no way to turn back the clock; the massive demonstrations of the "August days" had demonstrated that the population would accept nothing less than democracy. Gorbachev conceded power, realizing that he could no longer contain the power of the population. On December 25, 1991, he resigned. By January of 1992, by popular demand, the Soviet Union ceased to exist. In its place, a new entity was formed. It was called the "Commonwealth of Independent Republics," and was composed of most of the independent countries of the former Soviet Union. While the member countries had complete political independence, they were linked to other Commonwealth countries by economic, and, in some cases, military ties.

Now that the Soviet Union, with its centralized political and economic system, has ceased to exist, the fifteen newly formed independent countries which emerged in its aftermath are faced with an overwhelming task. They must develop their economies, reorganize their political systems, and, in many cases, settle bitter territorial disputes. A number of wars have developed on the peripheries of the former Soviet Union. Additionally, the entire region is suffering a period of severe economic hardship. However, despite the many hardships facing the region, bold steps are being taken toward democratization, reorganization, and rebuilding in most of the countries of the former Soviet Union.

The Soviet Economy to the mid-1960s

From the 1930s and into the 1970s, the Soviet economy had been geared for heavy industry and the military — production with a lot of steel and cement. It was a "command" economy, directed from a central planning commission. Agriculture was mainly collective, with farm workers allowed small private plots. Technical education was vast, with the Soviet Union graduating engineers, scientists, doctors and persons of other professions in great number. Soviet manufacturing had grown to 17.6 percent of the world share in 1938 (behind a 28.7 percent share for the United States), but in 1960s the question remained concerning future growth.

The Soviet Union had lost 26 million people in World War II, but by 1970 its population would be 228 million, up from 190 million in 1937. The Soviet Union was one-sixth of the land area of the world. Its arable land was equal to that of the United States and Canada combined. The Soviet Union had an abundance of natural resources, and it had been producing more oil, natural gas, iron, coal, lead, nickel, silver, copper and zinc than any other country. It had the largest long-range fishing fleet. It was second in the production of gold and chromium.

In the mid-fifties the Soviet Union was the most advanced nation in rocketry. In 1957 it was the first nation to send a satellite into space, and in 1961 the Soviet Union sent the first man into space. The Soviet leader from 1955 to 1964, Nikita Khrushchev, predicted that the Soviet Union would bury (surpass) the West economically in twenty years or so (around 1980). In this period, the Soviet economy, as measured in Gross National Product (GNP), was growing at about 6 percent a year. But in this period growth was high around the world. In 1960 the Soviet Union was producing 12.5 percent of the world's goods (from farm and factory), just under half that of the United States (25.9 percent) and the European Economic Community (26 percent). These figures would change little by 1970, while Japan's share jumped from 4.5 percent in 1960 to 7.7 percent in 1970. But the Soviet Economy was not the economic engine that Khrushchev had imagined.

Decline during the Brezhnev Years

From the 1960s a shift had been taking place in work. It was more toward the production of consumer items such as automobiles, electronic devices, pharmaceuticals, civilian aircraft—a production that was more knowledge intensive, more plastic and less cement. And it was more production for consumers — away from the kind of heavy industrial production that had developed under Stalin. From 1966 to 1970, under Leonid Brezhnev, the GNP held around 5.3 per year. Then during 1971 to 1975 the

GNP fell, averaging 3.7 growth per year. And after 1975 the GNP fell to a growth of between 2.6 and 2.7 percent per year. In these years production around the world was growing rapidly, rising to an average annual rate for the world of 6.2 percent in 1973. The Soviet Union was keeping up with the United States in the production of steel, pig iron, cement and oil, but the future lay in electronics and specialty chemicals.

Brezhnev and his colleagues wished Soviet citizens to be as prosperous as those in the capitalist nations, and to produce more for consumers they tried to incorporate innovations from the West, including innovations involving chemicals and computers. The Soviet Union was not keeping up with sophisticated techniques in computers, software and communications electronics or the design and manufacturing of automobiles — as were Taiwan and Korea. The Soviet Union lost its second place standing in manufacturing, falling behind the losers of World War II, Japan and Germany, and falling behind Britain and Italy. The Soviet Union's biggest customer for its manufactured goods was its military, and manufacturing for the military continued to use the Soviet Union's most skilled people, to the detriment of production for civilians.

The rigid command economy created by Stalin in the 1930s was not suited for the rapid changes that were a part of technological development outside the Soviet Union in the 1970s. The Soviet Union had no independently wealthy individuals looking to bankroll a new business with a new idea. In the Soviet Union it was the central government that was doing the investing, not only in the military but also in social programs, including spending money to keep bread available and at a low price. Money to modernize manufacturing was often lacking.

In the Soviet Union, the managers at various production plants were protected from international competition, and they had no competition from within the Soviet Union. Their thinking was not geared to consumer choice, and without a free market they had little notion of what was in demand and what was not. Rather than consumers, bureaucrats were deciding what was to be manufactured. And at the centre of the Soviet economy, planners could not keep up with the changing needs of various areas, which resulted in poor economic co-ordination, sometimes seen in the form of metal goods rusting away at railway sidings. By the 1970s, low morale of the Soviet Union's work force was hurting its economy. Workers were given goals that seemed abstract or remote from tangible benefits. Common people were criticizing people in power for not responding to their needs. Common people still lived in cramped housing and were seeing little material progress for themselves. Cynicism was high among Soviet workers and alcoholism prevalent. People were taking less pride in their work than people did in some other nations.

Skilled workers were also demoralized. The massive effort in the Soviet Union in education to create a skilled work force could not compensate for an economy that functioned poorly. Instead, education was producing poorly employed talent.

The agricultural sector of the Soviet economy was also functioning inefficiently. Under Brezhnev, most farming remained collectivized, with four percent of the Soviet Union's arable land being farmed on the side, as privately owned plots-with this four percent producing around twenty-five percent of the Soviet Union's agricultural output. Before World War I, Russia had been one of the greatest food exporters in the world, but now it had become one of the world's greatest importers of food. After decades of collective farming, agricultural workers in the Soviet Union had developed poor work habits. And with distribution and transportation a problem, some harvests rotted on their way to market, and sometimes as much as forty or fifty percent of a crop might rot in the fields.

During the Brezhnev years supplies of oil and natural gas were becoming more costly, these supplies now deeper in the ground or located in permafrost regions. The Soviet Union had not been using its energy efficiently, and scarcer supplies of fuel were now adding to the cost of production. A decline in sales of its oil abroad and the purchasing of food from abroad was a trade imbalance that was costing the Soviet Union hard currency and gold. Within the Soviet Union, government agencies were involved in more deficit spending than bureaucrats were admitting. And increases in the printing of money were contributing to the declining value of Soviet money — the ruble.

What grew during the Brezhnev years were bureaucracy and the size of the Communist Party — with many Party members working in bureaucracies. And growing too were the number of vacation residences, pensions, perks and privileges for Party members. In the eyes of the common Soviet citizen, corruption was growing alongside economic stagnation.

And the Brezhnev years included aggressive moves to defend the Soviet Union's position with its neighbours. Brezhnev was concerned that the Communist regime in Czechoslovakia was becoming too liberal — the Communist leader in Prague, Alexander Dubcek, having talked of creating a "socialism with a human face." Brezhnev saw Soviet hegemony in East Europe as threatened. He spoke of all the sacrifices that the Soviet people had made in World War II and, in August 1968, he sent tanks into Czechoslovakia to quell liberalization.

Brezhnev wanted to maintain the Soviet Union's standing in Europe and to maintain good relations with the West. He made himself a champion of Détente, and as a sign of his desire for good relations with the U.S. he kissed President Carter on the cheek. Then in December 1979, Brezhnev sent troops into Afghanistan, to support a friendly socialist regime there against guerrilla insurgents.

Gorbachev and Glasnost (Openness)

Brezhnev died in November 1982 and was replaced as Party leader by Yuri Andropov, a "no nonsense" disciplinarian who had been in charge of the Soviet police (the KGB). Andropov attacked what he saw as moral rot. He launched a campaign against corruption and alcoholism. People were arrested who should have been at work but were in drinking places. And Andropov criticized industry managers for poor supervision of their work force. Andropov knew of the underground economy and corruption that was interfering with government economic organization — corruption that had reached into the upper ranks of the Communist Party itself — to Brezhnev's daughter — and he wished to do something about it.

Large companies were more like welfare institutions than they were enterprises concerned with productivity and the costs of production. Andropov explored the issue of incentives and decision-making for enterprise managers, but little came of it, and he died after only thirteen months in office. He was replaced by

Konstantin Chernenko, who continued Andropov's objective of reforming the economy but he also died, and only after a year in office. The day after Chernenko's death — March 15, 1985 — the Politburo and a few others elevated the Party's second-in-command, Mikhail Gorbachev, to the position of Partly leader — his official title being General Secretary of the Central Committee. Like Chernenko, Gorbachev had also been associated with Andropov's desire for economic revitalization — to be known as *perestroika*.

However oppressive the Soviet system, the Soviet Union's communists still believed in the kind of democracy that Karl Marx had wanted. The goal of Marxism was the masses ruling themselves and eventually producing an abundance that allowed "to each according to his needs and from each according to his abilities." The Communists did not believe in the authoritarian state as had the fascists, and after Stalin's death, the more liberal Khrushchev denounced Stalin's authoritarian ways. With Gorbachev, the Soviet Union had a leader who believed that more liberalism was the answer to the Soviet Union's economic and social problems.

By now the Soviet economy had a negative GNP. In other words, rather than the Soviet economy growing more slowly than others, it was in decline. Gorbachev and his allies in the Party felt compelled to do something to reverse the economic decline and decay. Gorbachev believed that the Soviet Union needed, as he put it, "radical change." Like his predecessors he wanted his nation to catch up with the economic advances being made in the capitalist nations. Gorbachev wanted to prove that socialism could adapt, innovate, and be as productive as capitalism.

Gorbachev's *perestroika* was a command, or top-down, process, lacking the power of imagination rising from individuals outside of government bureaucracy — imagination that was sometimes lacking in the United States by the CEOs of the largest of corporations, but overcome by newcomers such as Steve Jobs of Apple Computer or Bill Gates of Microsoft. The Soviet economy was not giving opportunity to start up enterprises. Sticking to his belief in socialism, rather than radically change the Soviet economy Gorbachev tried tinkering with it. He denounced "unearned incomes." To improve the Soviet work force he began another crackdown against alcohol, and orders were given that embassy receptions and parties had to be alcohol free. He raised the price of alcohol, reduced supplies and the hours of sales. Then Gorbachev tried to create greater incentives for people of talent — scientific and technical personnel — whose wages were increased fifty percent. And in August 1985 the salaries of others were adjusted to the quality of their work.

Still believing in central planning, Gorbachev wished to increase the efficiency in central planning management. To make economic planning more effective and efficient, new super-agencies were created to oversee economic developments. In October 1985, Gorbachev published his plan to increase production of consumer's goods and to increase services. His plan called for a 30 percent increase by 1990 and an 80 to 90 per cent increase by the year 2000. He estimated that labor productivity in this period would more than double. With diminishing natural resources for energy, the Soviet Union had been looking toward the nuclear, and Gorbachev was planning to increase the production of nuclear power by 400 and 500 percent.

Gorbachev believed that advancing the Soviet Union's economy required mass participation, higher morale among the Soviet Union's work force, and more freedom and openness — *glasnost*. He likened the economy to a family's home, and democracy to ownership of the home.

"A house," he said, "can be put in order only by a person who feels that he owns this house." He spoke of the goodwill necessary in making an economy work. And regarding corruption versus worker morale, he complained of leaders having placed themselves beyond the reach of criticism and of some who had become accomplices in, if not the organizers of, criminal activities.

As a part of freedom to express oneself, Gorbachev started releasing political prisoners. The Soviet Union's most outspoken dissident, Andrei Sakharov (the father of the Soviet Union's hydrogen bomb) was allowed to return to Moscow from the city of Gorky, where he had been exiled for speaking out against Soviet troops being sent to Afghanistan. The Gorbachev regime allowed more openness in newspapers and on television. Gorbachev's popularity with the Soviet masses was rising.

Gorbachev Confers with Reagan

A part of Gorbachev's plan to improve the economy was to reduce military spending. He believed that the Soviet military was absorbing too much wealth and scarce resources, and he believed that one way to reduce military spending was to make an arms agreement with the United States. The President of the United States at this time happened to be Ronald Reagan. He had been calling the Soviet Union an evil empire. He was afraid of nuclear war and was committed to developing a perfect defence system called Star Wars. Reagan's critics complained it would seem to the Russians to give the U.S. a first strike capability — a perfect defence eliminating the possibility of retaliation. But Reagan did not scare Gorbachev. Gorbachev had a different view about defence than had Khrushchev and Brezhnev. Khrushchev and Brezhnev had believed that Soviet military prowess was necessary to restrain the capitalist powers from attacking the Soviet Union and its satellites. They believed that foreign policy should be a part of the class struggle. Gorbachev saw U.S. leaders as rational, as not interested in destroying the Soviet Union through war and as wanting to avoid a nuclear holocaust. Gorbachev believed that the capitalist powers were not in need of restraint provided by the Soviet Union. He remained a Marxist but rejected applying the class struggle to foreign policy. There were many who had favoured belligerence and threats against the Soviet Union in order to diminish communism. But the opposite was happening. It was a friendly U.S., represented by Reagan, that was producing what the anti-communists wanted.

Some were to describe Reagan as having forced Gorbachev to adopt his new policy toward the Cold War — in other words, to back down because of the Soviet Union's inability to keep up with U.S. advances in military spending. But no evidence exists that Gorbachev's policies were motivated by this. It was his military that wanted to keep up with the U.S., and Gorbachev argued with them. Reagan's Star Wars idea and his hostile attitude toward the "evil empire" made Gorbachev's arguments more difficult, but Gorbachev remained convinced that reductions in military spending were necessary to improve the Soviet economy, and Gorbachev let military spending decline with the decline of the Soviet economy in general.

Back in April, 1985 — his first month in office — Gorbachev had announced his first unilateral initiative: a temporary freeze on the deployment of intermediate-range missiles in Europe. Gorbachev met Reagan at Geneva a few months later, in November 1985, and again in October 1986 at Reykjavik in Iceland, and yet again in May 1988 at a summit meeting in Moscow. Gorbachev and Reagan became friends, Gorbachev recognizing that Reagan sincerely wanted to avoid a nuclear holocaust, that he was a man of decency and sincerity, a former actor who was not faking it. And Reagan saw Gorbachev as something other than an evil communist robot. Gorbachev convinced Reagan that he was sincere in wanting to end the arms race and in collaborating with the West in restructuring relations. Reagan became the leading "dove" in his administration while anti-communist Republican hardliners called Reagan "a useful idiot for Soviet propaganda" and "an apologist for Gorbachev."

Gorbachev stunned Reagan's advisors by agreeing to disarmament proposals that these advisors had put forth merely as a bargaining ploy. Meanwhile, Gorbachev's attitudes were making him popular in Western Europe and the United States, where people were calling him "Gorbie." And soon Gorbachev would win the Nobel prize for peace.

More Economic Troubles

On April 25 1986, the nuclear power plant at Chernobyl (in the Ukraine 90 kilometres north of Kiev) exploded, the radiation killing hundreds of women and children, contaminating rivers and streams and ruining local agriculture. A French satellite photographed it, and the French transmitted news of the blast to the world, including the Soviet Union. The damage measured in dollars was in the billions. In the Soviet Union, public mistrust of nuclear plants dashed hopes of nuclear energy as an inexpensive source of power, and plans were laid instead for building new natural gas pipelines.

Grain harvests were good in the Soviet Union in 1986 and 1987, allowing the Soviet Union to reduce grain imports, but the economy continued to decline. Gorbachev's policy on alcohol was of little help. People were now waiting in longer lines for the diminished supply of drink. Retail stores sold less alcohol, the government was receiving less from sales taxes, and brewing booze at home was increasing.

In response to reduced oil sales abroad, the government reduced the importation of consumer goods. This left soviet citizens with less to buy and reduced revenues from sales taxes. The incomes of consumers had been rising, but with too little on the shelves for people to buy, and too much money chasing too few goods, prices were rising. It was the opposite of what capitalist nations had faced in the Great Depression, when too little money was in the hands of consumers compared to what was available for purchase.

Deficit spending — government spending more money than it was acquiring in revenue — was a disaster for the Soviet economy. To make up for the insufficient tax revenues the government continued to print more money, increasing inflation. People were putting the money they could not spend into state savings banks-a bad place for money during inflation and a waste in that it was money not being invested in worthy enterprises.

Monetary policy was of little concern to Gorbachev and his advisors. New bureaucracies were created to oversee planning and investing at a more local level. Decrees were issued on quality production and completing projects on time. New laws were passed allowing managers to have more initiative. Producer cooperatives were allowed. Some joint ventures with foreign companies were authorized. But none of these were destined to turn the economy around.

The government tried to increase private farming by offering land to farmers for that purpose — land that could be farmed but not sold. But, unlike China, few people in the Soviet Union were interested in venturing into independent farming, some not sure that government favour toward private enterprise in agriculture was permanent. In 1987 the number who accepted the land grants increased, but many who accepted failed to make a success of it. Many of those who did succeed merely produced enough for their own subsistence. Overall, the move toward private farming remained unsubstantial, and the Soviet Union's agriculture remained largely collective.

More Failures and Political Reform, 1986-88

With Gorbachev's new bureaucracies the Soviet economy was even more of a tangle of confusion. After fifty years of being told what to do in petty detail, and afraid of initiative and risk, managers were not ready to take full advantage of production opportunities. There was ineptitude in investing. Demands made by planners were not in tune with production capabilities. Growth targets were missed by wide margins and projects remained uncompleted.

Until 1986 the Soviet Union had been criticizing China's economic reforms, but Soviet economists were now wondering why Chinese reforms were working better than Soviet reforms. One Soviet economist complained that the Chinese worked hard and that the Russians talked hard. One difference between China and the Soviet Union was that reforms in China began in the countryside with peasants taking to free enterprise with confidence.

In 1987 individual enterprises were given more freedom to make their own decisions regarding investments in production, hoping for a closer marriage between investment and production. In 1988, new priorities were given to the construction of housing and to modernizing industries that produced consumers goods.

Also in 1988, Gorbachev made new political moves. His reforms were being opposed and frustrated by opposition with the Communist Party and local bureaucracies, and Gorbachev responded by emasculating the power of the Central Committee Secretariat. He removed the Party from overseeing the economy, leaving this to local soviets. Meanwhile, Gorbachev was preparing to withdraw Soviet troops from Afghanistan.

Andrei Sakharov and the Reforms of 1989

Sakharov continued to agitate for the release of "prisoners of conscience." He wrote of "well-known prisoners" having been released, but he complained that people were still serving time in psychiatric hospitals and that people who were not well known were still serving time on "trumped-up charges." Soviet television helped to make Andrei Sakharov well known, and Sakharov was respected as he appeared to be without bitterness or political ambition. Sakharov worked with many others who were as dedicated to reforms as he, and he agitated for giving real political freedom to the various nationalities within the Soviet Union. To a degree, Gorbachev agreed. Gorbachev looked forward to "modernizing" the relationship between the nationalities and central Soviet power, hoping to make that association more genuine.

Sakharov called for an end to the Communist Party's monopoly of power and for freeing the economy from what he saw as excessive bureaucratic dictates. He praised Gorbachev's "courage" in reducing the Soviet Union's armed forces and for his new liberal attitude toward the rest of Eastern Europe. But Sakharov believed that greater cuts would be beneficial, and he advocated a fifty-percent reduction in military spending.

In May 1989, Sakharov attended the Soviet Union's newly created legislative body, a 2,250 member Congress of People's Deputies — an event that was televised and presided over by Gorbachev. There, Sakharov and a few others argued for more reform. Sakharov spoke of his being "increasingly troubled" by the government's domestic policies and by the gap between word and deed. He spoke against real power being in the hands of the Communist Party, against retreats in freedom of information and of ideology being turned over to men who were "enemies of *perestroika*."

Sakharov spoke of the economic crisis in the Soviet Union. He observed that the crisis was accompanied by distrust, and he described the public's confidence in Gorbachev as having fallen "to almost zero." Despair, he said, was a barrier to evolutionary development. He complained that moves toward a market economy had been half-measures and "impractical." People, he said, cannot wait any longer with nothing but promises to sustain them. A middle course in a situation like this, he said, "is almost impossible." Either accelerate reforms toward economic freedom, he complained, or retain administration of the command economy in all its aspects. Gorbachev answered, saying that "many big leaps" had been taken and that the results had always been "tragedy and backtracking." As for public support, Gorbachev said that he expected the people to understand his policies.

Sakharov and his allies were a minority at the Congress. One delegate who spoke against him was a veteran who had lost his legs in Afghanistan. The delegate spoke of problems veterans were having, and referring to words Sakharov had spoken recently during a visit to Canada, he described Sakharov as having committed slander. Sakharov had described the Soviet Union as waging a cruel and horrible war in Afghanistan and had called for a negotiated settlement of the war. The veteran ended his criticism of Sakharov by saying there were three matters that "we must all fight to protect." These were, "state power, our motherland, and Communism." This appeal to patriotism brought the delegates to their feet, and applause rocked the hall.

At the Congress, Sakharov's allies listed their complaints. Economic reforms were described as only cosmetic, and the complaint was lodged that reforms were being stalled by a wave "of retrograde measures." A complaint was voiced against agricultural subsidies and against inflation, against "a bureaucracy that rules without accountability." A complaint was lodged against the economy's focus: the production of too little in plastics, the dearth of computers and of scientists still using the abacus. Someone proposed investing only in things that would satisfy consumer demand in the near term. Someone also proposed a one-shot importation of consumer goods to achieve a balance between supply and demand. Also suggested was a cut in the importation of grain, allowing farmers to sell part of their produce for hard currency and allowing them to spend their hard currency as they wished. And it was suggested that the six to eight billions being spent in Latin America — mainly subsidies to Cuba — be stopped.

A biologist complained that 20 percent of the population lived in areas that were ecological disasters and that another 35 to 40 percent lived under unsatisfactory ecological conditions. He spoke of the infant mortality rate in the Soviet Union being higher than in many African countries, of the average life span in the Soviet Union being four to eight years less than it was in developed nations. And he spoke of one-fifth of the sausages and 42 percent of children's dairy products produced in the Soviet Union in 1987 containing a dangerous amount of chemicals.

Conditions at the End of the 1989

In December, 1989, Sakharov died, at the age of sixty-eight. Four days of national mourning were declared. Sakharov's popularity had been bolstered by his death. A poll taken in the

Soviet Union shortly after Sakharov's death placed him as the most popular person in the Soviet Union in the twentieth century.

By now Gorbachev had withdrawn troops from Afghanistan. By the end of 1989 each of the Soviet republics had acquired its own parliament, with its own president. But tensions in the Soviet Union had increased. The declining economy was producing strikes by labor — something that would not have been tried under Stalin. There were episodes of ethnic violence, with people in some of the Soviet republics blaming their misery on the Russians. In Latvia, Lithuania and Estonia a move toward independence was underway. All those years of Russian control had failed to erase a desire for self-rule among these peoples. And by now, Soviet hegemony was evaporating in Eastern Europe.

Freedom in Poland, Hungary, Czechoslovakia and East Germany

The socialist economies in Eastern Europe had been suffering along with that of the Soviet Union, with Gorbachev looking toward *glasnost* (openness) as a remedy for their economic troubles. In Hungary, one of the more economically advanced satellite nations, twenty-five percent of the population was living in dire poverty. In December 1988, Gorbachev announced in a speech to the United Nations General Assembly that by 1991 he intended to pull Soviet tanks and troops out of East Germany, Czechoslovakia and Hungary. For Hungarians this was encouraging news, and the Hungarians demonstrated for the freedom to create a political party, or parties, independent of Hungary's Communist Party.

1989 began in Czechoslovakia with the Communist government's judicial system prosecuting the playwright Vaclav Havel for his having incited illegal protests. The court sentenced Havel to remain in prison until September or October. Others dissidents in Czechoslovakia were also being tried and sentenced. But with the populace restive and in sympathy with the dissidents, the government thought that leniency would be prudent, and in May they released Havel.

In Poland the Communist regime had been compromising with public opinion. Failing to crush the dissident movement called Solidarity, the government tried to absorb Solidarity into a legitimate part of national affairs. The leaders of Solidarity agreed to cooperate with the Communist regime, and the regime allowed Solidarity to run candidates in coming elections. Some dissidents opposed collaboration with the Communists. They wanted to boycott the elections on the grounds that the elections were not entirely free. But Solidarity argued for participation, and at the polls Solidarity won an overwhelming victory, becoming the first freely elected opposition party in a country with a Communist regime.

Some anti-Communists in the United States had argued that Communists would never liberalize. They had claimed that Communism had to be overthrown by force. Now they were being proved wrong.

In early July, Gorbachev pledged that the Poles and Hungarians were free to determine their own future. Gorbachev believed that Communist leaders in the Warsaw Pact countries should try hanging onto power by being good Communists, that is, by winning the support of the masses. It may also be that Gorbachev believed that the Warsaw Pact countries were not worth hanging onto, that they were costing the Soviet Union more money than value being received in return.

In Hungary, Communist leaders were seeing "the handwriting on the wall." Conservative Party leaders were being replaced by younger, more liberal Communists. The Communist Party in Hungary recognized the rising in 1956 as legitimate, and the Communist leader who supported Hungarian national aspirations then, Imre Nagy, who had been executed by Khrushchev's regime, was exonerated and given a proper burial.

The Hungarian Communist Party changed its name to Socialist Party, to bridge a gap between doctrinaire Marxists and European Social Democrats. Hungary declared itself a republic, and Hungarians were free to travel abroad without the special permission that had been previously required. President Bush (the elder), who had been visiting Poland and celebrating developments there, also visited Hungary, and he promised the Hungarians economic help. And a U.S. company, General Electric, bought into lightbulb manufacturing in Hungary — the largest western investment in Hungary since World War II. Advances in freedom in Poland and Hungary was encouraging people in neighbouring Czechoslovakia. On August 21, the twenty-first anniversary of Soviet tanks rolling into that city, people in Prague demonstrated. The former Communist leader, Alexander Dubcek, who in 1968 had led what was called the *Prague Spring*, spoke encouraging words to the crowd.

Communist Party leaders in Czechoslovakia were more conservative than were those in Hungary. They had risen with the Soviet invasion and Dubcek's fall, and now they were slow in adjusting to what was taking place. Under the illusion that more repression would work, they began jailing demonstrators and rounding up dissidents, including Vaclav Havel.

The hope for more freedom had also spread to East Germany. The regime there, led by Eric Honneker, had been appalled by Gorbachev's liberalizations, and since 1988 Soviet publications had been banned in East Germany. But it was to no avail.

East Germans had been free to travel within the Warsaw bloc. That is where many of them went for their annual vacation. And with freedom of travel within Hungary, some from East Germany were fleeing across the Hungarian border into Austria — the slow-thinking East German regime having failed to block travel to Hungary. Many Germans wanting to flee to West Germany crowded into the West German embassies in Prague and Hungary, demanding entry to West Germany. The flight of Germans from Hungary into Austria increased to the thousands, and the Communist regime in East Germany panicked as its economy became threatened by the loss of educated and talented young people.

In mid-October 1989, mounting dissent in East Germany was followed by the Politburo there replacing Eric Honneker, hoping this would quiet dissent. But Honneker was replaced with another hardliner, and the dissent continued. On October 25, Gorbachev announced that the Warsaw Pact nations "were doing it their way," described by some as the Sinatra Doctrine — as opposed to the Brezhnev Doctrine. Under pressure from a more rebellious public, the East German regime tried appeasing public opinion. To reduce the "contradiction" between the Party line and public perceptions, and the Party admitted publicly that its regime was not popular.

On November 9, 1989, the Communist regime in East Germany went further in appeasing public opinion by announcing liberalized travel regulations. Inept in its communications, the regime led people in East Berlin to believe that this meant they could journey freely into West Berlin. A hoard of people massed at border crossing points, overwhelming the guards, who let the joyous crowds pass. The happy East Germans flocked to West German stores to make purchases and they rejoiced with West Berliners.

The freedom to cross into West Germany further encouraged people in East Germany, and the Communist regime surrendered to an aroused populace. In November, Berliners began what would become weeks of tearing down the wall that separated East and West Berlin — to Gorbachev's surprise. President Reagan had called on Gorbachev to "tear down this wall," but Gorbachev had left that as the business of the East Germans.

In Prague, the strategy of Communist leaders remained that of repression, despite what was happening in Berlin. In mid-November, 1989, on the fourth consecutive day of demonstrations, the police in Prague attacked demonstrators. Thirteen were admitted to hospitals and dozens were arrested. The following day the number of demonstrators increased, to approximately 10,000 persons. This inspired a greater demonstration the following day: an estimated 200,000 demonstrators. The leader of Czechoslovakia's Communist Party, Milous Jakes, known and ridiculed for his awkward use of language, resigned. Encouraged, an estimated 500,000 people marched for the end of Communist Party rule. And millions of Czechs went out on a two-hour general strike to express solidarity with the demand for political freedom. It was a demonstration too massive for the Communist regime, and the regime responded with a pledge of free elections within a year.

In early December, the Politburo of the Communist Party of Czechoslovakia declared the Soviet invasion to have been a mistake. And rather than waiting months for elections, the promised elections were held after only a few days. By the end of December, Czechoslovakia had a new parliament. Its president was Vaclav Havel, and the chairman of parliament was Alexander Dubcek. By the end of 1989 the Berlin Wall had been torn down. A reform-minded communist, Hans Modrow, had risen to power within East Germany's Communist Party, and Party officials continued to appeal to the public. In mid-December marchers in Leipzig held a candlelight vigil commemorating Stalin's victims. And in a Party Congress, many Communists made speeches of confessions and demanded an absolute break with the Stalinist past. Hans Modrow promised the public multi-party elections for May, and the Communist Party (originally the coalition party, or SED) created by Stalin, changed its name to the Reformed Party of Democratic Socialism. Then the elections were moved up to March, and in these elections the Reformed Party of Democratic Socialism suffered a crushing defeat. A new government was formed in East Germany, and it began lobbying for unification with West Germany — a move that was to be formally achieved in October, 1990, not with great enthusiasm by the government or people of West Germany.

Economic Depression and Disintegration

The economy in the Soviet Union was not a good argument for Soviet republics to stay in the Soviet Union. Instead, some were eager to break with Moscow on the ground that their republic could organize their economy better than could bureaucrats in Moscow. Also, nationalism was alive within the republics — where many Russians lived and considered home. There was some hostility towards these local Russians, who tended to be opposed to breaking away from Moscow. Gorbachev was on their side. He wished to keep the Soviet Union together. On the other hand, in 1990, elections in Estonia, Latvia and Lithuania gave overwhelming victories to political parties favouring independence. And the biggest republic in the Soviet Union, Russia, was also threatening to break away.

The President of the Russian Republic's parliament was Boris Yeltsin — a former Communist who had been dismissed from the Party's Politburo by Gorbachev and others in 1987. Yeltsin had been described by Sakharov as a man he liked but of a "different caliber" than Gorbachev — meaning lesser. Of a different calibre he may have been, but he appealed to the Russian people, and he took advantage of the new freedom in the Soviet Union to denounce the Communist Party and the policies of Gorbachev. As a rival to Gorbachev, Yeltsin owed at least some of his popularity to Gorbachev's unpopularity. In July, 1990, Yeltsin convened the Russian Republic's Supreme Soviet and called for economic sovereignty for the republic, in other words, taking control of the economy away from Gorbachev. Other republics wished to follow suit. The Ukraine called for the return of all Ukrainian soldiers from the Soviet military and the creation of an independent Ukrainian military. In the new atmosphere of freedom and democracy, the Soviet Union was unravelling.

The Communist Party was split between reformers and conservatives, and both were critical of Gorbachev, who was trying to steer a middle ground between state control of the economy and free enterprise. Gorbachev spoke of his belief in socialism and of his being a Communist. He was holding Lenin's New Economic Policy of the early 1920s as his model for what should be done.

To many in Russia, Gorbachev seemed weak and unable to make up his mind. One moment Gorbachev was praising a conservative Communist such as Ligachev, and another moment he was praising the liberal Yakovlev. People were wondering whether he knew where he stood, and they were holding him responsible for the continuing failure of the economy.

In 1991 Gorbachev's popularity in the West was at an all time high, but his approval rating in the Soviet Union was at an all-time low — not only because of the economy but also because of the fall of Communism in the satellite countries. Many in the Soviet Union were angry with Gorbachev for having allowed Germany to unite again. Some, including conservative and patriotic Communists, saw Gorbachev as having disarmed the Soviet Union. They saw him as having thrown away the victory in World War II that had cost twenty million lives.

In 1991 more Soviet factories were closing down. The parliament in the Russian Republic passed a few reforms in the direction of a market economy, and Yeltsin cut funding to various Soviet agencies based on Russian soil. Gorbachev was being destroyed by the new freedoms he had helped to create. He saw the power of the Soviet government as falling away, and he turned his strategy in the direction of preservation — what some would call a turn to the right. Gorbachev's ally, Foreign Minister Shevardnadze, resigned, warning that "a dictatorship is coming."

Around this time Gorbachev suggested to the conservatives around him, including the leader of the Soviet Union's military, that they were free to take whatever extraordinary action was necessary to preserve the Union of Soviet Socialist Republics (USSR). In August, 1991, they obliged him and staged what appeared to be a coup, while Gorbachev and his wife, Raisa, were vacationing in the Crimea. Leaders of the coup claimed that Gorbachev was ill. Gorbachev played along. He was, it appeared, under house arrest, but he had a telephone with which he could call anyone he wished.

The coup was a shock to Russians, who saw their nation as something different from what they thought was a Latin American banana republic, and many of them went into the streets to protest. Their cry was for the protection of what people in the United States believed they had never had: democracy. Yeltsin stood with people who were in the streets against the coup. Ideologically, the masses were much respected in the Soviet Union. Military men were easily persuaded to side with Yeltsin and the people in the streets. Coup leaders did not believe in the coup to the extent that they would commit themselves to a military takeover. Gorbachev's turn to the right and the coup were colossal failures. Gorbachev pretended to be liberated, and Yeltsin was more of a hero, overshadowing the hapless Gorbachev. In triumph, Yeltsin, by presidential decree, banned the Communist Party in the Russian Republic and seized all its property.

At the end of the year, the other former Soviet Republics followed the Russian Republic into independence. Abroad, all Soviet embassies and consulates became Russian embassies and consulates. The Soviet Union had ceased to exist as a legal entity, and Gorbachev was now out of a job, and bitter, blaming Yeltsin for breaking up his beloved Soviet Union.

The collapse had come after years of attempts by non-Communist governments to "peacefully coexist," to negotiate, sign agreements and to have cultural exchanges with the Soviet Union — opposed by those who demonized the Communists and falsely equated bargaining and befriending the Soviet with appeasing Hitler at Munich. Relaxed tensions between the Soviet Union and the capitalist West had paid off. The Cold War was over. Communism had not died, but it had declined dramatically.

The Soviet Union fell apart not at a height in belligerence by the United States but when relations were good.

Politics of the Soviet Union

The political system of the Soviet Union was characterized by the superior role of the Communist Party of the Soviet Union (CPSU), the only party permitted by Constitution. As authorized by Constitution, the Soviet government, called the Council of People's Commissars until 1946 and the Council of Ministers of the USSR afterwards, executed decisions of CPSU pertaining primarily to economy but also to security affairs and social issues. Constitutionally highest organ of legislative authority was the Congress of Soviets until 1936 and the Supreme Soviet of the Soviet Union from 1936 to 1989. But it met only a few days annually, while its Presidium managed affairs throughout the year.

Background

The Bolsheviks who took power during the October Revolution, the final phase of the Russian Revolution, were the first Communist Party to take power and attempt to apply Marxism (to be more specific, the Leninist variant of Marxism) in a practical way. Although they grew rapidly during the Revolution, from 24,000 to 100,000 members, and had some support, 25% of the votes for the Constituent Assembly in November, 1917, the Bolsheviks were a minority party when they seized power in Petrograd and Moscow. Their advantages were discipline and a platform supporting the broad based movement of workers, peasants, soldiers and sailors who had seized factories, organized soviets, appropriated the lands of the aristocracy and other large landholders, deserted from the army and mutinied against the navy during the Revolution. Karl Marx made no detailed proposals for the structure of a socialist or communist government and society other than the replacement of capitalism with socialism, and eventually communism, by the victorious working class. Lenin, the leader of the Bolsheviks, had developed the theory that a Communist Party should serve as the *vanguard of the proletariat,* ruling in their name and interest, but, like Marx, had not developed a detailed economic or political program. The new Communist government of the Soviet Union faced daunting concrete problems:

extending practical control beyond the major cities, combatting counter-revolution and opposing political parties, coping with the continuing war, and setting up a new economic and political system. Despite their relative discipline, the Bolsheviks were not of one mind, the Party being a coalition of committed revolutionaries, but with somewhat differing views as to what was practical and proper. These diverging tendencies resulted in lively debates within the Party over the next decade, followed by a period of consolidation of the Party as definite programs were adopted.

Soviet State

Communist Party

Organization

The CPSU controlled the government apparatus and took decisions affecting economy and society. The Communist Party followed the ideology of Marxism-Leninism and operated on the principle of democratic centralism. The primary CPSU bodies were the Politburo, the highest decision-making organ; the Secretariat, the controller of party bureaucracy; and the Central Committee, the party's policy forum. CPSU membership reached more than 19 million (9.7 percent of the adult population) in 1987, and was dominated by male Russian professionals. Party members occupied positions of authority in all officially recognized institutions throughout the country. Single party rule, combined with democratic centralism, which, in practice, consisted of a hierarchal structure which with the aid of a secret police organization enforced decisions made by the ruling party as well on the personnel of all governmental institutions, including the courts, the press, cultural and economic organizations and labor unions. The Soviet Union is considered by many to have been a totalitarian state for much of its existence. Critics include Western authors such as Robert Conquest and Russian critics such as Alexander Yakovlev.

Ideology

Education and political discourse proceeded on the assumption that it was possible to mold people using collectivist institutional forms into an ideal Soviet man or woman. The validity of ideas, public discourse, and institutional form were evaluated in terms of the official ideology of Marxism-Leninism, as interpreted by the Communist Party.

Government

As authorized by the 1977 Soviet Constitution, the fourth since 1918, the government executed decisions of the CPSU pertaining primarily to the economy but also to security affairs and social issues. The Congress of People's Deputies created in 1988 by amendment to Constitution was the highest organ of legislative and executive authority, consisting of 2,250 deputies, about 87 percent of whom were CPSU members or candidate members and some of whom were elected in the first multicandidate (although not multiparty) elections since the early Soviet period. It was slated to meet once a year for a few days. It met for the first time in May 1989; deputies openly discussed issues, elected a chairman, and selected about 542 deputies from among its membership to constitute a reorganized, bicameral Supreme Soviet of the Soviet Union, a standing legislature slated to remain in session six to eight months annually. Prior to 1989, the former Supreme Soviet was constitutionally the highest organ of legislative and executive authority but met only a few days annually; its Presidium managed affairs throughout the year. The Council of Ministers administered party decisions, mainly regarding economic management, by delegating authority to its Presidium; the chairman of Council of Ministers also sat on CPSU Politburo.

Ministries of Soviet Union

Judicial System

The Supreme Court, the highest judicial body, had little power, lacking authority to determine constitutionality of laws, to interpret laws, or to strike laws down. A large secret police organization monitored public activities closely; substantial efforts were made to discover expressions of dissent especially by government employees and Communist Party members and their families using a network of informers. Control over overt expressions of dissent was achieved through imprisonment, commitment to mental hospitals, and especially during establishment of the regime by death. During the first decades of the regime an extensive system of labor camps was maintained, the Gulag. The judicial system was controlled by the Party. Travel was tightly controlled with borders closed to both entrance or exit. All publications and electronic media were censored, use of copying machines was rigidly controlled, imports of written material tightly controlled, foreign electronic media jammed. Access to government documents and press archives was strictly limited.

Internal Politics

Perestroika and Glasnost

In the final years of the Soviet Union attempts were made by the Politburo under the leadership of Mikhail Gorbachev to reform the political system (first instigated by Yuri Andropov, successor of Leonid Brezhnev). Calls were made for *glasnost* (transparency or openness) and *perestroika* (rebuilding), which also included economic reforms. A somewhat representative legislative body was created, the Congress of People's Deputies, and major reform of the executive branch of the government and the economy attempted. These reforms were resisted by conservative forces within the Communist Party and interrupted by an attempted coup, followed by the outlawing of the Communist Party and the collapse of the Soviet Union.

External Politics

Diplomatic relations with majority of world's nations. Main foreign policy objectives as determined by CPSU Politburo: enhance national security, maintain presence in Eastern Europe, continue "peaceful coexistence" with free world democracies, and seek increased influence in Third World. The regime maintained close relationships on a world wide basis with revolutionary parties continuing support for an international movement to supplant capitalism with communism. It saw itself as subject to attack by developed capitalist countries and maintained massive defensive forces over many decades in anticipation of war.

International Agreements and Memberships

Dominant partner in Council for Mutual Economic Assistance (Comecon) and Warsaw Pact. Active participant in United Nations and its specialized agencies. Signatory to Final Act of Conference on Security and Cooperation in Europe (Helsinki Accords) and many other multilateral and bilateral agreements.

Secretariat of the CPSU Central Committee

The Secretariat of the CPSU Central Committee was a key body within the Communist Party of the Soviet Union and was responsible for the central administration of the party as opposed to drafting government policy which was usually handled by the Politburo. Its members were elected by the Communist Party's Central Committee, although in all but the first years of its existence the elections were a formality since decisions were made by the senior leadership before the voting. The General Secretary of the CPSU, who was also a Politburo member, was the leader of the Secretariat and the Party. Dual membership in the Secretariat and the Politburo was reserved for two or three very senior members of the Soviet leadership and in the post-Stalin era was a stepping stone to the ultimate power. The last 4 Soviet leaders (Leonid Brezhnev, Yuri Andropov, Konstantin Chernenko and Mikhail Gorbachev) were all senior Secretaries before becoming General Secretaries.

The Secretariat was established by the Central Committee on August 6, 1917 and was initially composed of Felix Dzerzhinsky, Matvei Muranov and Yakov Sverdlov as full members and Adolph Joffe and Elena Stasova as candidate members (or alternates). Following the October Revolution of 1917, Sverdlov and Stasova became the de facto Secretariat as other members of the body assumed other duties. At the time, the Secretariat was responsible for technical issues such as coordination of the activities of regional party organizations and handling routine administrative affairs of the Party.

By 1922, the body had been transformed from a technical committee to one of the most important components of the party and from that point on it was responsible for day to day operations of the Communist Party. Also in 1922, the position of General Secretary was created, the General Secretary became the head of the Secretariat and, in the years following Lenin's death, became the most important figure in the party and the country.

7

The Chinese Political System

China Political System

The Constitutional System

The Constitution is the fundamental law of the state.

The existing Constitution was adopted for implementation by the 5th Session of the 5th National People's Congress on December 4, 1982. Amendments were made to the Constitution respectively at the 1st Session of the 7th National People's Congress on April 12, 1988, the 1st Session of the 8th National People's Congress on March 29, 1993 and the 2nd Session of the 9th National People's Congress on March 15, 1999.

I. Major stipulations in the Constitution in regard to China's political system

1. Major political principles in China

(1) The Communist Party of China is the country's sole political party in power.

The People's Republic of China was founded by the Communist Party of China which is the leader of the Chinese people.

(2) The socialist system

The socialist system led by the working class and based on the alliance of the workers and farmers is the fundamental system of the People's Republic of China

(3) All rights belong to the people

All the power in the country belongs to the people who exercise their power through the National People's Congress and local people's congresses at all levels.

The people manage the state, economy, culture and other social affairs through a multitude of means and forms.

(4) The fundamental task and goals of the state

To concentrate on the socialist modernization drive along the road of building socialism with Chinese characteristics; to adhere to the socialist road, persist in the reform and opening up program, improve the socialist system in all aspects, develop the market economy, expand democracy, and improve the rule of law; to be self-reliance and work hard to gradually realize the modernization of the industry, agriculture, national defence, science and technology so as to build China into a strong and democratic socialist country with a high degree of cultural development.

(5) Democratic centralism

The organizational principle for the state organs is democratic centralism.

(6) The armed forces of the people

The armed forces of the People's Republic of China belong to the people.

The tasks of the armed forces are to consolidate national defence, resist invasion, defend the country, safeguard the people in their peaceful work and life, take part in the country's economic construction and strive to serves the people.

(7) To govern the country through the rule of law

All individuals, political parties and social organizations must abide by the Constitution in all their actions and shall not be privileged to be above the Constitution or the law.

All acts in violation of the Constitution and law must be investigated.

The rule of law is practiced to build China into a socialist country with the rule of law.

(8) The system of ethnic regional autonomy

All ethnic groups are equal. All prejudice and oppression against any ethnic group is forbidden. All behaviors harmful to ethnic unity and aimed at ethnic separation are forbidden.

2. The position and rights of the citizen in the political life of the country

(1) All citizens are equal before the law.

(2) The right to vote and stand for election

All citizens who have reached the age of 18 have the right to vote and stand for election, regardless of ethnic status, race, sex, occupation, family background, religious belief, education, property status or length of residence, except persons deprived of political rights according to law.

(3) The freedom of speech and thought

All citizens enjoy freedom of speech, of the press, or assembly, of association, of procession and of demonstration

(4) The freedom of religious belief

Citizens enjoy the freedom of religious belief.

No state organ, public organization or individual may compel citizens to believe in, or not to believe in, any religion.

(5) Inviolable freedom of the person

No citizen may be arrested except with the approval or by decision of a people's procuratorate or by decision of a people's court, and arrests must be made by a public security organ.

Unlawful detention or deprivation or restriction of citizens' freedom of the person by other means is prohibited, and unlawful search of the person of citizens is prohibited.

The personal dignity of citizens is inviolable, so are their residences.

(6) Freedom of correspondence

The freedom and privacy of correspondence of citizens are protected by law.

No organization or individual may, on any ground, infringe upon citizens' freedom and privacy of correspondence, except in cases where, to meet the needs of state security or of criminal investigation, public security or procuratorial organs are permitted to censor correspondence in accordance with procedures prescribed by law.

(7) The right to criticize and make suggestions

Citizens have the right to criticize and make suggestions

regarding any state organ or functionary. They have the right to make to relevant state organs complaints or charges against, or exposures of, any state organ or functionary for violation of the law or dereliction of duty.

(8) The right to compensation

Citizens who have suffered losses as a result of infringement of their civic rights by any state organ or functionary have the right to compensation in accordance with law.

(9) The right to work

Citizens have the right as well as duty to work.

The state should, through various channels, create conditions for employment, enhance occupational safety and health, improve working conditions and, on the basis of expanded production, increase remuneration for work and welfare benefits.

(10) The right to welfare

Citizens have the right to material assistance from the state and society when they are old, ill or disabled.

The state and society ensure the livelihood of disabled members of the armed forces, provide pensions to the families of martyrs and give preferential treatment to the families of military personnel.

The state and society help make arrangements for the work, livelihood and education of the blind, deaf-mutes and other handicapped citizens.

(11) The right to receive education

Citizens have the right and duty to receive education.

(12) The freedom to engage in academic studies and literary creation

Citizens have the freedom to engage in scientific research, literary and artistic creation and other cultural pursuits.

(13) The equality of men and women

Women enjoy equal rights with men in all spheres of life, in political, economic, cultural, social and family life.

(14) Both husband and wife have the duty to practice family planning.

(15) Citizens have the obligation to pay taxes in accordance with the law.

(16) Citizens have the obligation to perform military service and join the militia in accordance with the law.

II. The interpretation and revision of the Constitution and the system of supervision of its implementation

1. The right of interpretation of the Constitution

The right to interpret the Constitution rests with the Standing Committee of the National People's Congress.

2. The amendment of the Constitution

The National People's Congress holds the right to make amendments to the Constitution.

The revision of the Constitution shall be proposed by the Standing Committee of the National People's Congress or more than one-fifth of the delegates to the National People's Congress and it must be approved by a two-thirds majority of a session of the National People's Congress.

3. The system of supervision

The National People's Congress has the duty to supervise the enforcement of the Constitution.

The National People's Congress has the right to change or withdraw interpretations to the Constitution by the Standing Committee of the National People's Congress.

The System of People's Congress

The Nature and Position of the System of People's Congress

The system of people's congress is an organizational form for the state power in China. It is China's fundamental political system.

The power in the People's Republic of China belongs to the people and the organ for the people to exercise state power is the National People's Congress and local people's congresses at all levels.

The National People's Congress (NPC) and local people's congresses are established through democratic elections, responsible to and supervised by the people.

State administrative, judicial and procuratorial organs are created by, responsible to and supervised by the people's congresses.

The National People's Congress is the highest organ of state power. Local people's congresses are local organs of state power.

The National People's Congress

1. The composition and term of office of the NPC

The NPC is composed of deputies elected from the provinces, autonomous regions and municipalities directly under the Central Government and deputies elected by the armed forces.

Deputies to the NPC are organized into delegations according to the units they are elected from. Each delegation is headed y a chairman and vice chairmen.

All the ethnic minorities are entitled to appropriate representation.

The NPC is elected for a term of five years.

The Standing Committee of the NPC must ensure the completion of election of deputies to the succeeding NPC two months prior to the expiration of the term of office of the current NPC. Should extraordinary circumstances prevent such an election, it may be postponed and the term of office of the current NPC extended by the decision of a vote of more than two-thirds of all those on the Standing Committee of the current NPC. The election of deputies to the succeeding NPC must be completed within one year after the termination of such extraordinary circumstances.

The NPC meets in session once a year and is convened by its Standing Committee.

A session of the NPC may be convened at any time the Standing Committee deems it necessary or when more than one-fifth of the deputies to the NPC so propose.

2. The functions and powers of the NPC

The NPC exercises the following functions and powers:

(1) to amend the Constitution;

The amendment of the Constitution shall be proposed by the Standing Committee of the NPC or more than one-fifth of the deputies to the NPC and can only be adopted by a majority of no less than two-thirds of the deputies to the NPC.

(2) to supervise the enforcement of the Constitution;

(3) to enact and amend basic laws governing criminal offences, civil affairs, the state organs and other matters;

(4) to elect the President and the Vice President of the People's Republic of China;

(5) to decided on the choice of the Premier of the State Council upon nomination by the President, and on the choice of the Vice Premiers, State Councilors, Ministers in charge of ministries or commissions, the Auditor-General and the Secretary-general of the State Council upon nomination by the Premier;

(6) to elect the Chairman of the Central Military commission and, upon nomination by the Chairman, to decide on the choice of all other members of the Central Military Commission;

(7) to elect the President of the Supreme People's Court;

(8) to elect the Procurator-General of the Supreme People's Procuratorate;

(9) to examine and approve the plan for national economic and social development and the report on its implementation;

(10) to examine and approve the state budget and the report on its implementation;

(11) to alter or annul inappropriate decisions of the Standing Committee of the NPC;

(12) to approve the establishment of provinces, autonomous regions, and municipalities directly under the Central Government;

(13) to decide on the establishment of special administrative regions and the systems to be instituted there;

(14) to decide on questions of war and peace; and

(15) to exercise such other functions and powers as the highest organ of state power should exercise.

(16) The NPC has the right to remove the following functionaries:

1) The Chairman and Vice Chairman of the People's Republic of China;

2) The Premier of the State Council, the Vice Premiers, State Councilors, Ministers in charge of the ministries or commissions, the Auditor-General and the Secretary-general of the State Council;

3) The Chairman, Vice Chairman and other members of the Central Military Commission;

4) The President of the Supreme People's Court; and

5) The Procurator-General of the Supreme People's Procuratorate.

The Standing Committee of the NPC

The Standing Committee of the NPC is the permanent organ of the NPC. When the NPC is not in session, the Standing Committee performs the right of the highest organ of state power. It is responsible to and reports to the NPC.

1. The composition and term of office of the Standing Committee of the NPC

The Standing Committee of the NPC is composed of the Chairman, Vice Chairmen, Secretary-general and members.

Ethnic minorities are entitled to appropriate representation on the Standing Committee.

The NPC elects and has the power to recall members of the Standing Committee.

Those on the Standing Committee shall not serve in state administrative, judicial and procuratorial organs.

The term of office of the Standing Committee corresponds with that of the NPC and it shall exercise its power until a succeeding Standing Committee is elected by the succeeding NPC.

The Chairman and Vice Chairmen of the NPC shall not serve more than two consecutive terms.

2. The functions and powers of the Standing Committee

The Standing Committee of NPC exercises the following functions and powers:

(1) to interpret the Constitution and supervise its enforcement;

(2) to enact and amend laws, with the exception of those which should be enacted by the NPC;

(3) to partially supplement and amend, when the NPC is not in session, laws enacted by the NPC provided that the basic principles of these laws are not contravened;

(4) to interpret laws;

(5) to review and approve, when the NPC is not in session, partial adjustments to the plan for national economic and social development or to the state budget that prove necessary in the course of their implementation;

(6) to supervise the work of the State Council, the Central Military Commission, the Supreme People's Court and the Supreme People's Procuratorate;

(7) to annul those administrative rules and regulations, decisions or orders of the State Council that contravene the Constitution or the law;

(8) to annul those local regulations or decisions of the organs of state power of provinces, autonomous regions, and municipalities directly under the Central Government that contravene the Constitution, the law or the administrative rules and regulations;

(9) to decide, when the NPC is not in session, on the choice of Ministers in charge of ministries or commissions, the Auditor-General or the Secretary-general of the State Council upon nomination by the Premier of the State Council;

(10) to decide, upon nomination by the Chairman of the Central Military Commission, on the choice of other members of the Commission, when the NPC is not in session;

(11) to appoint or remove, at the recommendation of the President of the Supreme People's Court, the Vice Presidents and Judges of the Supreme People's Court, members of its Judicial Committee and the President of the Military Court;

(12) to appoint or remove, at the recommendation of the Procurator-General of the Supreme People's Procuratorate, the Deputy Procurators-General and the procurators of the Supreme People's Procuratorate, members of its Procuratorial Committee and the Chief Procurator of the military procuratorate, and to approve the appointment or removal of the chief procurators of the people's procuratorates of provinces, autonomous regions, and municipalities directly under the Central Government;

(13) to decide on the appointment or recall of plenipotentiary representatives abroad;

(14) to decide on the ratification or abrogation of treaties and important agreements concluded with foreign states;

(15) to institute systems of titles and ranks for military and diplomatic personnel and of other specific titles and ranks;

(16) to institute state medals and titles or honor and decide on their conferment;

(17) to decide on the granting of special pardons;

(18) to decide, when the NPC is not in session, on the proclamation of a state of war in the event of an armed attack on the country or in fulfillment of international treaty obligations concerning common defence against aggression;

(19) to decide on general mobilization or partial mobilization;

(20) to decide on the imposition of martial law throughout the country or in particular provinces, autonomous regions, or municipalities directly under the Central Government; and

(21) to exercise such other functions and powers as the NPC may assign to it.

3. Organs of the Standing Committee

The Chairman of the Standing Committee of the NPC directs the work of the Standing Committee and convenes its meetings. The Vice Chairmen and the Secretary-general assist the Chairman in his work.

The Chairman, Vice Chairmen and Secretary-general constitute the Council of Chairmen which handles the important day-to-day work of the Standing Committee of the NPC.

The Standing Committee of the NPC establishes a deputy credentials examination committee to examine the credentials of the deputies to the current NPC through by-elections and those newly elected to the succeeding NPC.

The credentials examination committee is composed of the chairman, vice chairman and members, nominated from among the members of the Standing Committee by the Council of Chairmen and agreed upon by the plenary session of the Standing Committee.

The NPC establishes special committees to examine, discuss and draw up relevant bills and draft solutions under the direction of the NPC and its Standing Committee.

When the NPC is not in session, its special committees work under the direction of the Standing Committee of the NPC.

The 9th NPC has established nine special committees, namely the ethnic groups committee, the law committee, the finance and economic committee, the education, science, culture and health committee, the foreign affairs committee, the overseas Chinese committee, the civil and judicial affairs committee, the environment and resources protection committee and the agriculture and rural areas committee.

Normally, the special committees are chaired by Vice Chairmen or members of the Standing Committee of the NPC.

The NPC and its Standing Committee may, when they deem it necessary, appoint committees of inquiry into specific questions and adopt relevant resolutions in the light of their reports.

Local People's Congresses and their Standing Committees

People's congresses are established in provinces, autonomous regions, municipalities directly under the Central Government, autonomous prefectures, counties, autonomous counties, cities, municipal districts, townships, ethnic townships and towns. Standing committees are established at people's congresses at and above the county level.

1. *The term of office of local people's congresses*

The term of office of people's congresses of provinces, autonomous regions and municipalities directly under the Central Government and cities divided into districts is five years.

The term of office of the people's congresses of counties, autonomous counties, cities not divided into districts, municipal districts, townships, ethnic townships, and towns is three years.

2. *The functions and powers of local people's congresses*

Local people's congresses at various levels ensure the observance and implementation of the Constitution and the law and the administrative rules and regulations in their respective administrative areas. Within the limits of their authority as prescribed by law, they adopt and issue resolutions and examine and decide on plans for local economic and cultural development and for the development of public services.

Local people's congresses at and above the county level shall examine and approve the plans for economic and social development and the budgets of their respective administrative areas and examine and approve the reports on their implementation. They have the power to alter or annul inappropriate decisions of their own standing committees.

The people's congresses of provinces, autonomous regions, municipalities directly under the Central Government, of cities which are capitals of the provinces or autonomous regions as well as large cities approved by the State Council have the right to adopt local regulations in the light of their regional political, economic and cultural characteristics.

Local people's congresses at their respective levels elect and have the power to recall governors and deputy governors, or mayors and deputy mayors, or heads and deputy heads of counties, districts, townships and towns.

Local people's congresses at and above the county level elect and have the power to recall presidents of people's courts and chief procurators of people's procuratorates at the corresponding level.

The election or recall of chief procurators of people's procuratorates shall be reported to the chief procurators of the people's procucratorates at the next higher level for submission to the standing committees of the people's congresses at the corresponding level for approval.

3. The composition, functions and powers of the standing committees of local people's congresses

The standing committee of a local people's congress at and above the county level is composed of a chairman, vice chairmen and members, and is responsible and reports on its work to the people's congress at the corresponding level.

A local people's congress at or above the county level elects and has the power to recall members of its standing committee.

No one on the standing committee of a local people's congress at or above the county level shall hold office in state administrative, judicial and procuratorial organs.

The standing committee of a local people's congress at or above the county level discusses and decides on major issues in all fields of work in its administrative areas; supervises the work of the people's government, people's court and people's procuratorate at the corresponding level; annuls inappropriate decisions and orders of the people's government at the corresponding level; annuls inappropriate resolutions of the people's congress at the next lower level; decides on the appointment or removal of functionaries of state organs within the limits of its authority as prescribed by law; and, when the people's congress at the corresponding level is not in session, recalls individual deputies to the people's congress at the next higher level and elects individual deputies to fill vacancies in that people's congress.

The standing committees of people's congresses of the provinces, autonomous regions, municipalities directly under the Central Government, cities which are capitals of provinces or autonomous regions as well as large cities approved by the State Council have the power to adopt local regulations in the light of the local regional political, economic and cultural characteristics, when the people's congresses at the corresponding level are not in session.

People's Congresses of Townships, Ethnic Townships and Towns

The term of office of people's congresses of townships, ethnic townships and towns is three years. Such a people's congress establishes a presidium headed by the chairman and vice chairmen. The presidium is responsible for convening the meetings of the people's congress.

The functions and powers of the people's congresses of townships, ethnic townships and towns mainly include the following:

1. *The power to examine and decide on major issues*

To decide on the plans for the construction of local economy, cultural undertakings and public understandings, in accordance with national plans; to examine and approve local financial budgets and report on the implementation of the budgets; and to decide on the implementation plans for civil work in their own regions.

2. *The power to elect, appoint and remove local functionaries*

To elect or recall the heads and deputy heads of the townships, ethnic townships and towns.

Candidates for the heads and deputy heads of the townships, ethnic townships and towns are to be nominated by the presidiums of the people's congresses or no less than ten deputies.

The presidiums or more than one-fifth of the deputies to the people's congresses of the townships, ethnic townships and towns may propose the removal of the above-mentioned functionaries when the people's congresses are in session. The proposal of removal are submitted to the congresses by the presidiums.

All elections are by secret ballot.

3. The power of supervision

To examine the work report of the governments of the townships, ethnic townships and towns, annul their inappropriate decisions and decrees, and recall or remove functionaries making up the governments of the townships, ethnic townships and towns.

Deputies to the People's Congresses

1. The election of deputies

Deputies to the NPC are elected by the people's congresses of the provinces, autonomous regions and municipalities directly under the Central Government and by the armed forces.

Deputies to the people's congresses of the provinces, autonomous regions, municipalities directly under the Central Government and cities divided into districts are elected by the people's congresses at the next lower level.

Deputies to the people's congresses of counties, cities not divided into districts, municipal districts, townships, ethnic townships and towns are elected directly by the electorates.

2. The rights of the deputies

(1) During the session

1) Right to draft proposals for bills;

2) Right to raise suggestions, criticisms and put forward opinions;

3) Right to vote in election and decide on appointment;

4) Right to examine issues;

5) Right to propose the recall of functionaries;

6) Right to raise bills for questioning and conduct hearings;

7) Right to draft suggestions;

8) Right to vote; and

9) Right to impunity.

(2) Not in session

1) Right to maintain contact with original voting units;

2) Right to inspect;

3) Right to propose provisional sessions;

4) Right to audit other meetings;

5) Right to participate in committees for investigating specified issues;

6) Right to sit in meetings of the people's congress and its standing committee of the original unit the deputy is elected from;

7) Right of special protection of the person; and

8) Right to privileges for deputies.

The Party in Power

The Communist Party is the sole party in power in China.

Founded in 1921, the Communist Party of China (CPC) established the People's Republic of China in 1949 through years of armed struggle.

The CPC now has more than 60 million members in more than 3 million grassroots organizations.

The CPC has established formal (through elections within the Party) and informal (appointed by the organization of the higher level) organizations within the Chinese government and various levels and walks of life in the country.

The Nature of the CPC

The CPC is the vanguard of the Chinese working class, the faithful representative of the interests of the Chinese people of all ethnic groups and the core of leadership over the socialist cause of China. CPC's maximum program of long objective is to realize the Communist social system and the minimum program at present is to build socialism with Chinese characteristics.

The CPC takes Marxism-Leninism, Mao Zedong Thought and Deng Xiaoping Theory as the guidance of its actions.

The CPC's basic line for the primary stage of socialism is to unite with and lead the people of all ethnic groups in the endeavour to build China into a prosperous, strong, democratic and highly civilized modern socialist state by taking economic development as the central task, adhering to the Four Cardinal Principles (adherence to the socialist road, the people's democratic dictatorship, the leadership of the Communist Party, and Marxism-Leninism and Mao Zedong Thought), persisting in reform and opening up, developing the spirit of self-reliance and pioneering enterprises with painstaking efforts.

Four Basic Demands for the Building of the Party

First, uphold the Party's basic line;

Second, adhere to the principle of emancipating he mind and seeking truth from facts;

Third, persist in serving the people wholeheartedly; and

Fourth, uphold democratic centralism.

The Political and Organizational Principle of Democratic Centralism

1. *The basic principle of democratic centralism*

(1) The individual Party member is subordinate to a Party organization, the minority is subordinate to the majority, the lower level organization is subordinate to the higher level, each organization and all members of the whole Party are subordinate to the Party's National Congress and the Central Committee.

(2) Leading bodies at various levels of the Party, except for their agencies and for leading Party groups in non-Party organizations, shall all be elected.

(3) The Party's supreme leading organ is the National Party Congress and the Central Committee it elects. The Party's leading bodies at all levels in the localities are the Party congresses at these levels and the committees they elect. Party committees at all levels are accountable and report work to the congresses at their respective levels.

(4) Party organizations at a higher level shall frequently listen to the opinions of lower organizations and Party members in general and solve their problems without delay. Lower Party

organizations shall ask for instructions from and report on their work to higher organizations, and also be responsible for solving problems independently within the scope of their official duties. Lower and higher organizations shall keep each other informed, and support and supervise each other. Party organizations at all levels shall help Party members to have a better understanding of and more participation in inner-Party affairs.

(5) Party committees at all levels carry out a system that combines collective leadership with divisions of work and personal responsibility. Major issues shall be discussed and decided collectively by the Party committee; and committee members shall earnestly perform their duties in accordance with the collective decisions and divisions of work.

(6) The Party prohibits personality cult in any form. There must be a guarantee for the activities of Party leaders to be placed under the supervision of the Party and people, while at the same time safeguarding the prestige of all leaders representing the interests of the Party and people.

2. *Organizational principles*

(1) The election of delegates to Party congresses at all levels and of committees is by secret ballot.

No organization or individual shall use any method to force voters to elect or not to elect a certain person.

If anything in violation of the Party Constitution occurs during the election of local Party congresses at various levels and grassroots congresses, a Party committee at the next higher level, after investigation and verification, shall make a decision invalidating the election and adopting appropriate measures; the decision then shall be reported to the Party committee at a still higher level for examination and approval, and its implementation formally declared.

(2) The party Central Committee and local committees at various levels, when necessary, call a representative conference to discuss and decide on major issues needing timely solutions. The number of delegates to a representative conference and the method of election of delegates to a representative conference and the method of electing them shall be decided by the committee which convenes the conference.

(3) Establishment of a new Party organization or dissolution of an existing one must be decided by a Party organization at the next higher level.

(4) The Party Central Committee and local committees at various levels may set up agencies.

(5) When the Party congresses at various levels and grassroots congresses are not in session, the Party organization at the next higher level, when it deems necessary, may transfer or assign responsible members to the leading Party group at a lower level.

(6) When Party leading bodies at various levels make decisions on important issues related to lower organizations, under normal conditions they shall solicit the opinions of the latter. They shall ensure that lower organizations can normally exercise their function and powers. Unless under special conditions, the leading bodies at a higher level shall not interfere in matters which should be handled by lower organizations.

(7) Only the Party Central Committee has the right to decide on major issues of national policy; Party organizations of various departments and localities may put forward their suggestions to the Central Committee, but must not make decisions without authorization or publish their own proposals in public.

(8) Lower Party organizations must firmly carry out the decisions of higher organizations.

Lower organizations may request a change in the decision of the higher organization if they think it does not conform to conditions in their locality or department; if the higher organization insists on its original decision, the lower organizations must carry it out and shall not openly publicize differing opinions, but they have the right to report the matter to the organizations at a still higher level.

(9) The newspapers, magazines and other mass media of Party organizations at various levels must publicize the Party's line, principles, policies and resolutions.

(10) In discussing and deciding issues, a Party organization must apply the principle of subordinating the minority to the majority. Decisions on important issues shall be put to the vote. Serious consideration shall be given to the different opinions of a few people. If a dispute over an important issue arises and the

number of people on both sides is approximately the same, except when in an emergency the opinions of the majority must be carried out, finalizing a decision shall be deferred. Under special circumstances, a report of the case under dispute may be referred to the organization at the next higher level for a ruling.

(11) If an important proposal published by an individual Party member on behalf of a Party organization exceeds the scope of the original decision, the matter shall be submitted to the Party organization for discussion and decision, or instructions shall be sought from the Party organization at the next higher level. No Party member, whether of high or low position, can individually decide on a major issue; if, in an emergency, a decision must be made by an individual, the matter must be promptly reported to the Party organization afterwards.

Organizations of the Party

Central organizations of the Party

(1) The National Party Congress and the Central Committee

The central leading organ of the Party is the National Party Congress and the Central Committee it elects. The Central Committee is accountable to and reports its work to the National Congress.

The National Party Congress, held once every five years, is convened by the Central Committee. If the Central Committee deems it necessary, or over one-third of the provincial-level organizations express a demand, the congress may be held ahead of schedule; and if there is no special situation, its convening shall not be postponed.

The number of delegates to the National Party Congress and the method of election are decided by the Central Committee.

The Central Committee is elected for a term of five years. If the National Congress is held ahead of schedule or deferred, its term of office shall be changed accordingly.

The functions and powers of the National Party Congress are:

1) To hear and examine the report of the Central Committee;

2) To hear and examine the report of the Central Commission for Discipline Inspection;

3) To discuss and decide on major issues of the Party;

4) To revise the Party Constitution;

5) To elect the Central Committee; and

6) To elect the Central Commission for Discipline Inspection.

When the National Congress is not in session, the Central Committee implements the resolutions of the National Congress, leads all the work of the Party, and represents the CPC outside the Party.

Members and alternate members of the Central Committee must have a Party standing of at least five years.

The number of members and alternate members of the Central Committee is decided by the National Congress. If posts of members of the Central Committee fall vacant, the vacancies shall be filled in proper order by alternate members in accordance with the number of votes they gain.

A plenary session of the Central Committee is held at least once a year by the Political Bureau of the Central Committee.

(2) The Political Bureau, its Standing Committee, the General Secretary, the Central Military Commission and the Secretariat

The leading organs of the Central Committee are the Political Bureau, its Standing Committee and general secretary of the Central Committee.

The Political Bureau of the Party Central Committee, the Standing Committee of the Political Bureau and the general secretary of the Central Committee are elected by the plenary session of the Central Committee.

The general secretary of the Central Committee must be elected from among members of the Standing Committee of the Political Bureau of the Central Committee.

When the plenum of the Central Committee is not in session, the Political Bureau of the Central Committee and its Standing Committee exercise the functions and powers of the Central Committee.

The general secretary of the Central Committee is responsible for calling sessions of both the Political Bureau of the Central Committee and its Standing Committee, and is in charge of the work of the Secretariat of the Central Committee.

The central military leading organ of the Party is the Central Military Commission.

Members of the Central Military Commission of the Party are decided on by the Central Committee.

The Secretariat of the Central Committee is the administrative body of the Political Bureau and its Standing Committee. Its members are nominated by the Standing Committee of the Political Bureau of the Central Committee and approved by the plenary session of the Central Committee.

Leading bodies and leaders of the Central Committee elected by each Central Committee shall continue to take charge of the day-to-day work of the Party while the next National Congress is in session, until a new central leading body and central leaders are elected by the next Central Committee.

2. *Local organizations of the Party*

Party congresses of various provinces, autonomous regions, municipalities directly under the central government, cities with districts and autonomous prefectures are held once every five years.

Local Party congresses at various levels are called by Party committees at the same level. Under special conditions, they may be held ahead of time or postponed with approval from the committee at the next higher level.

The number of delegates of local Party congresses at various levels and the method of election are decided by the Party committees at the same level and reported to the Party committee at the next higher level for approval.

The functions and powers of local Party congresses at various levels are:

1) To hear and examine the report of the committee at the same level;

2) To hear and examine the report of the discipline inspection commission at the same level;

3) To discuss major issues within the scope of the region and pass resolutions; and

4) To elect Party committees and party discipline inspection commissions at the same level.

When congresses are not in session, local Party committees at various levels carry out directions of the Party organizations at the next higher level and the resolutions of Party congresses at the same level, lead the work of the locality, and report work regularly to the higher Party committee.

Party committees of various provinces, autonomous regions, municipalities under the Central Government, cities divided into districts and autonomous prefectures are elected for a term of five years. Members and alternate members of these committees must have a Party standing of at least five years.

Party committees of counties (banners), autonomous counties, cities without districts and districts under the jurisdiction of a city are elected for a term of five years. Members and alternate members of these committees must have a Party standing of at least three years.

If local Party congresses at various levels are held ahead of time or postponed, the term of office of the committees they elect shall be changed accordingly.

The number of members and alternate members of the local Party committees at various levels shall be decided respectively by the committee at the next higher level. Vacancies of the posts for members of local Party committees at various levels shall be filled in proper order by alternate members in accordance with the number of votes gained.

Plenary sessions of local Party committees at various levels shall be held at least twice a year.

The plenary sessions of local Party committees at various levels elect their standing committees, secretaries and deputy secretaries, and report the results to the Party committee at the next higher level for approval.

The standing committees of local Party committees at various levels exercise the functions and powers of the committees when the plenums of the committees are not in session.

They continue to be in charge of the day-to-day work while the next congress is in session, until the new standing committees are elected.

Regional Party committees and organizations equivalent to regional committees are Party agencies of provinces and autonomous regions within the scope of several counties, autonomous counties and cities. Authorized by provincial and autonomous regional committees, they lead the work of the areas concerned.

3. Grassroots organizations of the Party

A grassroots Party organization shall be set up in enterprises, rural areas, organizations, schools, scientific research institutes, neighborhoods, People's Liberation Army companies and other basic units on the mainland in which there are three or more full Party members.

The grassroots Party organizations are combat bastions of the Party among grassroots social organizations and the foundation of all the Party's work and combat effectiveness.

Grassroots Party organizations respectively set up grassroots Party committees, general Party branch committees and Party branch committees in accordance with the requirements of the work and the number of Party members, after approval by the next higher level Party organization. Grassroots Party committees are elected by meetings or congresses of Party members. General Party branch committees and Party branch committees are elected by meetings of Party members.

The grassroots Party committees are elected for a term of three or four years. The general Party branch committees and the Party branch committees are elected for a term of two or three years.

The names of the secretaries and deputy secretaries elected by grassroots Party committees, general branch committees and branch committees shall be submitted to the Party organization at the next higher level for approval.

4. Leading Party groups

A leading Party group can be established in the leading bodies of central and local state organs, people's organizations, economic and cultural organizations and other non-Party organizations.

The tasks for the leading Party groups are to take as their main responsibility the realization of the Party's line, principles and policies; discuss and decide on major issues of their own department; unite with non-Party officials and masses in fulfilling the tasks assigned by the Party and the state; and direct the work of the Party organizations of the organs and the work units directly under them.

Members of a leading Party group are appointed by the Party committee that approves the establishment of the leading Party group. The leading Party group consists of a secretary and deputy secretaries.

The leading Party group must follow the leadership of the Party committee which approves its establishment.

5. Discipline inspection organizations of the Party

Discipline inspection organizations of the Party consist of the Central Commission for Discipline Inspection, local Party commissions for discipline inspection at various levels and the grassroots Party commissions for discipline inspection.

The Central Commission for Discipline Inspection works under the leadership of the Party Central Committee.

The local Party commissions for discipline inspection at various levels and the grassroots Party commissions for discipline inspection work under the dual leadership of the Party committee at the same level and Party commission for discipline inspection at the next higher level.

The term of each Party commission for discipline inspection is the same as that of the Party committee at the same level.

The plenary session of the Central Commission for Discipline Inspection elects its standing committee, secretary and deputy secretaries and reports this to the Party Central Committee for approval.

The plenary sessions of local Party commissions for discipline inspection at various levels elect the standing committee and secretary and deputy secretaries, and the results are passed by the Party committee at the same level and reported to the Party committee at the next higher level for approval.

Whether a discipline inspection commission or discipline inspection members for a grassroots Party committee shall be established or put into position is to be decided by a Party organization at the next higher level in light of specific conditions.

A general Party branch committee and a Party branch committee shall include discipline inspection members.

The Central Commission for Discipline Inspection may, if needed, accredit a discipline inspection group or discipline inspectors to central Party and state organs.

Leaders of the discipline inspection group or discipline inspectors may attend, as non-voting members, related conferences organized by Party leaders of the organ concerned.

Their work must be supported by the Party leaders and organizations of the organ concerned.

Party Members

Members of the CPC are vanguard fighters of the Chinese working class with communist consciousness.

Chinese workers, farmers, soldiers, intellectuals and other revolutionaries at 18 full years of age, who accept the Party Program and Party Constitution, are willing to participate in one Party organization and actively work in it, carry out Party resolutions and pay regular Party dues, may apply for membership in the CPC.

Party members must be admitted through a Party branch according to the principles of admitting members individually only, without exception.

Under special circumstances, the Party Central Committee, and provincial, autonomous regional and municipal Party committees can directly accept Party members.

An applicant must fill in the form for Party membership and have two full Party members as sponsors. The applicant can become a full Party member only when his or her application has been passed by the Party branch meeting and approved by the Party organization at the next higher level, and only after assessment over a probationary period.

Each Party member, regardless of whether his or her post is high or low, must be entered into a Party branch, group or other specific organization, and must participate in the Party's regular organizational activities.

Leading Party officials must also participate in democratic meetings of Party committees or leading Party groups.

Party members are free to withdraw from the Party. When

a Party member asks to withdraw from the Party, following discussion at a general meeting of the Party branch concerned, his or her name must be declared struck from the rolls, and the matter reported to the next higher level Party organization for the record.

When a Party member neglects to perform the duties of a Party member and fails to meet the requirements for a Party member, the Party branch shall educate him or her and require that he or she correct his or her shortcomings within a time limit; if after education he or she still shows no change, the Party branch shall persuade him or her to withdraw from the Party.

The matter of persuading a Party member to withdraw shall be discussed and decided by a general meeting of the Party branch concerned and reported to the Party organization at the next higher level for approval.

If the Party member persists in refusing to withdraw from the Party after being advised, the matter shall be referred to the Party branch for discussion at a general meeting, a decision taken to have his or her name struck from the rolls, and a report made to the Party organization at the next higher level for approval.

When a Party member has a difference of opinion concerning a Party resolution or policy, he or she may declare reservations on the premise of resolute implementation, and may forward his or her opinion to a higher organization up to the Central Committee.

CPC's Leadership of the Country

CPC's leadership over the country is mainly political, ideological and organizational, as reflected mainly in the following aspects:

First, organize and exercise leadership over the country's legislative and law enforcement activities.

Second, maintain leadership over the armed forces.

Third, provide leadership and manage the work of officials.

Fourth, organize and mobilize the society, and

Fifth, give importance to ideological and political work.

China's Political System

The Constitutional System

The fundamental law of the state. The current constitution was adopted by the 5th National Peopleâ€™s Congress on December 4, 1982.

The System of People's Congress

China's fundamental political system; an organizational form for the state power.

The National People's Congress (NPC) is the highest authority of state power while local peopleâ€™s congresses are the local authorities. Both authorities are elected by the people.

The Party in Power

The Communist Party. Founded in 1921, the Communist Party of China (CPC) established the Peopleâ€™s Republic of China in 1949.

The System of Multi-Party Cooperation and Political Consultation

The CPC is the only power in the People's Republic of China, but the eight other political parties may take part in state affairs under the recognized leadership of the CPC.

The Central Administrative System

Composed of the central administrative organs under the National People's Congress and the central administrative organs leadership over local administrative organs.

Central administrative organ: State Council of the People's Republic of China. Highest administrative organ of the state: State Council

The Local Administrative System

Makes local administration possible by establishing administrative regional divisions and local administrative organs.

The System of the Head of State

The head of state is the President of the Peoples Republic of China. The term lasts five years and no more than two consecutive terms can be served. Duties include various domestic powers as well as handling foreign affairs.

The System of Civil Servant

Civil servants are those that instigate power in state administrative organs. Duties include the execution of laws and public services.

The Election System

How citizens choose the state's public servants. Includes the peoples right to vote and stand for election, function of the powers that oversee the election, procedures of direct and indirect election, election expenditure and punishment of violations.

The System of Self-Government of Ethnic Autonomous Areas

Areas heavily populated with ethnic minorities are managed by self-government under national leadership. The administrative status of these areas is determined by size and population.

Autonomous regions are equal to provinces, autonomous prefectures are equal to prefectural-level cities, and autonomous counties are equal to counties.

Special Administrative Regions

When needed, the state establishes special administrative regions according to the law enacted by the National Peoples Congress.

The political system includes a chief executive, administrative organs, a legislative council, and judicial organs.

8

Socioeconomic Dimensions of the Chinese Political System

Structure of the State: China

The Communist Party of China (CPC) is the party in power in the country. The CPC has both central and local organizations. At the top is the Central Committee and, while when it is not in session, the Political Bureau and its Standing Committee exercise the power of the Central Committee. Both the Political Bureau and its Standing Committee are elected by the plenary session of the Central Committee. The CPC is a unified entity organized according to its program, constitution and the principle of democratic centralism. The Constitution of the Communist Party of China stipulates that any Chinese worker, farmer, member of the armed forces, intellectual and any advanced element of other social strata who has reached the age of 18 and who accepts the program and constitution of the CPC and is willing to join and work in one of the Party organizations, carry out the Party decisions and pay membership dues regularly may apply for membership in the CPC.

The Military

The Central Military Commission of the People's Republic of China is the highest state military organ with the responsibility of commanding the entire armed forces in the country. Led by a chairman and consisting of vice chairmen and members, the Commission is elected for a term of five years and can stand for reelection.

The Head of the State

The presidency of the People's Republic of China, as the head of the state, is an independent organ of the state which as an office of state power itself does not decide on state affairs, but exercises its power according to decisions of the National People's Congress and its Standing Committee.

The Organ of State Power

The National People's Congress (NPC) of the People's Republic of China is the highest organ of state power. The Standing Committee of the NPC is the permanent organ of the NPC. The term of office of the NPC and its Standing Committee is five years. The NPC and its Standing Committee are empowered with the rights of legislation, decision, supervision, election and removal.

The State Administrative Organ

The administrative branch of the state power is the Central People's Government and local people's governments. The State Council, another term for the Central People's Government, is the supreme administrative organ of state power.

The State Trial Organ

The people's courts are the trial organs of the state. The trial system consists of the Supreme People's Court, local people's courts and special people's courts such as the military court.

The State Prosecution Organ

The people's procuratorates are the legal supervision organs of the state. The prosecution system consists of the Supreme People's Procuratorate, local people's procuratorates and special people's procuratorates such as the military procuratorate.

The Political Consultative Organ

The Chinese People's Political Consultative Conference is a united front organization under the leadership of the Communist Party of China and an organ for various other political parties, mass organizations and personages of various social circles to take part in the running of the state.

Social Organizations

Mass organizations are an important component in the political life in China. Despite the fact that they are non-governmental organizations, the All-China Federation of Trade Unions, the Communist Youth League of China and the All-China Women's Federation exercise, to a fairly large extent, some of the functions of the government. As a result, the tasks, the organizational setup and posts of leaders of some mass organizations are decided by organs of the central authorities. For the same reason, these organizations receive appropriations from the state treasury for funding.

Communist Party of China

The Communist Party of China (CPC), also known as the Chinese Communist Party (CCP), is the founding and the ruling political party of the People's Republic of China (PRC) and the world's largest political party. While not a governing body recognized by the PRC's constitution, the Party's position as the supreme political authority and power in the PRC is realized through its control of all state apparatuses and of the legislative process.

The Communist Party of China was founded in May 1920 in Shanghai, and came to rule all of mainland China after defeating its rival the Kuomintang (KMT) in the Chinese Civil War. The party's 70 million members constitute 5.5% of the total population of mainland China.

Organization

The party's organizational structure was destroyed during the Cultural Revolution and rebuilt afterwards by Deng Xiaoping, who subsequently initiated "Socialism with Chinese characteristics" and brought all state apparatuses back under the control of the CPC.

Theoretically, the party's highest body is the National Congress of the Communist Party of China, which meets at least once every five years. The primary organization of power in the Communist Party which is detailed in the party constitution include:

- Central Committee, which includes:

  - o The Politburo Standing Committee, which currently consists of nine members; see current members of the Politburo Standing Committee for a complete list.
  - o The Politburo, consisting of 24 full members (including the members of the Politburo Standing Committee) and one alternate; see current members of the Politburo for a complete list.
  - o The Secretariat, the principal administrative mechanism of the CPC, headed by the General Secretary of the Communist Party of China;
  - o The Central Military Commission (a parallel organization of the government institution of the same name);
- The Central Discipline Inspection Commission, which is directly under the National Congress and on the same level with the Central Committee, charged with rooting out corruption and malfeasance among party cadres.

Other central organizations include:

- General Office
- Central Organization Department;
- Propaganda Department
- International Liaison Department; and
- United Front Department.

In addition, there are numerous commissions and leading groups, the most important of which are:

- Central Political and Legislative Affairs Committee
- Work Committee for Organs under the Central Committee
- Work Committee for Central Government Organs
- Central Financial and Economic Leading Group
- Central Leading Group for Rural Work
- Central Leading Group for Party Building
- Central Foreign Affairs Leading Group
- Central Taiwan Affairs Leading Group
- Commission for Protection of Party Secrets
- Leading Group for State Security
- Party History Research Centre

- Party Research Centre
- Central Party School.

Every five years, the Communist Party of China holds a National Congress. The latest happened on October 15, 2007. Formally, the Congress serves two functions: to approve changes to the Party constitution regarding policy and to elect a Central Committee, about 300 strong. The Central Committee in turn elects the Politburo. In practice, positions within the Central Committee and Politburo are determined before a Party Congress, and the main purpose of the Congress is to announce the party policies and vision for the direction of China in the following few years.

The party's central focus of power is the Politburo Standing Committee. The process for selecting Standing Committee members, as well as Politburo members, occurs behind the scenes in a process parallel to the National Congress. The new power structure is announced obliquely through the positioning of portraits in the *People's Daily*, the official newspaper of the Party. The number of Standing Committee members varies and has tended to increase over time. The Committee was expanded to nine at the 16th Party National Congress in 2002.

There are two other key organs of political power in the People's Republic of China: the formal government and the People's Liberation Army.

There are, in addition to decision-making roles, advisory committees, including the People's Political Consultative Conference. During the 1980s and 1990s there was a Central Advisory Commission established by Deng Xiaoping which consisted of senior retired leaders, but with their passing this has been abolished since 1990.

Internal or External Groupings

Political scientists have identified two groupings within the Communist Party leading to a structure which has been called "one party, two factions". The first is the "elitist coalition" or *Shanghai clique* which contains mainly officials who have risen from the more prosperous provinces. The second is the "populist coalition" or "Youth League faction" which consists mainly of officials who have risen from the rural interior, through the

Communist Youth League. The interaction between these two factions is largely complementary with each faction possessing a particular expertise and both committed to the continued rule of the Communist Party and not allowing intra-party factional politics threaten party unity. It has been noted that party and government positions have been assigned to create a very careful balance between these two groupings.

Within his "one party, two factions" model, Li Chen has noted that one should avoid labeling these two groupings with simplistic ideological labels, and that these two groupings do not act in a zero-sum, winner take all fashion. Neither group has the ability or will to dominate the other completely.

Membership

The party was small at first, but grew intermittently through the 1920s. Twelve voting delegates were seated at the 1st National Party Congress in 1921, as well as at the 2nd (in 1922), when they represented 195 party members. By 1923, the 420 members were represented by 30 delegates. The 1925 4th Congress had 20 delegates representing 994 members; then real growth kicked in. The 5th Congress (held in April-May 1927 as the KMT was slaughtering communists) comprised 80 voting delegates representing 57,968 members. It was at October 3, 1928 6th Congress that the now-familiar 'full' and 'alternate' structure originated, with 84 and 34 delegates, respectively. Membership was estimated at 40,000. In 1945, the 7th Congress had 547 full and 208 alternate delegates representing 1.21 million members, a ratio of one representative per 1,600 members as compared to 1:725 in 1927. After the Party defeated the Nationalists, participation at National Party Congresses became much less representative. Each of the 1026 full and 107 alternate members represented 9,470 party members (10.73 million in total) at the 1956 8th Congress. Subsequent congresses held the number of participants down despite membership growing to more than 60 million by 2000.

History

Criticism and Support

Opinions about the Communist Party of China often create unexpected political alliances and divisions, e.g: divisions among conservatives in the United States. Many of the unexpected opinions about the CPC result from its rare combination of attributes as a party formally based on Marxism which has eventually overseen a market economy, yet maintains an authoritarian political system.

Critics

- Trotskyists argue that the party was doomed to its present character, that of petty-bourgeois nationalism in the 1920s, because of the near-annihilation of the workers' movement in the KMT betrayal of 1927, which was made possible by Stalin's order that the Communists join with the KMT in a centrist coalition, effectively disarming it, which opportunity the KMT swiftly exploited to defeat the communist revolution. This slaughter forced the tiny surviving Party to switch from a workers' union-to a peasant, guerrilla-based organization, and to seek the aid of the most heterodox sources: from "patriotic capitalists" to the dreaded KMT itself, with which it openly sought to participate in a coalition government, even after the Japanese general surrender in 1945. Chinese Trotskyists from Chen Duxiu onward have called for a political revolution against what they see as an opportunist, capitalist leadership of the CPC.
- Supporters of the International Tibet Independence Movement, Falun Gong, the Republic of China (Taiwan), Taiwan independence, East Turkestan Independence Movement, neoconservatives in the United States and Japan, international human rights groups, proponents of civil liberties and freedom of expression, advocates of democracy, anarchists, along with many democratic and anti-authoritarian left-wing forces in those same countries, are among the groups which have opposed the PRC government because it is said to be a repressive single-party state regime.
- Some of the opponents of the Party within the Chinese democracy movement have tended not to argue that a strong Chinese state is inherently bad, but rather that the Communist leadership is corrupt. The Chinese New Left,

meanwhile, is a current within China that seeks to "revert China to the socialist road" – i.e., to return China to the socialist system that existed before Deng Xiaoping's reforms.

Self-criticism

Leaders of the Communist Party of China are aware that there are serious problems with corruption and with maintaining the trust of the Chinese people. However, attempts made in closed-door sessions at Fourth Plenary Session of the 17th Communist Party of China Central Committee in September 2009 to grapple with these problems produced inconclusive results although a directive which requires disclosure of investments and property holdings by party and governmental officials was passed.

Supporters

- Another school of thought argues that the worst of the abuses took place decades ago, and that the current leaders were not only unconnected with them, but were actually victims of that era. They have also argued that, while the modern Communist Party may be flawed, it is comparatively better than previous regimes, with respect to improving the general standard of living, than any other government that has governed China in the past century and can be seen in a more favourable light compared with most governments of the developing nations. As a result, the CPC has recently taken sweeping measures to regain support from the countryside, with limited success.
- In addition, some scholars contend that China has never operated under a decentralized democratic regime in its several thousand years of history, and therefore it can be argued that the present structure, albeit not up to western moral standards, is the best possible option when compared to its alternatives. A sudden transition to democracy, they contend, would result in the economic and political upheaval that occurred in the Soviet Union in the 1990s, and that by focusing on economic growth, China is setting the stage for a more gradual but sustainable transition to

a more liberal system. This group sees Mainland China as being similar to Spain in the 1960s, and South Korea and Taiwan during the 1970s. This school of thought also brings together some unlikely political allies. Not only do most intellectuals within the Chinese government follow this school of thinking, but it is also the common belief held amongst pro-free trade liberals in the West.

- Many observers from both within and outside of China have argued that the CCP has taken gradual steps towards democracy and transparency, hence arguing that it is best to give it time and room to evolve into a better government rather than forcing an abrupt change. However, other observers (like Minxin Pei) question whether these steps are genuine efforts towards democratic reform or disingenuous measures by the CCP to retain power.

Current Leadership

The Members of the Politburo Standing Committee of the Communist Party of China are:

1. Hu Jintao: President of the People's Republic of China, General Secretary of the CPC, Chairman of the Central Military Commission.
2. Wu Bangguo: Chairman of the Standing Committee of the National People's Congress
3. Wen Jiabao: Premier of the State Council of the People's Republic of China
4. Jia Qinglin: Chairman of the People's Political Consultative Conference
5. Xi Jinping: Vice President of the People's Republic of China, top-ranked member of CPC Secretariat
6. Li Keqiang: Executive Vice Premier
7. Li Changchun: "Propaganda Chief"
8. He Guoqiang: Head of Central Commission for Discipline Inspection
9. Zhou Yongkang: Head of Political and Legislative Affairs Committee.

Members of the Politburo of the CPC Central committee:

Wang Lequan, Wang Zhaoguo, Hui Liangyu, Liu Qi, Liu Yunshan, Li Changchun, Wu Yi, Wu Bangguo, Wu Guanzheng, Zhang Lichang, Zhang Dejiang, Luo Gan, Zhou Yongkang, Hu Jintao, Yu Zhengsheng, He Guoqiang, Jia Qinglin, Guo Boxiong, Cao Gangchuan, Zeng Qinghong, Zeng Peiyan, Wen Jiabao.

Alternate member of the Politburo of the CPC Central Committee: Wang Gang

Members of Secretariat of the CPC Central Committee: Zeng Qinghong, Liu Yunshan, Zhou Yongkang, He Guoqiang, Wang Gang, Xu Caihou, He Yong.

Leaders

Between 1921 and 1943 the Communist Party of China was headed by the General Secretary:

- Chen Duxiu, General Secretary 1921–1922 and 1925–1927
- Qu Qiubai, General Secretary 1927–1928
- Xiang Zhongfa, General Secretary 1928–1931
- Li Lisan, acting General Secretary 1929–1930
- Wang Ming, acting General Secretary 1931
- Bo Gu, a.k.a. Qin Bangxian, acting General Secretary 1932–1935
- Zhang Wentian a.k.a. Luo Fu, acting General Secretary 1935–1943.

In 1943 the position of Chairman of the Communist Party of China was created.

- Mao Zedong, Chairman 1943–1976
- Hua Guofeng, Chairman 1976–1981
- Hu Yaobang, Chairman 1981–1982.

In 1982, the post of Chairman was abolished, and the General Secretary, at this time held by the same man as the post of Chairman, once again became the supreme office of the Party.

- Hu Yaobang, General Secretary 1982–1987
- Zhao Ziyang, General Secretary 1987–1989
- Jiang Zemin, General Secretary 1989–2002
- Hu Jintao, General Secretary since 2002.

National Congress of the Communist Party of China

The National Congress of the Communist Party of China (simplified Chinese:-NýVqQ§NZQhQýVãNh^'YO; pinyin: *Zhôngguó GòngchÎndÎng Quánguó DàibiÎo Dàhuì*) is a party congress that is held about once every five years. The National Congress is theoretically the highest body within the Communist Party of China, but in practice important decisions are made before the meeting. Since 1987 the National Congress has always been held in the months of October or November. The venue for the event, beginning in 1956, has always been the Great Hall of the People in Beijing. In the past two decades the National Congress of the CPC has been pivotal at least as a symbolic part of leadership changes in the People's Republic of China, and therefore has gained international media attention.

Overview

The National CPC Congress should not be confused with the National People's Congress which is the legislature of the People's Republic of China. In contrast with the NPC which has become more assertive since the 1990s, the National Congress of the Communist Party has shown no signs of becoming a deliberative assembly with independent power. In addition the National Congress should not be confused with the Chinese People's Political Consultative Conference. While leadership changes in the government usually occur at the National People's Congress sessions, now held every March, leadership changes in the party occur at the Party's National Congress.

Since the mid-1980s, the Communist Party has attempted to maintain a smooth and orderly succession and avoiding a cult of personality, by having a major shift in personnel every ten years in even number party congresses, and by promoting people in preparation for this shift in odd number party congresses.

In addition, as people at the top level of the party retire, there is room for younger members of the party to move up one level. Hence the party congress is a time of a general personnel reshuffle, and the climax of negotiations that involve not only the top leadership but practically all significant political positions in China. Because of the pyramid structure of the party and the existence of mandatory retirement ages, cadres who are not promoted at a party congress are likely to face the end of their political careers. In addition to making leadership changes, the Congress also reviews and changes, if necessary, the Party's Constitution, and selects the Central Committee, a powerful decision making body. Each five-year cycle of the National People's Congress also has a series of plenums of the Central Committee which since the mid-1990s have been held more or less regularly once every year.

Since the establishment of PRC, the Congresses have occurred approximately every five years and since 1956, they have always taken place in the capital, Beijing. Each Party Congress lasted for five to ten days. Unlike Central Committee meetings which have on occasion been the focus of shifts in Party policy, Congresses have been occasions in which personnel decisions made beforehand have been announced, and ideologies and doctrines which have already been introduced are entrenched into the Party Constitution.

Similar to the practice of the NPC, the delegates to the Congress are formally selected from grassroot party organizations, and like the NPC, the system of staggered elections in which one level of the party votes for the delegates to the next higher level allows the party centre to control the election of delegates.

Deng Xiaoping

Deng Xiaoping was a prominent Chinese politician, statesman, theorist, and diplomat. As leader of the Communist Party of China, Deng became a reformer who led China towards a market economy. While Deng never held office as the head of state or the head of government, he nonetheless served as the Paramount leader of the People's Republic of China from 1978 to the early 1990s.

Born into a farming background in Guang'an, Sichuan, Deng studied and worked abroad in France in the 1920s, where he would come under the influence of Marxism. He joined the Communist Party of China in 1923. Upon his return to China he worked as a political commissar in rural regions and was considered a "revolutionary veteran" of the Long March. Following the founding of the People's Republic of China in 1949, Deng worked in Tibet and other southwestern regions to consolidate Communist control. He was also instrumental in China's economic reconstruction following the Great Leap Forward in the early

1960s. His economic policies came to odds with the political ideologies of Chairman Mao Zedong. As a result, he would be purged twice during the Cultural Revolution but regained prominence in 1978 by outmaneuvering Mao's chosen successor, Hua Guofeng.

Inheriting a country wrought with social and institutional woes left over from the Cultural Revolution and other mass political movements of the Mao era, Deng became the core of the "second generation" of Chinese leadership. He is called "the architect" of a new brand of socialist thinking, having developed Socialism with Chinese characteristics and led Chinese economic reform through a synthesis of theories that became known as the "socialist market economy". Deng opened China to foreign investment, the global market, and limited private competition. He is generally credited with advancing China into becoming one of the fastest growing economies in the world and vastly raising the standard of living.

Early Life

Deng Xiansheng, the former paramount leader of China, was born into a Hakka family in Guang'an County in Sichuan province. Deng's ancestors could be traced back to Meixian. He was educated in France, as were many notable Asian revolutionaries (such as Ho Chi Minh, Zhou Enlai, and Pol Pot), where he discovered Marxism-Leninism.

His first wife, one of his schoolmates from Moscow, died when she was 24, a few days after giving birth to Deng's first child, a baby girl, who also died. His second wife, Jin Weiying, left him after he came under political attack in 1933.

His third wife, Zhuo Lin, was the daughter of an industrialist in Yunnan Province. She became a member of the Communist Party in 1938, and a year later married Deng in front of Mao's cave dwelling in Yan'an. They had five children: three daughters (Deng Lin, Deng Nan, Deng Rong) and two sons (Deng Pufang, Deng Zhifang).

Early Career

In the summer of 1919, Deng Xiaoping graduated from the Chongqing Preparatory School. He and 80 schoolmates, participating in a work-study program for Chinese students, were to board a ship for France (traveling steerage). Deng, the youngest of all the Chinese students, had just turned 15. The night before his departure, Deng's father took his son aside and asked him what he hoped to learn in France. He repeated the words he had learned from his teachers: "To learn knowledge and truth from the West in order to save China." Deng Xiaoping had been taught that China was weak and poor, and that the Chinese people must have a modern, Western education to save their country.

In October, they arrived in Marseille. He briefly attended middle schools in Bayeux and Chatillon, but he spent most of his time in France working; first at the Le Creusot Iron and Steel plant in central France, then later as a fitter in the Renault factory in the Paris suburb of Billancourt, as a fireman on a locomotive and as a kitchen helper in restaurants. He barely earned enough to survive. Many of these jobs had brutal working conditions, with workers frequently being injured. Deng would later claim that it was here where he got an initial feel for the evils of the capitalist society.

In France, under the influence of his seniors (Zhao Shiyan, Zhou Enlai among others), Deng began to study Marxism and did political propaganda work. In 1921 he joined the Chinese Communist Youth League in Europe. In the second half of 1923 he joined the Chinese Communist Party and became one of the leading members of the General Branch of the Youth League in Europe. During 1926 Deng studied at Moscow in the then-USSR. He returned to China in early 1926.

In 1928 Deng led the Baise Uprising in Guangxi province against the Kuomintang (KMT) government. The uprising soon failed and Deng went to the Central Soviet Area in Jiangxi province.

He was a veteran of the Long March, during which Deng served as General Secretary of the Secretariat of the Communist Party. While acting as political commissar for Liu Bocheng, he organized several important military campaigns during the war with Japan and during the Civil War against the Kuomintang. In late November 1948, Deng led the final assault on the Kuomintang forces, who were under the direct command of Chiang Kai-shek in Sichuan. The city of Chongqing fell to the PLA on 1 December and Deng was immediately appointed mayor and political commissar. (Chiang Kai-shek, who had moved his headquarters to Chongqing in mid-November, fled to the provincial capital of Chengdu. This last mainland Chinese city to be held by the KMT fell on 10 December and Chiang fled to Taiwan on the same day.) When the PRC was founded in 1949 Deng was sent to oversee issues in the Southwestern Region, and acted as its First Secretary.

Political Rise

Policymaker following the Great Leap Forward

As a supporter of Mao Zedong, Deng was named by Mao to several important posts in the new government.

After officially supporting Mao Zedong in his Anti-Rightist Campaign of 1957, Deng became General Secretary of the Secretariat and ran the country's daily affairs with then President Liu Shaoqi. Having failed to advance the "social productive forces" in the Great Leap Forward through the "communist wind" and the "exaggeration wind", Liu and Deng moved from an "ultra-leftist" approach to a "pragmatic" or right opportunist approach.

In the rural areas, they allowed the peasants to have bigger private plots and sell their outputs on free markets, diverting peasants' labour effort away from the collective work. The collective work itself was partially privatised as a result of the "contracting production to the family" policy. This new partial privatisation had led to rising inequality among peasants as well as growing corruption among the rural cadres.

In the cities, the industrial sector was reorganised to concentrate power and authority in the hands of managerial and technical experts. Bonuses and piece rates were widely introduced to promote economic efficiency, leading to a rising economic and social inequality. Then, Deng and Liu used growing disenchantment with Great Leap Forward, and gained influence within the CCP. They embarked on economic reforms that bolstered their prestige among the party technocrats and apparatus bureaucrats. Deng and Liu advocated more rightist policies, as opposed to Mao's leftist ideas.

In 1961, at the Guangzhou conference, Deng uttered what is perhaps his most famous quotation: "I don't care if it's a white cat or a black cat. It's a good cat so long as it catches mice." This was interpreted to mean that being productive in life is more important than whether one follows a communist or capitalist ideology.

Two Purges

Mao grew apprehensive that the right-wing politics of Deng and Liu could lead to restoration of capitalism and end the Chinese Revolution achievements for workers and peasants. For this amongst other reasons, Mao launched the Cultural Revolution in 1966, during which Deng fell out of favour and was forced to retire from all his offices. He was sent to the Xinjian County Tractor Factory in rural Jiangxi province to work as a regular worker. While there Deng spent his spare time writing. He was purged nationally, but to a lesser scale than Liu Shaoqi.

During the Cultural Revolution, Deng Xiaoping and his family were targeted by Red Guards. Red Guards imprisoned Deng's son, Deng Pufang. Deng Pufang was tortured and forced out of the window of a four-story building, becoming a paraplegic.

Nonetheless, when Maoist rebels were defeated, and after Lin Biao attempted an abortive coup and was killed in an air crash, Deng Xiaoping (who had led a large field army during the civil war) became the most influential among the remaining army leaders. When Premier Zhou Enlai fell ill from cancer, Deng Xiaoping became Zhou's choice for a successor, and Zhou was able to convince Mao to bring Deng Xiaoping back into politics in 1974 as First Vice-Premier, in practice running daily affairs. Deng focused on reconstructing the country's economy and stressed unity as the first step to raising production. He remained careful, however, of not intruding the basic Maoist line of thinking, at least on paper.

In reality, the Cultural Revolution was not yet over, and a radical leftist political group known as the Gang of Four, led by Mao's wife Jiang Qing, competed for power within the Communist Party. The Gang saw Deng as their greatest challenge to power. Mao, too, was suspicious that Deng would annul the positive reputation of the Cultural Revolution, what Mao considered one of his greatest policy initiatives. Beginning in late 1975, Deng was asked to draw up a series of self-criticisms. Although Deng admitted to having taken an "inappropriate ideological perspective" while dealing with state and party affairs, he was reluctant to admit that his policies were wrong in essence. Deng's antagonism with the Gang of Four became increasingly clear, and Mao seemed to swing in the Gang's favour. Mao refused to accept Deng's self-criticisms and asked the party's Central Committee to "discuss Deng's mistakes thoroughly".

Zhou Enlai died in January 1976, to an outpouring of national grief. Zhou was a very important figure in Deng's political life, and his death eroded the little support within the Party's Central Committee that Deng had left. After delivering Zhou's official eulogy at the state funeral, the Gang of Four, with Mao's permission, began the so-called *Criticize Deng and Oppose the Rehabilitation of Right-leaning Elements* campaign. Hua Guofeng, not Deng, was selected to become Zhou's successor. On 2 February, the Central Committee issued a Top-priority Directive, officially transferring Deng to work on "external affairs", in reality removing Deng from the party's power apparatus. Deng stayed at home for the subsequent months, awaiting his fate. The political turmoil had brought the economic progress Deng had laboured for in the past year to a halt. On 3 March, Mao issued a directive reaffirming the legitimacy of the Cultural Revolution and specifically pointed to Deng as an internal, rather than external, problem. This was followed by a Central Committee directive issued to all local party organs to study Mao's directive and criticize Deng.

Deng's political fortunes were dealt another blow following Qingming Festival, when the mass mourning of Premier Zhou on the traditional Chinese holiday sparked the Tiananmen Incident of 1976, an event the Gang of Four branded as counterrevolutionary and threatening to their power. Furthermore, the Gang deemed Deng the mastermind behind the incident, and Mao himself wrote that "the nature of things has changed". This prompted Mao's decision to remove Deng from all leadership positions but keep his party membership.

Re-emergence

Deng gradually emerged as the de-facto leader of China in the few years following Mao's death in 1976. Prior to Mao's death, the only governmental position he held was that of First Vice-Premier of the State Council. By carefully mobilizing his supporters within the Chinese Communist Party, Deng was able to outmaneuver Mao's appointed successor Hua Guofeng, who had previously pardoned him, and then oust Hua from his top leadership positions by 1980. In contrast to previous leadership changes, Deng allowed Hua to retain membership in the Central Committee, to quietly retire, and helped to set a precedent that losing a high-level leadership struggle would not result in physical harm.

Deng then repudiated the Cultural Revolution and, in 1977, launched the "Beijing Spring", which allowed open criticism of the excesses and suffering that had occurred during the period. Meanwhile, he was the impetus for the abolishment of the class background system. Under this system, the CCP put up employment barriers to Chinese deemed to be associated with the former landlord class; its removal therefore effectively allowed Chinese capitalists to join the Communist Party.

Deng gradually outmaneuvered his political opponents. By encouraging public criticism of the Cultural Revolution, he weakened the position of those who owed their political positions to that event, while strengthening the position of those like himself who had been purged during that time. Deng also received a great deal of popular support. As Deng gradually consolidated control over the CCP, Hua was replaced by Zhao Ziyang as premier in 1980, and by Hu Yaobang as party chief in 1981. Deng remained the most influential of the CCP cadre, although after 1987 his only official posts were as chairman of the state and Communist Party Central Military Commissions.

Originally, the president was conceived of as a figurehead of state, with actual state power resting in the hands of the premier and the party chief, both offices being conceived of as held by separate people in order to prevent a cult of personality from forming (as it did in the case of Mao); the party would develop policy, whereas the state would execute it.

Deng's elevation to China's new number-one figure meant that the historical and ideological questions around Mao Zedong had to be addressed properly. Because Deng wished to pursue deep reforms, to continue Mao's hard-line "class struggle" policies and mass public campaigns was unreasonable. In 1982 the Central Committee of the Communist Party released a document entitled

On the Various Historical Issues since the Founding of the People's Republic of China. Mao retained his status as a "great Marxist, proletarian revolutionary, militarist, and general", and the undisputed founder and pioneer of the country and the People's Liberation Army. "His accomplishments must be considered before his mistakes", the document declared. Deng personally commented that Mao was "seven parts good, three parts bad." The document also steered the prime responsibility of the Cultural Revolution away from Mao (although it did state that "Mao mistakenly began the Cultural Revolution") to the "counter-revolutionary cliques" of the Gang of Four and Lin Biao.

Opening up

Under Deng's direction, relations with the West improved remarkably. Deng travelled abroad and had a series of amicable meetings with western leaders, and became the first Chinese leader to visit the United States in 1979, meeting with President Carter at the White House. Shortly before this meeting, the U.S. had broken diplomatic relations with the Republic of China (Taiwan) and established them with the People's Republic of China (PRC).

Sino-Japanese relations also improved significantly. Deng used Japan as an example of a rapidly progressing economic power that sets a good example for China's future economic directions.

Another achievement was the agreement signed by United Kingdom and China on 19 December 1984 (Sino-British Joint Declaration) under which Hong Kong was to be handed over to the PRC in 1997. With the 99-year British lease on the New Territories expiring, Deng agreed that the PRC would not interfere with Hong Kong's capitalist system for 50 years. A similar agreement was signed with Portugal for the return of Macau. Dubbed "one country, two systems", this fairly unprecedented approach has been touted by the PRC as a potential framework within which Taiwan could be reunited with the Mainland in more recent years.

In October 1987, at the Plenary Session of the National People's Congress, Deng Xiaoping was re-elected as Chairman of Central Military Commission, but Deng resigned as Chairman of the Central Advisory Commission and he was succeeded by Chen

Yun. He continued to chair and developed the reform and opening up as the main policy, put forward the three-step suitable for China's economic development strategy within 70 years: the first step, to double the 1980 GNP and ensure that the people have enough food and clothing, was attained by the end of the 1980s; second step, to quadruple the 1980 GNP by the end of the 20th century, was achieved in 1995 ahead of schedule; the third step, to increase per capita GNP to the level of the medium-developed countries by 2050, at which point, the Chinese people will be fairly well-off and modernization will be basically realized.

Deng, however, did little to improve relations with the Soviet Union, continuing to adhere to the Maoist line of the Sino-Soviet split era that the Soviet Union was a superpower equally as "hegemonist" as the United States, but even more threatening to China because of its geographical proximity.

Changing China: Economic Reforms

Improving relations with the outside world was the second of two important philosophical shifts outlined in Deng's program of reform termed *Gaige Kaifang* (*lit.* Reforms and Openness). The domestic social, political, and most notably, economic systems would undergo significant changes during Deng's time as leader. The goals of Deng's reforms were summed up by the Four Modernizations, those of agriculture, industry, science and technology and the military.

The strategy for achieving these aims of becoming a modern, industrial nation was the socialist market economy. Deng argued that China was in the primary stage of socialism and that the duty of the party was to perfect so-called "socialism with Chinese characteristics", and "seeking truth from facts." This interpretation of Maoism reduced the role of ideology in economic decision-making and deciding policies of proven effectiveness. Downgrading communitarian values but not necessarily the ideology of Marxism-Leninism himself, Deng emphasized that "socialism does not mean shared poverty". His theoretical justification for allowing market forces was given as such:

Planning and market forces are not the essential difference between socialism and capitalism. A planned economy is not the definition of socialism, because there is planning under capitalism;

the market economy happens under socialism, too. Planning and market forces are both ways of controlling economic activity."

Unlike Hua Guofeng, Deng believed that no policy should be rejected outright simply because it was not associated with Mao. Unlike more conservative leaders such as Chen Yun, Deng did not object to policies on the grounds that they were similar to ones which were found in capitalist nations.

This political flexibility towards the foundations of socialism is strongly supported by quotes such as:

We mustn't fear to adopt the advanced management methods applied in capitalist countries (...) The very essence of socialism is the liberation and development of the productive systems (...) Socialism and market economy are not incompatible (...) We should be concerned about right-wing deviations, but most of all, we must be concerned about left-wing deviations.

Although Deng provided the theoretical background and the political support to allow economic reform to occur, it is in general consensus amongst historians that few of the economic reforms that Deng introduced were originated by Deng himself. Premier Zhou Enlai, for example, pioneered the Four Modernizations years before Deng. In addition, many reforms would be introduced by local leaders, often not sanctioned by central government directives. If successful and promising, these reforms would be adopted by larger and larger areas and ultimately introduced nationally. An often cited example is the household-responsibility system, which was first secretly implemented by a poor rural village at the risk of being convicted as "counter-revolutionary." This experiment proved very successful. Deng openly supported it and it was later adopted nationally. Many other reforms were influenced by the experiences of the East Asian Tigers.

This is in sharp contrast to the pattern in the *perestroika* undertaken by Mikhail Gorbachev in which most of the major reforms were originated by Gorbachev himself. The bottom-up approach of the Deng reforms, in contrast to the top-down approach of *perestroika*, was likely a key factor in the success of the former.

Deng's reforms actually included the introduction of planned, centralized management of the macro-economy by technically proficient bureaucrats, abandoning Mao's mass campaign style of economic construction. However, unlike the Soviet model, management was indirect through market mechanisms. Deng sustained Mao's legacy to the extent that he stressed the primacy of agricultural output and encouraged a significant decentralization of decision making in the rural economy teams and individual peasant households. At the local level, material incentives, rather than political appeals, were to be used to motivate the labor force, including allowing peasants to earn extra income by selling the produce of their private plots at free market.

In the main move toward market allocation, local municipalities and provinces were allowed to invest in industries that they considered most profitable, which encouraged investment in light manufacturing. Thus, Deng's reforms shifted China's development strategy to an emphasis on light industry and export-led growth. Light industrial output was vital for a developing country coming from a low capital base. With the short gestation period, low capital requirements, and high foreign-exchange export earnings, revenues generated by light manufacturing were able to be reinvested in more technologically-advanced production and further capital expenditures and investments.

However, in sharp contrast to the similar but much less successful reforms in Yugoslavia and Hungary, these investments were not government mandated. The capital invested in heavy industry largely came from the banking system, and most of that capital came from consumer deposits. One of the first items of the Deng reforms was to prevent reallocation of profits except through taxation or through the banking system; hence, the reallocation in state-owned industries was somewhat indirect, thus making them more or less independent from government interference. In short, Deng's reforms sparked an industrial revolution in China.

These reforms were a reversal of the Maoist policy of economic self-reliance. China decided to accelerate the modernization process by stepping up the volume of foreign trade, especially the purchase of machinery from Japan and the West. By participating in such export-led growth, China was able to step up the Four Modernizations by attaining certain foreign funds, market, advanced technologies and management experiences, thus accelerating its economic development. Deng attracted foreign companies to a series of Special Economic Zones, where foreign investment and market liberalization were encouraged.

The reforms centred on improving labor productivity as well. New material incentives and bonus systems were introduced. Rural markets selling peasants' homegrown products and the surplus products of communes were revived. Not only did rural markets increase agricultural output, they stimulated industrial development as well. With peasants able to sell surplus agricultural yields on the open market, domestic consumption stimulated industrialization as well and also created political support for more difficult economic reforms.

There are some parallels between Deng's market socialism especially in the early stages, and Lenin's New Economic Policy as well as those of Bukharin's economic policies, in that both foresaw a role for private entrepreneurs and markets based on trade and pricing rather than central planning. An interesting anecdote on this note is the first meeting between Deng and Armand Hammer. Deng pressed the industrialist and former investor in Lenin's Soviet Union for as much information on the NEP as possible.

Role in the Tiananmen Square Protests

The Tiananmen Square protests of 1989 culminating in the Tiananmen Square Massacre (referred to in Chinese as *the June Fourth Incident*, to avoid confusion with two other Tiananmen Square protests) were a series of demonstrations in and near Tiananmen Square in the People's Republic of China (PRC) between 15 April and 4 June 1989. Many socialist governments collapsed during the same year.

The protests were sparked by the death of Hu Yaobang, a reformist official backed by Deng Xiaoping and ousted by his enemies. Many people were dissatisfied with the party's slow response and relatively subdued funerary arrangements. Public mourning began on the streets of Beijing and elsewhere. In Beijing this was centred on the Monument to the People's Heroes in Tiananmen Square. The mourning became a public conduit for anger against perceived nepotism in the government, the unfair dismissal and early death of Hu, and the behind-the-scenes role of the "old men". By the eve of Yaobang's funeral, the demonstration had reached 100,000 people on the Tiananmen square. While the protests lacked a unified cause or leadership, participants were generally against the authoritarianism and some voiced calls for economic liberalization and democratic reform within the structure of the government while others called for a less authoritarian and less centralized form of socialism.

During demonstrations, Deng Xiaoping's pro-market ally General Secretary Zhao Ziyang supported demonstrators and distanced himself from the Politburo. Martial law was declared on 20 May by the socialist hardliner Li Peng, but no action was taken until 4 June. The movement lasted seven weeks. Soldiers and tanks from the 27th and 28th Armies of the People's Liberation Army were sent to take control of the city on 4 June. Many ordinary people in Beijing believed that Deng Xiaoping had ordered the intervention, but political analysts do not know who was the real person behind the order. However, Deng's daughter defends the actions that occurred as a collective decision by the party leadership.

To purge sympathizers of Tiananmen demonstrators, the Communist Party initiated a one and half year long program similar to Anti-Rightist Movement. It aimed to deal "strictly with those inside the party with serious tendencies toward bourgeois liberalization" and more than 30,000 communist officers were deployed to the task.

Zhao Ziyang was placed in house arrest by socialist hardliners and Deng Xiaoping himself was forced to make concessions to anti-reform communists. He soon declared that "the entire imperialist Western world plans to make all socialist countries discard the socialist road and then bring them under the monopoly of international capital and onto the capitalist road". A few months later he said that the "United States was too deeply involved" in the student movement referring to foreign reporters who had given financial aid to the student leaders and later helped them escape to various Western countries, primarily the United States through Hong Kong and Taiwan.

Although at first he made concessions to the socialist hardliners, he soon resumed his reforms after his 1992 southern tour. After his tour, he was able to stop the attacks of the socialist hardliners on the reforms through their "named capitalist or socialist?" campaign. Deng Xiaoping privately told the Canadian Prime Minister that factions of the Communist Party could have grabbed army units and the country had risked a civil war. Two years later, Deng Xiaoping endorsed Zhu Rongji, a Shanghai Mayor, as a vice-premier candidate. Zhu Rongji had refused to declare martial law in Shanghai during the demonstrations even though socialist hardliners had pressured him.

After Resignation and the 1992 Southern Tour

Officially, Deng decided to retire from top positions when he stepped down as Chairman of the Central Military Commission in 1989, and retired from the political scene in 1992. China, however, was still in the *era of Deng Xiaoping*. He continued to be widely regarded as the "paramount leader" of the country, believed to have backroom control. Deng was recognized officially as "The chief architect of China's economic reforms and China's socialist modernization". To the Communist Party, he was believed to have set a good example for communist cadres who refused to retire at old age. He broke earlier conventions of holding offices for life. He was often referred to as simply *Comrade Xiaoping*, with no title attached.

Because of the Tiananmen Square protests of 1989, Deng's power had been significantly weakened and there was a growing formalist faction opposed to Deng's reforms within the Communist Party. To reassert his economic agenda, in the spring of 1992, Deng made his famous southern tour of China, visiting Guangzhou, Shenzhen, Zhuhai and spending the New Year in Shanghai, in reality using his travels as a method of reasserting his economic policy after his retirement from office. On his tour, Deng made various speeches and generated large local support for his reformist platform. He stressed the importance of economic construction in China, and criticized those who were against further economic and openness reforms. Although there is debate on whether or not Deng actually said it, his perceived catchphrase, "To get rich is glorious", unleashed a wave of personal entrepreneurship that continues to drive China's economy today. He stated that the "leftist" elements of Chinese society were much more dangerous than "rightist" ones. Deng was instrumental in the opening of Shanghai's Pudong New Area, revitalizing the city as China's economic hub. His southern tour was initially ignored by the Beijing and national media, which were then under the control of Deng's political rivals. President Jiang Zemin showed little support. Challenging their media control, Shanghai's *Liberation Daily* newspaper published several articles supporting reforms authored by "Huangfu Ping", which quickly gained support amongst local officials and populace. Deng's new wave of policy rhetoric gave way to a new political storm between factions in the Politburo. President Jiang eventually sided with Deng, and the national media finally reported Deng's southern tour several months after it occurred. Observers suggest that Jiang's submission to Deng's policies had solidified his position as Deng's heir apparent. Behind the scenes, Deng's southern tour aided his reformist allies' climb to the apex of national power, and permanently changed China's direction toward economic development. In addition, the eventual outcome of the southern tour proved that Deng was still the most powerful man in China.

Deng's insistence on economic openness aided in the phenomenal growth levels of the coastal areas, especially the "Golden Triangle" region surrounding Shanghai. Deng reiterated that "some areas must get rich before others", and asserted that the wealth from coastal regions will eventually be transferred to aid economic construction inland. The theory, however, faced numerous challenges when put into practice, as provincial governments moved to protect their own interests. The policy contributed to a widening wealth disparity between the affluent coast and the underdeveloped hinterlands.

Death and Reaction

After being disconnected from life supporting machines, Deng Xiaoping died on 19 February 1997, at age 92 from a lung infection and Parkinson's disease, but his influence continued. Even though Jiang Zemin was in firm control, government policies maintained Deng's political and economic philosophies. Officially, Deng was eulogized as a "great Marxist, great Proletarian Revolutionary, statesman, military strategist, and diplomat; one of the main leaders of the Communist Party of China, the People's Liberation Army of China, and the People's Republic of China; The great architect of China's socialist opening-up and modernized construction; the founder of Deng Xiaoping Theory".

Although the public was largely prepared for Deng's death, as rumors had been circulating for a long time, the death of Deng was followed by the greatest publicly sanctioned display of grief for any Chinese leader since Mao Zedong himself. However, in contrast to Mao's death, Deng's death in the media was announced without any titles attached (Mao was called the Great Leader and Teacher, Deng was simply "Comrade"), or any emotional overtones from the news anchors that delivered the message.

At 10 A.M. on the morning of 24 February, from all walks of life in the entire nation, people were asked by Premier Li Peng to pause in silence in unison for three minutes. The nation's flags flew at half-staff for over a week. The nationally televised funeral, which was a simple and relatively private affair attended by the country's leaders and Deng's family, was broadcast on all cable channels. Jiang Zemin's tearful eulogy to the late reformist leader declared, "The Chinese people love, thank, mourn and cherish the memory of Comrade Deng Xiaoping because he devoted his life-long energies to the Chinese people, performed immortal feats for the independence and liberation of the Chinese nation." Jiang vowed to continue Deng's policies.

After the funeral, his organs donated to medical research, the remains were cremated, and his ashes were subsequently scattered at sea, according to his wishes. For the next two weeks, Chinese state media ran news stories and documentaries related to Deng's life and death, with the regular 7 pm *National News* program in the evening lasting almost two hours over the regular broadcast time.

Domestically, in contrast to Zhou's death, during which people wept on the streets, the reaction to Deng's death was largely calm, with no stock market crashes, no business closures, no wearing special armbands of grief, and no interruption to life in general. Certain segments of the Chinese population, notably the modern Maoists and radical reformers (the far left and the far right), had negative views on Deng. In the year that followed, songs like "Story of Spring" by Dong Wenhua, which were created in Deng's honour shortly after Deng's southern tour in 1992, once again were widely played.

There was a significant amount of international reaction to Deng's death. UN Secretary-General Kofi Annan said Deng was to be remembered "in the international community at large as a primary architect of China's modernization and dramatic economic development". French President Jacques Chirac said "In the course of this century, few men have, as much as Deng Xiaoping, led a vast human community through such profound and determining changes"; British Prime Minister John Major commented about Deng's key role in the return of Hong Kong to Chinese control; Canadian Prime Minister Jean Chrétien called Deng a "pivotal figure" in Chinese history. The Taiwan presidential office also sent its condolences, saying it longed for peace, cooperation, and prosperity. The Dalai Lama voiced regret.

Legacy

"Deng Xiaoping, was one of the 20th century's greatest men. He ended Marxist dogma, releasing the energy of his long-suffering people whose nation had been raped by Western and Japanese imperialism, then ravaged by brutal civil wars and destructive Marxist policies. Deng's innocuous-sounding dictum, "it does not matter what color a cat is as long as it hunts mice", unleashed the greatest explosion of productivity and economic growth in history." — *Eric Margolis*

"And in 1978 China had its first piece of great good luck in a long, long time—perhaps the first time some important chance broke right for China since the end of the Sung dynasty. China acquired as its paramount ruler one of the most devious and effective politicians of this or indeed any age, a man who was quite possibly the greatest human hero of the twentieth century: Deng Xiaoping. Deng sought to maintain the Communist Party oligarchy's control over China's politics while also seeking a better life for China's people, and he is guided by two principles: (i) be pragmatic ("what matters is not whether the cat is red or white, what matters is whether the cat catches mice), and (ii) be cautious ("cross the river by feeling for the stones at the bottom of the ford with your feet")" — *J. Bradford DeLong*

Deng changed China from a country obsessed with mass political movements to a country focused on economic construction. In the process, Deng maintained the unrelenting political clout of the Communist Party of China, as evidenced by the 1989 Tiananmen Square Protests. Although some criticize Deng for his actions in 1989, China's significant economic growth in the 1980s and 1990s was largely credited to Deng's policies. Put into sharp contrast with Mikhail Gorbachev's *glasnost and perestroika*, Deng's socioeconomic model of a socialist market economy was a largely novel concept.

Deng Xiaoping's policies are among some of the most successful industrializations in human history, comparable to only the rapid industrialization of other East Asian countries, the Soviet Union and the home place of the industrial revolution itself, Britain. In a little over 30 years, his policies allowed China to move from the peasant society it once was to an industrial superpower with gross output second only to the United States. Despite controversial incidents such as the June 4th incident and the corruption of his son, Deng Xiaoping is largely remembered as a heroic and able leader.

The same policies, however, left a large number of issues unresolved. These issues, including unprofitable state-owned enterprises, regional imbalance, urban-rural wealth disparity and official corruption were exacerbated during Jiang Zemin's term (1993-2003). Although some areas and segments of society were notably better off than before, the re-emergence of significant inequality did little to legitimize the Communist Party's founding ideals, as the party faced increasing social unrest. Deng's emphasis in light industry, compounded with China's large population, created a large cheap labor market which became significant on the global stage. Favouring joint-ventures over domestic industry, Deng allowed foreign capital to pour into the country. While some see these policies as a fast method to put China on par with the west, Chinese hard line communists criticize Deng for abandoning the Party's founding ideals and selling out China.

Deng was an able diplomat, and he was largely credited with the successes of China in foreign affairs. Deng's time as China's leader saw agreements signed to revert both Hong Kong and Macau to Chinese sovereignty. Deng's era, set under the backdrop of the Cold War, saw the best Sino-American relations in history. Some Chinese nationalists assert, however, that Deng's foreign policy was one of appeasement, and past wrongs such as war crimes committed by Japan during the World War II were forgotten to make way for economic partnership.

Memorials

When compared to the memorials of other former CCP leaders, those dedicated to Deng have been relatively low profile, in keeping with Deng's pragmatism. Deng's portrait, unlike that of Mao, has never been hung publicly anywhere in China. Likewise, he was cremated after death, as opposed to being embalmed like Mao.

There are a few public displays of Deng in the country. A bronze statue of Deng was erected on 14 November 2000, at the grand plaza of Lianhua Mountain Park of Shenzhen. This statue is dedicated to Deng's role as a great planner and contributor to the development of the Shenzhen Special Economic Zone, starting in 1984. The statue is 6 metres (20 ft) high, with an additional 3.68-meter base. The statue shows Deng striding forward confidently. In addition, in many coastal areas and on the island province of Hainan, Deng is seen on large roadside billboards with messages emphasizing economic reform or his policy of One country, two systems.

Another bronze statue of Deng was dedicated 13 August 2004 in the city of Guang'an, Deng's hometown, in southwest China's Sichuan Province. The statue was erected to commemorate Deng's 100th birthday. The statue shows Deng, dressed casually, sitting on a chair and smiling. The Chinese characters for "Statue of Deng Xiaoping" are inscribed on the pedestal. The original calligraphy was written by Jiang Zemin, then Chairman of the Central Military Commission.

In Bishkek, capital of the Republic of Kyrgyzstan, there is a six-lane boulevard, 25 metres (82 ft) wide and 3.5 kilometres (2 mi) long, the *Deng Xiaoping Prospekt*, which was dedicated on 18 June 1997. A two-meter high red granite monument stands at the east end of this route. The epigraph in memory of Deng is written in Chinese, Russian and Kirghiz.

Bibliography

Adam, R.: *Elements of Government*, New York, Random House, 1960.

Ahmad, Imtiaz: *State and Foreign Policy: India's Role in South Asia*, New Delhi, Vikas, 1993.

Ashton, S.R.: *British Policy Towards the Indian States, 1905-1939*, London, Curzon, 1982.

Austin, Granville: *The Indian Constitution: Cornerstone of a Nation*, Oxford, Clarendon Press, 1966.

Baldwin, David, *Economic Development and American Foreign Policy, 1943-1966*, Chicago, 1966.

Barber B.R.: *Strong Democracy. Participatory Politics for a New Age*. Berkeley, University of California Press, 1984.

Bhatta, Sitesh: *Agricultural Price Policy and Production in India*, Delhi, Konark, 1991.

Chandra, R.: *Judicial System in India*, Lucknow, Print House (India), 1992.

Davies .A.: *Telecommunications and Politics. The Secentralised Alternative*, London, Pinter, 1994.

Foreman-Peck J. and Millward, R: *Public and Private Ownership of British Industry 1820-1990*, Oxford, Clarendon Press, 1994.

Giersch, H. : *Trade Policy and Demand Management*, Tübingen, J.S.B.Muhr, 1973.

Greer P.: *Transforming Central Government: the Next Steps Initiative*, Buckingham, Open University Press, 1994.

Hans J. : *Politics Among Nations: The Struggle for Power and Peace*, New York, Knopf, 1960.

Hauft, Ottomar: *Distribution of Stock of Money*, Effingham, London, 1892.

Jarillo, J.C.: *Creating the Borderless Organization*, Oxford, Butterworth-Heinemann, 1993.

Keane J.: *Democracy and Civil Liberty*, London, Verso, 1988.

Kegan, K. : *Money and the Mechanism of Exchange*, MacMillan, London, 1890.

Lipietz A.: *Mirages and Miracles*, London, Verso, 1987.

Lucian, W. : *Asian Power and Politics: the Cultural Dimensions of Authority*, Cambridge, Belknap Press, 1985.

Mackenzie, D.: *Knowing Machines: Essays on Technical Change*, London, Mit Press, 1996.

Manpong, C. M.: *District Administration in Arunachal Pradesh*, New Delhi, Omsons Publications, 1993.

Mary, W.: *Asian Power and Politics: the Cultural Dimensions of Authority*, Cambridge, Belknap Press, 1985.

Morris, W.H.: *The Government and Politics of India*, London, Hutchinson, 1971.

Ottomar, H.: *Distribution of Stock of Money*, Effingham, London, 1892.

Prahlad, K.: *Governance and Public Administration for Poverty Reduction*, Salvador, Brazil, 1997.

Raj, K.N.: *New Economic Policy*, Delhi, Oxford University Press, 1986.

Riggs, F.: *Administrative Reform and Political Responsiveness*, Beverly Hills, Sage Publications, 1970.

Robert, T.: *Practical Public Management*, New York, Marcel Dekker, 1995.

Rosen, P.: *Societies and Military Power: India and its Armies*, Ithaca, Cornell University Press, 1996.

Thompson, V.: *Public Administration*, New York, Knopf, 1950.

Simon, D. : *Public Administration*, New York, Knopf, 1950.

Victor G. : *Law as a Political Instrument*, New York, Random House, 1955.

Whitakar, A. C. : *Foreign Exchange. Appleton*, New York, 1920.

Index

♦♦♦